"Michele Ribeiro has put together a critical cont[...] the intersectionality of reference group identities i[...] I am not aware of any other book that provides s[...] apy approach to interventions within diverse group contexts. Examining Social Identities and Diversity Issues in Group Therapy *speaks to the experiences of veterans, mothers of young children, athletes, those who are incarcerated, adolescents involved with the court system, Lebanese women who suffer from depression, college and university students, and leadership among women of color. The intersectionality of reference group identities (e.g., ethnicity, religion, nationality, socioeconomic status, gender identity, chronic health and ability status, sexual identity, spirituality, power and privilege) within the context of group therapy are addressed in ways that extend our knowledge and its application. A must have resource for group therapists, supervisors, students, trainees, and anyone interested in group processes in the 21st century."*

Caroline S. Clauss-Ehlers, Ph.D., ABPP; Chair, American Psychological Association Task Force on Re-envisioning the Multicultural Guidelines for the 21st Century; Associate Professor, Rutgers, The State University of New Jersey

"Counseling centers cannot keep pace with the number of students seeking individual therapy on campus, which can lead to students not having access to timely services. While, many institutions struggle with underutilized group therapy programs for a variety of reasons, including not offering culturally relevant treatment. Group therapy programs work best when the groups match students' specific cultural needs. This is why this book is ground breaking, forward thinking, timely, and culturally relevant; it incorporates a multicultural strength approach integrated throughout the chapters. Its practical application is written for group practitioners who are invested in taking their group therapy program to another level! This book will appeal to practitioners who want to serve all of their students from privileged or marginalized identities. I commend Ribeiro for devoting an entire book on the intersectionality of group psychotherapy."

Shari A. Robinson, Ph.D, Director, Psychological and Counseling Services; University of New Hampshire

"In the olden days we were surprised when they talked on topics of 'culture and personality.' Society was coming to grips with how we were treating each other. First wave was like Leonard Cohen's light radiating through cracks in our own mindless, self-centered point of view. Edited volumes often had a dedicated chapter or section addressing diversity, social justice and privilege. We now know that diversity is diversely deconstructive to all our points of view and the best we can do is strive to mentalize, come to grips and adhere to our best practices. Here is an edited volume with accounts of self and other relating to the tasks of group psychotherapy and rooted in the struggle to make sense, compassion and engagement central to the healing endeavor. Ribeiro has woven together

a panoply of chapters that embody and encourage our desire to see more of what is going on and how we facilitate that process."

Joshua M. Gross, Ph.D., ABPP, CGP, FAGPA, FAAGP,
President Elect for the Society of Group Psychology and
Group Psychotherapy (APA Division 49);
Director of Group Programs, The University
Counseling Center, Florida State University;
Co-Editor of The College Counselor's Guide to
Group Psychotherapy

Examining Social Identities and Diversity Issues in Group Therapy

A unique blend of theory and practice within the world of group psychotherapy, this text discusses diversity issues in group contexts within the realm of teaching, consulting, and facilitating psychotherapy groups.

Chapters present a unique perspective on diversity issues within certain populations, such as prisoners, elite athletes, and high-risk youth, and examine questions around race, language, ability, gender, and the similarities and differences between the leader and their clients. Such examples provide an intricate look into the psychological dynamics that arise within these populations and the skill of group therapists in honoring their clients' humanity.

Readers will appreciate the practical examples of how to navigate difficult dynamics such as microaggressions and the role of compassion as a foundational principle of practice for group therapists.

Michele D. Ribeiro is a licensed psychologist and certified group psychotherapist at Oregon State University's Counseling and Psychological Services. She is co-editor of *The College Counselor's Guide to Group Psychotherapy* and a Fellow of the American Group Psychotherapy Association.

Examining Social Identities and Diversity Issues in Group Therapy

Knocking at the Boundaries

Edited by
Michele D. Ribeiro

NEW YORK AND LONDON

First published 2020
by Routledge
52 Vanderbilt Avenue, New York, NY 10017

and by Routledge
2 Park Square, Milton Park, Abingdon, Oxon OX14 4RN

Routledge is an imprint of the Taylor & Francis Group, an informa business

Library of Congress Cataloging-in-Publication Data
Names: Ribeiro, Michele D., editor.
Title: Examining social identities and diversity issues in group therapy : knocking at the boundaries / edited by Michele D. Ribeiro.
Description: New York, NY : Routledge, 2020. |
Includes bibliographical references and index. |
Identifiers: LCCN 2019059012 | ISBN 9780367077235 (hbk) |
ISBN 9780367077259 (pbk) | ISBN 9780429022364 (ebk)
Subjects: LCSH: Group psychotherapy--Cross-cultural studies. |
Minorities--Psychology.
Classification: LCC RC488 .E89 2020 | DDC 616.89/152--dc23
LC record available at https://lccn.loc.gov/2019059012

ISBN: 978-0-367-07723-5 (hbk)
ISBN: 978-0-367-07725-9 (pbk)
ISBN: 978-0-429-02236-4 (ebk)

Typeset in Goudy
by Taylor & Francis Books

I dedicate this book to my family who share in my interest to explore the diverse world we live in. Thank you Subbappa, Abhijat, and River.

Contents

SECTION VI
Other Perspectives and Endings

Illustrations

Contributors

Alexis D. Abernethy, PhD, CGP, FAGPA is a Clinical Psychologist and Professor of Psychology in the Graduate School of Psychology at Fuller Theological Seminary. She is also the Associate Provost for Faculty Inclusion and Equity. She received her MA and PhD in clinical psychology from the University of California, Berkeley. Her primary research interest is the intersection between spirituality and health. Dr Abernethy's Spirituality and Health Lab includes three research teams: Experience of Spirituality and Health-Related Outcomes; Spirituality, Cancer, and Health Disparities; and Spirituality, Culture, and Eating Disturbance. She has received grants from the following grantors: California Cancer Research Program, the National Cancer Institute, and the John Templeton Foundation. She has numerous research publications and has also written in two areas of clinical specialty, group therapy and cultural competency training. Dr Abernethy has a small private practice and is a Certified Group Psychotherapist and Fellow of the American Group Psychotherapy Association.

Massiel M. Abramson is a licensed Marriage and Family therapist who has worked in the clinical mental health field for over ten years in different capacities including direct care, management, and professional training. She is currently an Early Childhood Development Specialist and Clinician with Child First, Inc. where she provides dyadic therapy to infants, young children, and their parents providing attachment and trauma-based therapy. Massiel has certifications in Child-Parent Psychotherapy (CPP) and The Circle of Security (COS). Her systemic approach to psychotherapy focuses on themes of attachment, trauma processing, stages of human development, play therapy, and creativity. She earned her Master's in Human Development with a specialty in Marriage and Family Therapy from the University of Rhode Island in 2009.

Dr David F. Allen, MD, MPH is a board-certified psychiatrist and a distinguished life fellow of the American Psychiatric Association. He was trained in medicine at St. Andrews University, Scotland, and Psychiatry and Public Health at Harvard Medical School. He has held academic positions at Yale University and Georgetown Medical School. He has published widely in the Addictions, Public Health Issues, and General Psychiatry. David is the founder and director of The Family: People Helping People project, funded by the Templeton World Charity Foundation. He lives in The Bahamas where he is head of The Discovery Clinic at the Renascence Institute International.

Jenny Ambroise earned her MFA in painting from Indiana State University. After living on the Mississippi for several years, she returned home to Indianapolis where she works as an assistant professor of art. She shows her work in local, national, and international exhibitions. While her art ranges in subject matter from portraits to landscapes to still-lifes, its overarching theme is ultimately about understanding the human condition.

Cindy Miller Aron, LCSW, CGP, FAGPA was long time Director of Group Programs/Faculty at Samaritan Health Services, Department of Psychiatry, Corvallis, Oregon. Cindy recently transitioned to full-time private practice in Portland focusing on the treatment of elite athletes and group therapy consultation. She is consulting with and providing services to the OHSU Sports Medicine team at Portland State University and consults with several conferences regarding mental health protocols and practices.

Cindy has been a clinical member of AGPA since 1988. She has been on the annual faculty at AGPA as a workshop leader or institute instructor since 1996. She is a founding member and founding president of the Oregon Group Psychotherapy Society. She was a board member of AGPA, serving as Member at Large from the Affiliate, as well as elected to the Nominating Committee. She is a long-time member of the AGPA distance learning committee and was a participant for four years on the open session committee. Cindy received the National Affiliate Assembly Award for Outstanding Contribution to Affiliate Societies in 2006. Cindy is a fellow in the American Group Psychotherapy Association and has been a national presenter for 25 years on a variety of clinical and interventional topics.

Cindy was appointed to the NCAA Inaugural Mental Health Task Force, the NCAA Sexual Violence and Prevention Summit, the American Medical Society for Sport Medicine Task Force for Prevention and Treatment of Sexual Violence in Sport, and the NCAA Governors' Commission to Combat Sexual Violence. She has previously served as a consultant to the U.S. Center for Safe Sport. She is a founding member of the Alliance for Social Workers in Sport. Cindy is a member of the International Olympic Committee Consensus Meeting on Mental Health in Elite Athletes. This committee recently published its consensus document in the British Journal of Sports Medicine. Additionally Cindy contributed a subspecialty paper on PTSD and Other Trauma Related Disorders in Elite Athletes also published in the British Journal.

Kristin Bertsch, PhD graduated with her doctorate in Counseling Psychology in 2014 from Lehigh University and with her master's degree in counseling in 2007 from Arcadia University. Currently, she works as the New Jersey Area Health and Education Center (AHEC) Director, as an Assistant Professor (Course Director of the Community Service Learning and Leadership Curriculum), and a licensed psychologist at Rowan University, School of Osteopathic Medicine, in Stratford, NJ. She joined the Rowan School of Osteopathic Medicine after serving as the Coordinator for Diversity, Inclusion, and Outreach Programming at Drexel University's Counseling Center 2015–2019. Prior to that, she completed her doctoral internship and postdoctoral fellowship at the University of Pennsylvania's Counseling and Psychological Services. She has experience in a variety of settings including college counseling centers, inpatient hospitals, and outpatient therapy clinics. Within the psychology community Kristin is a recognized resource for working with those with multiple intersecting minoritized identities. She has taught at the graduate level, presented at numerous national conferences, and is a published author in her field. Her clinical interests include working with patients around life transitions, chronic illness, family relationships, LGBT identity, and the intersection of identities (e.g., race, gender, and sexual orientation), discrimination, trauma, and mood regulation.

Keva Bethell earned her Master's in Public Health from the University of Oklahoma in 2012. She has previously worked at the Oklahoma State Department of Health, in the Injury Prevention Services. In 2013, she spear-headed a suicide task force with Dr David Allen. In three months, Keva collaborated with the Central Detective Unit to abstract all suicide cases that occurred in a 14-year period. In addition to this, she carried out a national survey, concerning suicide, which had never been done before. This study was published in the *Global Journal of Human Social Sciences*. Currently, she is the Director of Research for 'The Family: People Helping People' project, a community-based program offering free group therapy in inner-city communities. She has ten published papers through her work with The Family Program.

Dr Marie Allen Carroll is a counseling psychologist, individual and group psychotherapist, researcher, trainer, teacher, and curriculum developer. Her degrees include a Master's in clinical community counseling with a specialization in child and adolescent psychology, and a PhD in psychology, with specialization in family psychology. Dr

Allen Carroll is the Director of Training and Curriculum Development for The Family Program. The Family Program is a research-driven, evidence-based program which provides free group therapy to marginalized communities throughout the Bahamas. A key component of The Family Program is training community members in the role of Family Group Facilitators. Dr Carroll developed, and is currently implementing, the Family Group Facilitator Training curriculum. Thus far, quantitative and qualitative data have demonstrated significant decrease in violence, anger, and need for revenge in persons attending The Family groups.

Wendy Freedman, PhD, CGP received a bachelor's degree from Cornell University and a doctorate in clinical and school psychology from the University of Virginia. She has worked in the field of college counseling since 2003 and is currently the Director of the Vassar College Counseling Service. Dr Freedman has a passion for working with individuals with disabilities and health conditions, has facilitated therapy groups for this population for over ten years, and has presented about this topic at national and regional conferences. Dr Freedman is a certified group psychotherapist and serves as co-chair of the Health and Medical Issues Special Interest Group of the American Group Psychotherapy Association (AGPA).

Denie Fountain has a Master's in Psychology and Counseling and is a coordinating psychotherapist at The Family: People Helping People project. She is the coordinator of the court-ordered adolescent program and also the court-ordered parent program. She teaches the participants effective communication, conflict resolution, anger management skills, healthy relationships (with parents and peers) as well as the importance of taking responsibility for their actions. She advises parents on the importance of listening to their adolescents. Denie is also the Office Administrator for The Family Program.

Leslie Klein, PhD received her bachelor's degree in 2000 from the University of California, Berkeley, and her doctorate in clinical psychology in 2011 from Gallaudet University, the world's only institution of higher education designed to accommodate deaf and hard of hearing students. Dr Klein trained in university counseling center as well as physical rehabilitation settings, and she worked as a staff psychologist at the University of Southern California until 2014 when she started an independent practice. Dr Klein is particularly passionate about work with people with disabilities and chronic health conditions. Dr Klein serves as co-chair of the Health and Medical Issues Special Interest Group of the American Group Psychotherapy Association (AGPA) and has presented on disability-related topics at national and regional conferences since 2015.

Katheryne Kopp-Miller, PsyD, HSPP received a bachelor's degree from Indiana University and a doctorate in clinical psychology from the University of Indianapolis. She was a staff psychologist at Purdue University and the Group Coordinator at the University of Pittsburgh before going into private practice in 2015. She currently works in private practice in Bloomington, IN, and specializes in eating disorders and autism spectrum disorders. Dr Kopp Miller has provided group and individual therapy for people with disabilities and health conditions since graduate school, and has presented about these topics at national and regional conferences. She is an adjunct instructor at the University of Indianapolis where she teaches courses in CBT, ACT, DBT, and interpersonal therapy approaches.

Dr Pratibha Kumar, PhD is an Assistant Professor of Communication at Mount St. Mary's University. Her teaching and research interests include interpersonal and intercultural communication, multiculturalism, and gender. Pratibha holds a PhD in Communication and Public Discourse from the University of North Dakota. Her research has focused on cultural differences among astronauts on the International Space Station, social change and reform in developing countries, immigration issues, Muslims and Islamophobia, etc. She has presented papers at regional, national, and international conferences as well as spoken at non-academic, community settings. She is also the founder of Sungh Consultancy LLC, a diversity and inclusion company and is a certified conflict mediator.

Dr Sydney LeFay is a consult-liaison psychiatrist and faculty member at Oregon Health & Science University where she cares for a diverse and largely underserved population through psychiatric emergency services. She graduated from medical school at the Texas College of Osteopathic Medicine in 2014 and went on to complete her psychiatry residency at Good Samaritan Regional Medical Center in Corvallis, Oregon, where she served as Chief Resident. During residency she sought training in group psychotherapy in both acute psychiatric inpatient settings as well as long-term outpatient settings, and co-led a workshop on narcissistic injury in group psychotherapy training at the American Group Psychotherapy Association annual meeting in February 2018. She completed her fellowship in consult-liaison psychiatry at Oregon Health & Science University in Portland, Oregon in June 2019 where she gained expertise in working with medically complex patients with psychiatric symptoms. Dr LeFay is an avid educator and has given lectures on a wide variety of topics with special interests in transgender health care, acute-care psychiatry, and trauma-related disorders.

Miguel Lewis, PsyD, CGP, ABPP completed his doctorate in clinical psychology from the Nova Southeastern University in 2005. He is currently a staff psychologist at the West Palm Beach, VA mental health clinic and provides individual, group, and couples therapy. He is an Acceptance and Commitment Therapy (ACT) VA National Consultant where he offers weekly consultation to training participants over a six-month period. He is a certified group psychotherapist and Board Certified in Couples and Family Psychology. He has served as President of the Florida Group Psychotherapy Association (FGPA) since 2017. His clinical interests include Acceptance and Commitment Therapy, Emotionally Focused Couples Therapy, Motivational Interviewing, Interpersonal Psychotherapy for Depression, Interpersonal Process Group Therapy, and men's issues.

Gaea Logan, LPC-S, CGP, FAGPA has offered contemporary psychoanalytic psychotherapy to individuals, couples, and groups as well as clinical consultation and supervision nationally and internationally for over 35 years. She is a Licensed Professional Counselor and approved supervisor in the states of Colorado and Texas. She is a Certified Group Psychotherapist, a Fellow of the American Group Psychotherapy Association and an alumna of the Harvard Refugee Trauma/ Global Mental Health Program. Her evidence-based trauma protocol, Contemplative-Based Trauma and Resiliency Training (CBTRT), has been adapted for utilization throughout UN bodies in the Middle East and Africa. In recognition of clinical excellence, social justice and international humanitarian outreach, Gaea was the 2015 recipient of the Social Responsibility Award of the American Group Psychotherapy Association.

Nan Narboe, MSW worked as a psychotherapist and trainer for 40 years, specializing in group and couples work. In 2017, she published *Aging: An Apprenticeship*, which continues to bring her invitations to speak, most recently at a film festival. She is currently developing a model that combines individual meditation with group exploration.

David W. Neal, PsyD graduated with his master's and doctorate in Clinical Psychology from George Fox University in Newberg, OR. He recently completed his internship at the Institute of Living in Hartford, CT, and he is currently a Post-Doc Clinical Psychology Fellow and psychoanalytic candidate at the Austen Riggs Center in Stockbridge, MA. His interests include metacognition, primitive affect states, and the intersection of psychoanalysis, culture, and society.

Dr Sheela Reddy, EdD is an Executive Leadership Coach and Psychologist in private practice since 2008. Sheela has a MS Counseling Psychology and EdD in Multicultural Systems Psychology and a Post-Doctoral Certificate in Trauma. She is certified in Neuro-Linguistic Programming (NLP), Mediation, Divorce Coaching, and Yogic Breathing. Her holistic approach to coaching combines motivational and systems psychology with yoga, meditation, and NLP. As a partner in a technology company for five years, she managed expats, created assessments, and implemented organizational change initiatives. Other leadership roles include Clinical Director of the Domestic Violence Center, the Director of a Children's Play Program at University of Maryland Medical Systems, and leading sub-committees for Maryland Psychological Association educational affairs committee. She is a seasoned presenter for the MPA. In addition, Sheela is known for her presentations on self-awareness, stress-management, women's empowerment, conflict management, executive functioning strategies, mental health, diversity, and domestic violence for corporate and health-care organizations.

Michele D. Ribeiro, EdD, ABPP, CGP, FAGPA graduated with her doctorate in Counseling Psychology at Rutgers, The State University of New Jersey in 2005 with an emphasis in multicultural counseling and education. Currently she works as a licensed psychologist and certified group psychotherapist at Oregon State University's Counseling and Psychological Services where she established the Group Therapy Internship and Practicum Training Program and served as the Group Coordinator from 2006 to 2013. Michele is a Fellow and an active member of the American Group Psychotherapy Association (AGPA) through service on the board; Diversity, Equity, and Inclusion Task Force; and as Conference Committee Co-Chair of Open Sessions for the Annual Meeting. Michele also serves on the executive board of The American Psychological Association's Society of Group Psychology and Group Psychotherapy (Division 49) and International Psychology (Division 52). She also co-edited the book *The College Counselor's Guide to Group Psychotherapy* (2018) with Routledge Press.

Miriam M. Ribeiro, LCSW earned her MSSW (Master's of Science in Social Work) from Columbia University in New York City. Miriam has been working in the field of Forensics as a clinical psychiatric social worker for approximately 13 years. She initially worked for the California Department of Mental Health at Coalinga State Hospital (CSH) before the department became known as the California Department of State Hospitals. She worked with the Sexually Violent Predator (SVP) population throughout her six years of employment at CSH. Miriam then began working for the California Department of Corrections, California Men's Colony, a medium security prison, and remained for just under seven years working with inmates diagnosed with a variety of mental illnesses. She recently returned to the State Mental Hospital System, and currently works at Atascadero State Hospital where she continues to work as a psychiatric social worker in the forensics arena. She currently works with inmates who fall under the classification of Mentally Disordered Offenders (MDOS), those incompetent to stand trial, and those who were found "guilty by reason of insanity." Miriam's therapeutic modality is Rogerian. She has found this modality to be beneficial when working with offenders. Over the years she has been humbled and feels fortunate to have witnessed many offenders finding their humanity through group work in particular. Group therapy is of specific interest to Miriam and is where she has observed the most healing and transformation among the incarcerated.

Carlos A. Taloyo, PhD graduated with his doctorate in Clinical Psychology, and an MA in Theology from Fuller Theological Seminary. He is in private practice in Salem, OR. His interests include group psychotherapy, multiculturalism, spirituality, and psychoanalytic psychotherapy.

Salaheddine Ziadeh, PsyD is a clinical psychologist with 15 years of post-doctoral experience in a variety of settings – universities, hospitals, community health centers, clinics – and with diverse populations. He holds both a doctorate and a master's degree in clinical psychology from Rutgers University, a master's degree in psychology from New York University, and two bachelor's degrees – one in psychology and social behavior – from the University of California. Dr Ziadeh trained in outpatient, inpatient, and emergency psychiatry at Montefiore Medical Center of The Albert Einstein College of Medicine, and practiced psychotherapy in Manhattan for six years, before moving to the West Coast. In 2017–2018, he co-trained Lebanese clinicians in Interpersonal Psychotherapy (IPT) – a joint project by Teachers College at Columbia and the Lebanese Ministry of Public Health – and he is currently training West-African clinicians in the provision of IPT-G, the group modality of IPT. Dr Ziadeh is a member of the American Psychological Association (APA), the Society for Clinical Psychology (Division 12), and the Society of Group Psychology and Group Psychotherapy (Division 49).

Foreword

This excellent book, well crafted by Michele Ribeiro and her colleagues, is one of the first group therapy texts devoted entirely to culture, diversity, and social identity. It addresses principles and techniques that promote therapeutic inclusivity through group therapist awareness, sensitivity, attunement, and skill. Prominent group therapy textbooks and journals from an earlier generation were relatively silent on the issues of race and diversity and until recently, our field has paid insufficient attention to this very important clinical focus.

This book advances our capacity to understand and utilize that understanding effectively in a variety of important client domains: race, culture, gender, sexual orientation, social identity, and disability. These impact all of the core domains of our work, from clinical care to clinical supervision and training, to consultation to organizations, and, our as yet, underdeveloped public voice regarding the dynamics of exclusion, discrimination, and social injustice in society at large.

My own clinical experience training group therapists in China for many years has brought to awareness my many blind spots with regard to the impact of culture on individual psychology, identity, and group dynamics. Being the ethno-racial minority in that environment made it impossible for me to ignore what I did not know. In that setting, I could readily work toward the requisite sensitivity needed to learn and to understand as fully as possible the role of culture in the groups that I was leading and supervising.

In our much more familiar settings, the great risk is that we neglect the role of culture, race, racial trauma, gender, sexual orientation, and disability as they intersect and shape our clients' identities. At the same time, it has never been more important for us to attend to these forces, and to promote the difficult dialogues that our group clients require. We need to become expert at understanding the impacts of culture and diversity. And we need to acknowledge our own defensiveness in avoiding a deep dive into this complex and important area.

Without that accountability, there is limited opportunity for repair or reconciliation. The authors in this textbook illuminate with great clarity the ways in which therapists block and defend themselves from full ownership of their responsibility to address the impact of hurt and trauma rooted in exclusion and discrimination of the "other." This book generates a painful confrontation regarding the impact of privilege on society and in our groups.

In a recent clinical supervision session, I was struck by the challenge of this task. The group therapist trainee I was supervising was distressed by criticism leveled at her by a racialized group member. The client protested that this group leader could not understand her own experience because the therapist's vision and sensitivity were obscured by her White privilege. Unbeknownst to the group, and to me until this supervision, this group therapist was the child of a Mexican father and Chinese mother. She was acutely aware throughout her life and professional training of the impact of race and culture on her own identity and acceptance in society but never spoke of it until that supervision session. This experience underscores the assumptions and projections that emerge in our therapeutic encounters; and the importance of being open and sufficiently courageous to look at both our client's and our own personal experience in its full complexity.

If we remain closed off, or defensive, in the interest of reducing our feelings of guilt or shame, we will be less effective in creating groups that provide safety and opportunity for healing and repair for our clients.

Our field has evolved substantially over the past 25 years. We are acutely aware of the negative effects of stigma and discrimination on mental health. We are aware of the changing cultural composition of our psychotherapy groups in the face of immigration and shifting demographics, as those who once felt unwelcome now feel some hope for proper care. For those who have the privilege of working with refugees, understanding the psychological impacts of forced migration, violence, and war-inflicted trauma on mental health has broadened our scope and capacity. We also live in a political and social environment that has become more polarized and tends to exclude rather than integrate. This is where the power of group therapy can be most clear. Group therapy can create a healing force within the social microcosm of the group. Our group therapy is either going to be part of our clients' solution or part of our clients' problem: If we do not create a healing environment then we run the grave risk of creating an injurious one.

We all seek to be evidence-based group therapists and mend the quality gap in the delivery of mental health care. The cornerstones of evidence-based practice are therapist empathy and group cohesiveness. Therapist multicultural orientation is also strongly correlated with significantly better clinical outcomes. Therapists should seek to create a treatment for each individual rather than force the client to adapt to us. This is not cookie cutter therapy. Understanding our clients' relationship to their culture and to the construction of their identities is an essential part of empathic attunement. It requires our cultural humility – our openness to learning without presumption or disrespect; and a willingness to be informed and educated by our clients. We must recognize the limits of our knowledge. We need to own our responsibility as part of a society that has all too often perpetuated and exacerbated discrimination and trauma. And we must do so in ways that elevate us into therapeutic action. These are important and difficult clinical and educational challenges and this book will help its readers to engage this challenge effectively.

It is heartening to see that many of the contributors to this excellent text are members of the American Group Psychotherapy Association (AGPA). As Dr Ribeiro notes, some of the inspiration for this work emerged from her work with colleagues within AGPA who are committed to advance inclusion and diversity in our clinical work and in our organization. Other organizations, including the American Psychological Association, are addressing these issues and have produced clinical guidelines for working with clients for whom diversity considerations are central.

Engagement, acceptance, belonging, and reconciliation are key challenges in our work with clients from diverse backgrounds. We have every reason to be hopeful that we can be effective clinically, and in turn contribute to creating a more just society.

One of the most compelling lectures I have heard was given by Justice Albie Sachs at a group conference in London. Justice Sachs is one of the chief architects of South Africa's post-apartheid constitution. He has since served as a Constitutional Court judge in South Africa for many years. Justice Sachs described in his lecture meeting later in his life the South African government agent who had been ordered to assassinate him. The government sought to silence his anti-apartheid advocacy. Justice Sachs lost an arm and an eye in a car bombing, but survived. The dialogue between the hired assassin and Sachs, brought them both to tears of grief and healing. They lamented the society that first brought them into collision. But, beyond that, they shared an overriding sense of hope that they could now reconcile together in a new and better society.

Molyn Leszcz, MD, FRCPC, CGP, DFAGPA Professor of Psychiatry, University of Toronto. President, The American Group Psychotherapy Association October 21, 2019

Preface

Introductory Considerations

I grew up White with Austrian, Portuguese, and Norwegian heritage in a military town that was ethnically and racially diverse, and in a family where education was limited to high school and our social class was lower. Experiencing life in a racially diverse and educationally limited context afforded me experiences but no theoretical understanding of my experience and socialization (Harro, 2008). I also identify as cis-gendered, female, pansexual, currently able-bodied, Catholic, U.S. born, and the daughter of an immigrant. Having lived in Seattle prior to graduate school and living on Capitol Hill, a neighborhood known as the gay district, I started examining issues of race with gender and sexual orientation, but at the time not linking them. Although Crenshaw (1989, 1991) had already begun to advocate for the case of intersectionality, I had not been exposed to her work. Again, I was living and learning from my experiences. Theory became my guide in graduate school.

I was first exposed to multicultural counseling theory in the early 1990s when I was working on my Master's degree in community counseling and reading Sue and Sue's (1990) book *Counseling the Culturally Different*. I remember feeling drawn to the field of multicultural counseling/family systems. Through exposure to and learning from Helms (1995), I understood my personal process regarding my White racial identity development, for the first time. At the same time, I took my first graduate course in group theory and dynamics. Issues of culture were not brought into the group dynamics course, and group psychotherapy, a counseling intervention, was not part of the multicultural counseling course. This book attempts to merge culture and group psychotherapy.

Since the 1990s, the well-being of millions has been impacted by global issues like terrorism, genocide, and massive migration. A resurgence of White supremacist ideologies continues to gain momentum and is reappearing in the policies and practices of big government institutions as well as smaller NGOs, thereby impeding the well-being of millions of lives. As therapists, we have the privilege of listening, attuning, and assisting in the healing of lives that are affected by ecological changes happening in our world.

Each of us is born into a group, our family and a subsequent community. This initial group membership can be a vital component to our growth or a destructive one. As therapists, we have the ethical and moral responsibility to understand not just the theories that guide our work (e. g. CBT, ACT, psychodynamic, etc.) but also the nuances within our work that are the hallmarks of what make us unique and fundamentally connected. We all come from a place, a culture, a home. Yet many of us have migrated to other states, territories, countries, and/or continents in search of a better life, to escape persecution, and/or as a means of survival. We consistently seek connection and the idea of home whether within ourselves or among others.

Group provides the vehicle to explore that which is both comfortable and uncomfortable within and to bear witness to this exploration with others. We are given the opportunity as group therapists to not only be a part of our sociocultural framework, but to also transcend it, by creating a safe space to courageously explore aspects of ourselves that are both familiar and unfolding. This book invites us to look at individuals in groups and the interplay of societal issues that are constantly influencing our clients' lives. It further encourages us to explore the intersections of identity within a group context.

In group therapy, we have an opportunity to explore the boundaries of what is familiar to us, and to go beyond the edge of those boundaries. We invite our clients to knock on the boundaries of another group member who may be different due to race, sexual orientation, religion, social class, etc. What do we do with this opportunity? Turn away, or presuppose we do not have enough in common? What would happen if curiosity led our behaviors and lives? What would happen if we took more steps in the direction of the unknown? Could we possibly make a new connection?

Navigating diversity issues in group is complex and dynamic. Before we, as group therapists, examine these issues with others, we must embark upon our own introspective journey. Cone-Uemura (2009/2018) provides an exercise that assists therapists to begin this journey around identity development. We have an obligation to ask ourselves what is our understanding of our race, culture, gender, class, sexual orientation, religion, and ability? With which identities are we most comfortable? What aspects of our identity trigger insecurity? In what areas are we wearing blinders? What aspects of our identity do we take for granted because they are rooted in privilege and are made easy for us by our society (e.g. health insurance for married couples if heterosexual, men in leadership positions if identifying as a male)? In areas where we are not challenged to think, we may hold dominance. On the opposite side, what aspects of our identity require us to think, plan or work harder, because society is structured in an exclusionary way (e.g. street curbs with no curb ramp for people with disabilities, few to no Professors of Color teaching at a public university for Students of Color)? This is where we may hold marginalized/targeted status.

Behaviors/Statements to Manage Dissonance

Societies are structured in a manner giving more privilege to some than others. This architectural design is carefully created. If someone holds a marginalized identity they may be unaware that the system is working against them and/or that inequities exist and contribute to discriminatory behaviors and prejudicial attitudes of inferiority. As a result, members of society unknowingly propagate and perpetuate these unexamined differences in power and access. There are many ways dominant groups have developed and maintained the status quo and/or managed their dissonance, feeling guilty for the inequities that exist while also not wanting to lose any privileges they enjoy. Olsson (2011) identified 28 behaviors or "detours" that White people do regularly to manage the dissonance they may feel regarding injustice and/or their own White privilege. A few examples of detouring behaviors/statements to manage dominant identity status and the consequences of these beliefs are included below (reprinted with permission from Jona Olsson):

> **I. *I'm Colorblind:*** "People are just people; I don't see color; we're all just human." or "I don't think of you as Chinese." or "We all bleed red when we're cut." or "Character, not color, is what counts with me."
>
> **Reality Check/Consequence:** Statements like these assume that people of color are just like me, White; that they have the same dreams, standards, problems, peeves that I do. "Colorblindness" negates the cultural values, norms, expectations, and life experiences of People of Color, and most importantly, their experience as a target of racism. Even if an individual White person could ignore a person's color, the society does not. By saying we are not different, that we don't see their color, we are also saying we don't see my whiteness. This denies their experience of racism and our experience of privilege. "I'm colorblind" can also be a defense when afraid to discuss racism, especially if one assumes all conversation about race or color is racist. Speaking of another person's color or culture is not necessarily racist or offensive. As one of my African American friends says, "I don't mind that you notice I'm Black." Color consciousness does not equal racism.
>
> **II. *BWAME:*** "But What About Me. Look how I've been hurt, oppressed, exploited …?"

Reality Check and Consequence: This diminishes the experience of People of Color by telling our own story of hardship. We lose an opportunity to learn more about the experience of racism from a Person of Color, while we minimize their experience by trying to make it comparable or less painful than ours.

III. *Innocence By Association:* "I'm not racist, because ... I have Vietnamese friends, or my lover is Black, or I marched with Dr King."

Reality Check and Consequence: (Perhaps, if every White person who says they marched with Dr King actually had, the current situation would look different!) This detour into denial wrongly equates personal interactions with People of Color, no matter how intimate they may be, with anti-racism. There is an assumption that our personal associations free us magically from our racist conditioning.

IV. *White on White, and Righteously So:* "What is wrong with those White people? Can't they see how racist they're being?" or "I just can't stand to be around White people who act so racist anymore."

And

You're preaching to the choir: "You're wasting your time with us, we're not the people who need this training."

Reality Check and Consequence: We distance ourselves from "other" White people. We righteously consider ourselves White people who have evolved beyond our racist conditioning. This is another level of denial. There are no "exceptional White people." We may have attended many anti-racism workshops; we may not be shouting racist epithets or actively discriminating against People of Color, but we still experience privilege based on our white skin. We benefit from this system of oppression and advantage no matter what our intentions are. This distancing serves only to divide us from potential allies and limit our own learning.

V. *Silence*

Reality Check and Consequence: Our silence may be a product of our guilt or fear of making People of Color or White people angry with us or disappointed in us. We may be afraid that speaking out could result in losing some of our privilege. We may be silenced by fear of violence. The reasons for our silence are many, but each time we are silent we miss an opportunity to interrupt racism, or to act as an ally or to interact genuinely with People of Color or other White people. And no anti-racist action is taken as long as we are silent.

VI. *Smoke and Mirrors:* We use the current politically correct language; we state the liberal line; we're seen at the right meetings with the right people. We even interrupt racist remarks when the right people are watching and when there is no risk to us. We look like anti-racists.

Reality Check and Consequence: This is the "Avon Ally," the cosmetic approach. People of Color and other White anti-racists see through this pretense quickly. This pseudo-anti-racist posturing only serves to collude with racism and weakens the credibility of sincere White anti-racists.

When leading trainings with White-identified educators at this author's university, faculty and staff typically feel they can relate to these examples. We are always humbled as we work on owning our privilege and our discomforts (including shame, sadness) particularly when examining how we enact many of these behaviors/detours.

Until recently, most books on group psychotherapy have had a handful of chapters, at most, that covered diversity issues in group psychotherapy. For this reason, a need existed for a book that is inclusive of diversity through multiple lenses. As such, this book, offers a personal and professional mosaic from a diverse contingency of group therapists. Talking about identity is personal. The authors within this book are in different places regarding their analysis of self in the context of society as a whole. Some have been exploring the aforementioned issues most of their life, others for the past few years, and still others have embarked on the journey more recently, and as a result of writing their chapter. We are all on our individual path to self-discovery and to learning how to be culturally sensitive and responsive to our clients who have placed their trust in us. The mental health system has done a great deal of damage to many marginalized communities. As group practitioners/therapists we have the responsibility to raise the bar on our practices; to learn, grow, and to change so as to meet our clients who courageously show up and share their vulnerability.

This book like so much scholarly work on identity is written through a social constructivist lens. This lens encourages the reader to understand that society has been constructed and structured, and that there are multiple ways to see and understand our work. As marginalized groups find ways to voice their experiences, our profession, language, and how we intervene psychologically will shift and change. This book seeks to expand beyond the Eurocentric theoretical framework in which many of us have been trained. Indigenous and international psychologies are slowly pushing the envelope for practitioners in the United States to broaden our perspectives (Morgan-Consoli, Inman, Bullock, & Nolan, 2018). This book attempts to be an aid in broadening our views.

Section I, Foundations of Practice, guide us through a history of domination while eliciting questions like who has freedom and liberty today? The first section invites the reader to reflect on the foundational components of intersectionality, privilege, and marginalization while illuminating the importance of the fundamental practice of compassion in diversity work.

Section II, Social Identities in Group Psychotherapy, invites the reader to explore social identities present in ourselves, as group therapists, and as members in our groups. The areas that are covered include gender identity, chronic health conditions/ability issues, sexual orientation, and race/nationality. These chapters encourage us to think more deeply about inclusivity in our groups and promote practices that allow our clients to take risks and be curious across differing identities.

Section III, Working with Specific Populations in Groups, provides a more in-depth look at specific populations. There are groups of people in our society that often are on the fringe, either adored or loathed, with their humanity lost in both extremes. Two of the three chapters in this section provide us important insights into working with these specialized populations with more clarity and effectiveness. The third chapter highlights the specific population of veterans and the destructive dynamic that occurs as a function of prejudices and biases. Microaggressions, defined, provide the reader with an understanding of a dynamic that can unfortunately happen with regularity in groups. This chapter highlights this dynamic with the specific population of veterans. Our goal as therapists is to learn to recognize these microaggressions, seek to minimize them, and actively pursue reparation when they occur. Finally, the fourth chapter in this section provides the reader a new way of understanding the power of group through non-traditional therapies, specifically art, and with women and Mothers of Color. This chapter is particularly important in that it informs the culturally sensitive therapist to expand beyond their standard talk therapy approach.

Section IV, Structural and Institutional Components of Groups, covers the institutions of religion, higher education, and leadership within organizations. Each is highly influential in shaping how our society functions. Within religion lies a deep connection to the spirit; within universities a passion for learning and teaching exists; and within corporations there lies the creation for mentorship and evolved leadership. These chapters provide us with insight into the fact that we need to show up in important ways for one another, for our students, our clients, and for our colleagues.

Section V expands our Eurocentric work to include dynamic psychological practices within a global context in two countries, Lebanon and the Bahamas. Navigating adjustment, loss, and opportunity will be highlighted in different developmental stages of clients' lives in these chapters. Additionally, the chapters will explore specific intersections of poverty, limited resources, and resilience as a result of compassionate and culturally attuned group leadership and larger systemic supports.

References

Cone-Uemura, K. (2009/2018). Identity exploration activity. In M. D. Ribeiro, J. M. Gross, & M. M. Turner (eds) *The college counselor's guide to group psychotherapy* (pp. 34–35). New York, NY: Routledge.

Crenshaw, K. (1989). Demarginalizing the intersection of race and sex: A Black feminist critique of antidiscrimination doctrine, feminist theory, and antiracist politics. *The University of Chicago Legal Forum*, 8, 138–167.

Crenshaw, K. W. (1991). Mapping the margins of intersectionality, identity politics and violence against Women of Color. *Stanford Law Review*, 43(6), 1241–1300, doi:10.2307/1229039.

Harro, B. (2008). The cycle of socialization. In M. Adams, W. J. Blumenfeld, C. R. Castañeda, H. W. Hackman, M. L. Peters, & X. Zúñiga (eds) *Readings for diversity and social justice* (2010) (2nd ed., pp. 45–51). New York, NY: Routledge Taylor & Francis.

Helms, J. E. (1995). An update of Helms White and People of Color racial identity models. In J. G. Ponterotto, J. M. Casas, L. A. Suzuki, & C. M. Alexander (eds) *Handbook of multicultural counseling* (pp. 181–198). Thousand Oaks, CA: Sage.

Olsson, J. (2011). Cultural Bridges to Justice. Retrieved on August 2, 2019 from: www.culturalbridgestojustice.org.

Morgan-Consoli, M. L., Inman, A. G., Bullock, M., & Nolan, S. A. (2018). Framework for competencies for U.S. psychologists engaging internationally. *International Perspectives in Psychology: Research, Practice, Consultation*, 7(3), 174–188, doi:10.1-37/ipp0000090.

Sue, D. W. & Sue, D. (1990). *Counseling the culturally different: Theory and practice* (2nd ed.). New York, NY: John Wiley & Sons.

Acknowledgments

I would like to acknowledge and thank Amanda Devine, our editor who solicited this topic for a book after I took us off course with the co-edited book I needed to work on first. I would also like to show appreciation to the significant contributions of our colleagues from the American Group Psychotherapy Association. From the professionals who run the organization (Marsha Block and Angela Stephens), the board who helps to steer it, and the colleagues and friends who have become like family, you have inspired and shaped me in the most meaningful ways personally and professionally.

I also want to particularly acknowledge the dedication of the authors of this text, who gave their time and talents even when their lives were filled with other things, including but not limited to having a baby, managing an illness, and transitioning jobs/working on tenure. You are all superstars and I thank you from the bottom of my heart!

Other appreciations go out to Dr Molyn Leszcz for writing a thoughtful and humble foreword for the book; to my sister, Miriam M. Ribeiro, who provided clarity, and helpful suggestions and edits in the writing of the Preface, and Chapters 1 and 7; and Dr Shaznin Daruwalla for feedback to Chapter 1. Thank you to one of my amazing mentors, Dr Josh Gross, who always tells me how much he believes in me and guides me into new professional adventures that aid in my growth! Thank you to Dr Marcey Bamba, my supervisor who is my anchor at work and encourages me to follow my heart! Thank you to my family who had to manage my busy days on the weekends when I could have been inner-tubing down the river this summer! Thank you once more to my sister who exposed me to traveling when I finished college, to my mother who is always an inspiration in everything I do, even if she only lives on in spirit, and to my father, Anthony J. Ribeiro, Jr., who taught me strong determination in my work ethic. Thank you to my 99-year-old neighbor and dear friend Patti Bird Kirkdoffer, who always inspires me to ponder on life, appreciate it fully, and to be love to others. Thank you finally to Honoka Mitsuishi, who provided assistance with checking for reference accuracy. This book is a testament to everyone's faith in me and a belief that clients deserve our best personal and professional selves.

– Michele

Section I
Foundations of Practice

1 Intersectionality, Social Identities, and Groups Examined

Michele D. Ribeiro

Introductory Thoughts on an Ecological Approach to Psychological Practice

Given the sociocultural context of the United States and the world, there is a great need to examine issues of race, culture, class, ability, sexual orientation, gender, gender expression, religion/spirituality, nationality, and language, and how these identities are negotiated within the group context. Although the above identities do not encompass all aspects of diversity that people can identify with or even find salience in, these tend to be the most common ways people can be marginalized and/or can operate through dominance. The counseling and psychology professions have taken steps to bring more awareness and direction to guiding practitioners in their roles as researchers, clinicians, and educators. Adherence to implementing directives can still be haphazard; however, due to how many of us were socialized growing up and continue to be socialized in our psychology training through a White supremacist ideology (Bonilla-Silva, 2012; Liu, Liu, Garrison, Kim, Chan, Ho, & Yeung, 2019). Many White therapists today can have a negative reaction to the notion of White supremacy guiding our field, but scholars (DiAngelo, 2011) continue to name a western-White dominated field within this purview. Further, adopting frameworks such as the matrix of domination (Andersen & Collins, 2007), which focuses on oppressive structural patterns that bind systems of discrimination, are useful in that they unveil other systemic, institutionalized forms of discrimination such as heteronormativity, class oppression, ableism, and religious discrimination (Shin, 2014). As therapists, we must be ready to embody a psychology of liberation which aims to increase people's awareness of oppression, ideologies, and inequitable structures that keep some marginalized and oppressed (Comas-Diaz, 2007; Shin 2014) and others in dominant social positions. This chapter explores a broader perspective of working within group psychotherapy by recognizing the importance of acknowledging with cultural humility, sensitivity, and inclusivity clients who present with marginalized identities. Further, group therapists are called to understand how intersectionality of social identities may have more salience to marginalized clients as well as increase the likelihood these clients may experience more oppression due to societal structures at play.

Adhering to Best Practices

The Task Force on re-visioning the multicultural guidelines for the 21st century (American Psychological Association, 2017) outlined ten practice guidelines for psychologists that included awareness and active implementation of key issues. For a thorough understanding, these guidelines can be found at: https://www.apa.org/about/policy/multicultural-guidelines. pdf. A brief overview of them is highlighted below, along with examples of how they can be practiced. These guidelines include an understanding that:

1 *Identity and self-definition are fluid and complex.* This guideline has specific implications when starting a therapy group. Since identities can be more fluid and complex, group therapists can invite members to identify their pronouns and any other salient identities that are important for that member to share with the group. Based on social conditioning, members may assume they know gender based on outward appearances. As an example, leaders can model sharing their gender pronouns and help limit microaggressions related to gender by creating space for members to self-identify their gender pronouns as well. The leader could start the group by saying: "Welcome to group everyone. We are going to start group by introducing ourselves along with any identities that may be salient to us and that you would like the group to know. This could also include what gender pronouns you identity with. I'll begin. My name is Michele, and I identity as White, spiritual, and I use the pronouns she/her/they. I am co-facilitating the group this term. Who would like to go next?"

2 *Beliefs influence our perceptions and clinicians/practitioners need to move past categorical assumptions/biases.* Beliefs are often shaped early on in many people's lives. This author was facilitating a group in which there were three Asian American women. Each shared her racial identity as being a Woman of Color except one of the women who stated that she was a daughter and a student. I assumed after hearing the other two women who identified as Asian American and Women of Color that the third woman would also identify in this way, but she didn't. I was reminded that categorical assumptions about identity are not useful and that actually hearing from clients regarding what is salient is an important step with group disclosures.

3 *Language and communication vary across people and cultures.* One example occurred with an Asian American male student who sat in a general interpersonal process group for ten weeks and barely said more than one sentence each group. Believing that if a member doesn't say anything they

likely are not getting as much out of group, this author found herself feeling frustrated with this member who didn't seem to be making any connections with other members in group. To my surprise, this member shared in the last group how much he learned from being in the group and went on to relay all the different things he appreciated from the various members throughout the term. I was humbled and shared with him how much I assumed about his silent communication and how wrong I was as a result of this assumption.

4 *Social and physical environments impact the lives of all clients.* An example related to this guideline includes this author's work with a PhD student who had grown up in poverty throughout her life. She shared how much she felt she didn't belong in higher education as a result of her past and even though she had made it into the program and was doing well, she couldn't stop feeling anxious about being at the university and in a doctoral program. This client had elevated her socioeconomics and class from what she grew up in, and yet she could not escape the idea that she did not deserve to be in graduate school based on this past.

5 *Historical and current experiences with power, privilege, and oppression need to be addressed as part of our role to promote justice.* An example: I was working with a student from an African country whose family moved to the U.S. when she was a teenager. She came to study public health in graduate school, and reported feeling excited and confident at the start. Within the first three years of the program, she described her advisor leading her into other projects, which took time away from her dissertation research. She then described how her advisor began to question her ability. The student's progress was impacted so much that she was put on academic warning. She later changed advisors and she explained how this new advisor was supportive and helped her to refocus on degree-related work. Our work together in counseling looked at the relationship to this first advisor and the system that permitted this experience as the cause of her delay and poor progress rather than internalizing that she wasn't capable of being in the program and finishing her degree.

6 *Culturally adaptive, flexible interventions, and advocacy within and across systems are necessary in our work.* A young Asian American woman invited the two group co-facilitators to attend her senior fashion show in which models would be showcasing her clothing designs. We, as group facilitators, knew that attending would give the message that we appreciated all her hard work and celebrate in her final success prior to graduating from college. We both attended the fashion show and shared our excitement and admiration for her designs after the show. She asked to take a photo with both of us and then later sent us an email sharing how much our attendance meant to her. We knew that speaking to her success in group would not have had the same impact as showing up for her in person at her fashion show. This flexible intervention was necessary to close the group experience with us despite the group having already ended. We had

become important figures that she would mentalize (Bateman & Fonagy, 2006) and carry with her. The fact that we both showed up also solidified our support of her.

7 *There are varied ways of working within an international context and culturally sensitive adaptations need to be practiced.* A U.S. psychologist on sabbatical, who was fluent in Italian, was working with an Italian non-profit organization that provides medical and psychological assistance to sub-Saharan refugees, immigrants, and asylum seekers in Italy. Because of his background in group therapy, he was asked to help the organization create a therapy group for refugees who were dealing with significant trauma. In order to be able to run the group in one language spoken by all of the members, they selected group members who were from sub-Saharan countries where English was a primary language (Nigeria, Sierra Leone, and The Gambia). They held the group in English, though his co-leaders were native Italian speakers. They also worked with a "cultural mediator"/translator who had emigrated from the Ivory Coast several years ago. He helped to bridge language and cultural barriers. Below is an excerpt of the outcome of sensitively adapting group practices to the local client context (Beecher, personal communication, September 28, 2019): "As I was thinking about how to best begin the group, I wanted to have group members introduce themselves in a way that was culturally meaningful to them. I asked our cultural mediator if there was any way we could introduce ourselves in such a way. He thought for a while and then suggested that nearly everyone in Italy who comes from an African country has a name that no one knows is their 'African name.' He explained that these names tend to be somewhat grandiose and may be somewhat embarrassing, but that sharing them would be a way to unite the group. After we had briefly gone over some rules and norms for the group, our cultural mediator began the session by introducing himself first, talking about his own African name, and explaining how it was embarrassing because it meant something like, 'King over all of Africa.' After sharing his own, he asked the other group members to each share their African name. Having them share their African name was a stroke of genius. It was amazing to watch all wariness in the group melt away as the members started talking about their African names. They seemed to brighten as they talked about Africa and this intimate detail about themselves. They laughed and joked with each other and shared common experiences. It was beautiful!"

8 *Developmental stages and life transitions intersect with the larger bio-socio-cultural context.* A first-year Mexican American graduate student shared his insecurity of being in a White-dominated field within higher education. This author specifically taught the course on positive psychology that he took through a multicultural lens. In presentations, I used phrases from the research such as "Tu eres mi otro yo" and then presented research on Latin American countries having the highest outcomes in

purpose well-being due to their focus on people over tasks. In response to this research, this student shared how he could intimately relate to the research and felt appreciative to know his cultural perspectives are valued in the literature and this course.

9 *Culturally appropriate and informed psychological practices need to be conducted across all domains of the profession.* An Internal Review Board (IRB for research programs) learns after community conversations with the local Indigenous people that recent research has identified burial sites of ancestors in digital dissertation research publications, and that ancestors that have passed on are considered human subjects in their culture. Action is taken to protect the burial site information outside of the Indigenous culture and practices are created for future research with new protections identified.

10 *A strength-based approach is necessary to build resilience and minimize trauma within a sociocultural context.* Yoga, as an intervention for trauma, is taught for seven days to 47 and 183 tsunami survivors, in separate studies and in two Southeast Asian countries. Outcomes showed significant reductions in self-rated symptoms in both studies (Telles, Naveen, & Dash, 2007; Descilo, Vedamurtachar, Gerbarg et al., 2010).

How practitioners within psychology operationalize these guidelines in our everyday practice as therapists will be germane in transforming a psychology that meets the needs of all people and culturally attunes to the unique needs both between and within diverse groups of people.

The group psychotherapist has an important role in navigating systems that parallel larger national and global dynamics but within the microcosm (Yalom & Leszcz, 2005) of the group. Because there are so many layers to one's identity, it is not surprising that there is a greater chance that misperceptions and inaccurate assumptions can occur among group members and between the leaders (Cone-Uemura & Bentley, 2018; Ribeiro & Turner, 2018). There is also the possibility of connection and a potential for healing between members and/or for the group as a whole. Leaders have salient identities that may either provide them with more privilege and dominance (such as being White, able-bodied) or marginalized (such as being a Woman of Color). When leaders hold one or more marginalized identities, this may actually flip the power structure where more power is possessed in some of the group members who hold dominant identities rather than the group leader (Petty John, Tseng, & Blow, 2019).

Manifestations of Oppression within Groups

There are five manifestations of oppression that can be displayed by practitioners in their various roles (e.g. teaching, administration, clinician, research). Having knowledge about these areas may assist the practitioner in understanding what a client or colleague may be experiencing and needing support/validation. These five areas include:

1   Exploitation – the steady process of transferring results of labor of one social group to benefit another
2   Marginalization – the process by which one social group is either limited or denied access to a system of labor
3   Powerlessness – experienced by those who lack recognized authority or power and are positioned to accept orders with rare, if any, rights of giving them
4   Cultural imperialism – the universalization of a dominant group's experience and culture and establishment of it as the norm
5   Violence – actions inflicted upon a group that subsequently elicit a fear-based response among certain social group members who live in fear of experiencing random, unprovoked attacks on their persons or property, without motive except to damage, humiliate, or destroy the person (Adams, Blumenfeld et al., 2000).

Group therapy leaders, educators, and/or leaders of organizations must be able to understand the various ways oppression manifests within an institutional context. By doing so, they can understand how clients may feel marginalized and why they may need to feel validated for their experiences of marginalization within the therapy group. Often group members or clinicians who lack cultural awareness of these manifestations of oppression may not understand why a group member is having a difficult time moving beyond an issue or feeling more sensitive to comments that may be said in the group. Helms (1990) outlined four relationship types, which refer to the match in racial identity attitudes, and may occur between leaders and members in therapy. These types include parallel, crossed, progressive, and regressive and have particular relevance in therapy groups. These types also are useful across other identity attitudes (e.g. class, gender, ability) outside of just racial identity. Helms' research demonstrated that when the therapist's racial identity status was more mature than that of the client, a progressive relationship was occurring and therapeutic work involving racial content was less conflicted. Similarly, when the counselor's racial identity status was less mature than that of the client, a regressive relationship type, the counselor tended to treat the issue of race as the client's problem. Interactions occurring between group members, at either similar or different states of racial identity, can heavily contribute to the dynamics of the group as well (McRae, 1994). Thus, it is imperative that group therapists build more awareness and learn skills to lessen the internalized and often unconscious biases so as to create more equitable practices and experiences for those who are marginalized.

Again, although Helms' work looked explicitly at racial identity, there is much overlap for group therapists and group members who hold dominant social identities to attribute the difficulties experienced to the marginalized group member, rather than understanding the societal structures that actually create the marginalization and inequity. Misattributing oppressive experiences can then lead to microaggressions that may cause further harm to already marginalized group members. When the leader and group members are able to acknowledge and attune to marginalized group members' experiences as existing and/or related to structural or institutionalized forms of oppression, healing can begin to occur instead.

Social Identities and Intersectionality

For the purposes of this chapter, we will use Tajfel's (1978) work on social identity theory to understand more about how concepts around "in and out group" or "othering" emerge. Social identity is defined as a person's sense of who they are based on their group membership(s). Tajfel (1978) proposed that the groups (e.g. social class, culture, etc.) that people belong to provide an important source of pride and self-worth. Groups provide a sense of belonging to the social world. In order to increase one's self-image, individuals enhance the status in which groups belong, causing discriminatory behaviors to emerge. This begins to divide the world into "us" and "them" based on a categorization of social identities.

Social identities are comprised of cognitive, evaluative, and emotional components (Van Dick, 2001) and are fluid in nature due to life span development changes and the changing contextual nature of communities and environments. Gender identity is one of the most recent fluid identities that have emerged in the United States in the past 10–15 years. The field of multicultural counseling/psychology and the ways in which we understand people, communities, nations, and the world is also ever evolving. One evolution is the continuous uncovering of historical trauma suffered by groups such as Native Americans/Indigenous peoples, Japanese-American nationals, Latinx, African Americans, and Middle Eastern and Northern Africa descendants (Hartmann, Wendt, Burrage, Pomerville, & Gone, 2019; Nagata, Kim, & Wu, 2019; Chavez-Duenas, Adames, Perez-Chavez, & Salas, 2019; Awad, Kia-Keating, & Amer, 2019). As these trauma narratives become more visible and validated, people, representing different lived realities, are able to voice their experiences of marginalization and resilience. One aspect of this trauma plays out or is demonstrated in how societies construct ideologies about individuals and groups of people. These ideologies can create divisions that cause inequities deeply rooted in the foundations of governments, societies, and ways of living in communities.

Specific and common identities that are constructed and used to socially categorize people are gender (Schneider, Gruman, & Coutts, 2016), race, and class, to name a few. These categorizations can then easily lead to prejudicial and discriminatory behaviors enacted toward an individual or group of people. Owen et al. (2017) reported that 53–81%

of minoritized racial and ethnic clients experienced either the therapists' tendency to avoid culturally appropriate discussions or the therapists' tendency to engage in common cultural stereotypes, without checking in with clients regarding their own perspectives. The Task Force on Diversity, Equity, and Inclusion through the American Group Psychotherapy Association, recently created the document *Creating Affirming Group Experiences* (American Group Psychotherapy Association, 2019) to assist clinicians in providing culturally sensitive and appropriate interventions in therapy and organizational group processes. Appendix A provides the document for reference.

Until recently, social identities were often researched through a dominant lens (e.g. White, male, Christian, able-bodied, etc.), and in isolation of each other, rather than through the lens of simultaneous and linked experiences (i.e. African American, Muslim woman). Intersectionality or "interlocking systems of oppression" are terms that came about to describe this phenomenon (Crenshaw, 1989; Crenshaw, 2015; Collins, 1990). For example, someone with particular multiple marginalized identities (e.g. Woman of Color) might be completely overlooked in terms of rights granted to other groups of people holding one common social identity to them. Mock (2008) defines intersectionality as "an individual's exposure to the multiple, simultaneous, and interactive effects of different types of social organization and their experiences related to prejudice and power or societal oppression" (p. 427). These intersecting identities that socially locate a person determine the power and privilege a person holds based on their relative position historically and in present-day society (Mock, 2008). Crenshaw specifically states:

> Intersectionality is an analytic sensibility, a way of thinking about identity and its relationship to power … Intersectional erasures are not exclusive to Black women. People of color within LGBTQ movements; girls of color in the fight against the school-to-prison pipeline; women within immigration movements; trans women within feminist movements; and people with disabilities fighting police abuse – all face vulnerabilities that reflect the intersections of racism, sexism, class oppression, transphobia, able-ism and more.
>
> (Crenshaw, 2015)

Figure 1.1 showcases how privilege works in direct opposition to oppression and resistance with domination being the line that cuts through the two. As a person or group has one or more marginalized status, there is also an increase in the chances that the person/group will experience inequitable treatment and even violence being enacted upon them. These violent enactments are based on historical and present-day beliefs that can play out when marginalized voices threaten the dominant discourse. The more removed one is from domination the higher the

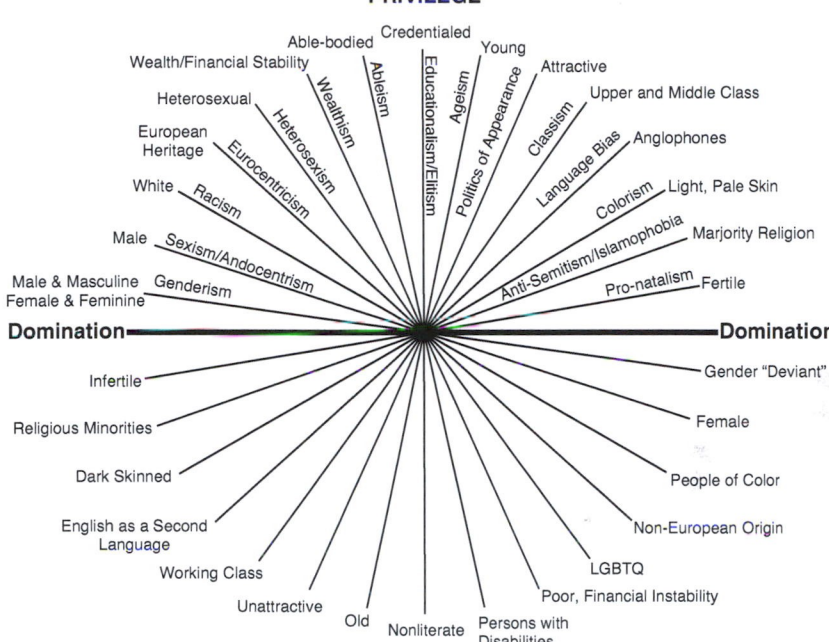

Figure 1.1 Oppression Wheel
Permission to use this work was provided by Kathryn Morgan and Chi-Fang Tseng.

chances that these privileged identity markers become seen as "normal" and anything outside of this "normality" is seen as deviant or less than. Individuals can also hold both a marginalized identity along with a privileged identity (e.g. Woman of Color who identifies as heterosexual) which speaks to the complexity of social identities and how they interplay with societal norms and treatment.

Research has suggested that therapists who are unaware of various dimensions of a client's multiple identities may be more likely to engage in microaggressions, or at a minimum may miss topics of identity that are important to the client (Owen, Drianne, Tao, DasGupta, Zhang, & Adelson, 2018). Just as important in recognizing and speaking to salient identities, however, is honoring when clients may not always want to elevate these issues in a group. An example includes a first appointment this author had with a student who was feeling socially isolated and was not doing well academically. During the initial assessment, the client highlighted coming from a Mexican American background in which she and her mother were sharing an apartment after her mother left the client's father due to domestic/interpersonal violence issues. The client reported having a brother who had moved out and was living in a large city north of the town in which we resided. The client shared that her mother did not work and was fearful to leave the house due to her undocumented status and the recent ICE raids that were happening all over the country, including their last city of residence, prior to moving to our town. The most salient issues in our individual work were staying on track academically when her mother did not want the client to leave her alone in the apartment and the client needed to go to class or study at the library. The client presented with severe generalized and social anxiety as a result of numerous environmental factors. After building trust, and a therapeutic alliance, we were able to discuss culturally sensitive ways to support her mother's well-being through resources like free English classes as well as other resources offered by the local Catholic Church, and the local foodbank. Eventually we discussed transitioning the client into an interpersonal process group. The client was made aware that she could share as much about herself and social identities as she felt comfortable. Although our individual sessions were full of social identity exploration, it was in the group that she examined her social anxiety. She found connection through others' stories of sibling support and she was able to share how she connected to these stories through her relationship with her own brother. She began to take risks, asking her fellow members how to socialize, and in believing she had something to offer and ultimately say in her relationships. Her social identities (race, gender, class, child of an undocumented parent, child of an IVS home) in individual therapy took center stage. In group, however, she shared how she just wanted to be a student who could learn how to connect with others. This therapist aimed to attune to the client's fluidity of identity issues and was able to support the client in leading with what was most salient for her in each therapeutic modality. The client stayed in the group for six months before she and her mother were evicted from their apartment and had to move in with family in another city. The client stayed in contact with this therapist sporadically, however, asking for support in terms of referrals and resources at the community college and eventually a four-year university to which she transferred. Three years after she transferred, she proudly emailed letting me know she was about to graduate with a degree in mathematics.

Petty John, Tseng, and Blow (2019) assert that transparency of the therapist in addressing intersectionality of social identities not only deepen the therapeutic alliance, but can also positively affect treatment outcomes. They further state that despite the relevant importance of identity in terms of how the client interacts with the world, depending on the presenting problem in therapy, every part of their identity may not be relevant and thus may not need to be explicitly addressed. The key for therapists is to assess the salience of identities for the client in the pregroup meeting and process what may be areas of exploration in the group that may or may not intersect with their presenting issues. Clients often feel validated knowing that even if their goals for therapy and/or group may not be specific to a particular social identity immediately, the group can be a place for exploration eventually.

Therapy Group Example

This scenario occurred when this White identified author was co-facilitating with a Woman of Color who had come to the U.S. for graduate school and thus maintained her native accent. We both started the first group as we normally would with introductions, identifying treatment goals, and group guidelines. One White male expressed that his prior group had had different leadership, specifically a male leader, and further stated he wasn't sure if the group would be useful or not for him. Based on our knowledge of the clinical staff demographics from his previous group, we knew the leader was a White male. Another White male joined in with this group member and shared a similar thought. My colleague and I were caught off guard initially. Recognizing that this was the first group that also had two additional Women of Color as members, we knew it was necessary that we model openness and strength to this feedback, in order to establish stability for the group. We presented the group with the possibility of learning something from this different gender and racial facilitator make-up. We opened the discussion to the group members, regarding the uncertainty the group may be feeling. This invitation to process allowed others to share their own cultural transference, noting their responses tended to demonstrate anxious, avoidant, and secure attachment styles (Marmarosh, Markin, & Spiegel, 2013). After the group, the two co-facilitators processed reactions to the power differential felt by my co-facilitator, a Woman of Color, and me, a White woman. We agreed that the potential intersectionality of her identities (Woman of Color, having an accent) may have heightened his feelings and thus increased his tendency to discount our leadership. Further, although this White writer had equal racial power with the student, there was still a negation experienced for her status as a woman. The co-facilitators also processed their respective desires to resist the projected negation so as to model strength for the other group members who may also have felt marginalized in their identities. Group practitioners have an elevated role in needing to understand how these dynamics can play out and thus how to respond if ruptures occur. The group therapist's aim then is to not only be sensitive to issues of diversity but also to the complexity of navigating members' and leaders' engagement across difference.

When we are sensitive, open to not knowing, and curious about learning, we are working within a framework of cultural humility (Hook, Davis, Owen, Worthington, & Utsey, 2013; Tervalon & Murray-Garcia, 1998). Cultural humility incorporates a life-long commitment to self-evaluation and self-critique. Active intention to correct power imbalances that are unjust, while growing partnerships by advocating beside individuals and groups to create positive change (Tervalon & Murray-Garcia, 1998), are also central to cultural humility's framework. Cultural humility takes on a greater responsibility than cultural competence in that group psychotherapists must be willing to listen with a deeper level of care and openness, understanding that learning is not merely an outcome-based experience.

Organization Example

The importance of intersectionality can be missed in therapy groups as well as in other types of groups such as in organizations. An organizational example follows that involved a group of employees engaging in a staff dialogue/in-service on gender and the impact it has on the organization. The dialogue in-service started with ground rules and boundaries on what the staff would be focusing on that day in terms of social identities, and the group of about 20 staff were told they would focus on gender. When one of the staff raised the issue of intersectionality being left out of the focus especially since Women of Color may have a different experience than White women in the organization, one of the facilitators of the in-service refocused the topic to be on gender without the need to hone in on race for this discussion. The dialogue then stayed on gender only. What the group began to notice, however, is that no Women or Men of Color spoke up. When these voices were invited into the dialogue, one of the Women of Color began to cry, sharing how she didn't know where her place had gone in the group. Two other Women of Color specifically stated that once they heard that they had to leave out their salient identity of race as Women of Color, they no longer felt they had a place in the group either. The facilitators (two White women and one Woman of Color) of the in-service shared how they discussed opening it up but then agreed they wanted the focus to be isolated to gender. They then highlighted their frustration to the group, with how men in the room were now getting off the hook because the women couldn't unify around their gender. The dialogue ended up shutting down without a productive ending because two of the facilitators could not see their own privilege as White women and rather wanted to solely focus on their marginalization as women. But, what would have happened if the facilitators were open to learning and curious to hear how others felt with the request to include intersectionality? What if, in the beginning, intersectionality was welcomed? Likely, the conversation would have been nuanced, so that all voices could have been heard rather than narrowing the discourse and essentially silencing already marginalized voices.

As group therapists or leaders in an organization, we must understand that the composition of a group is diverse on multiple visible and invisible levels. Communicating the importance of honoring discussions across all aspects of identity can at least set the stage for members by reinforcing that they have a voice in the group and that the sharing of their narratives is welcomed.

Kaklauskas and Nettles (2019) identify that "integrating culturally sensitive approaches into proven models of therapy is considered a best contemporary practice" (p. 42). This practice includes implementing a culturally adapted, empirically supported protocol (if available), increasing cultural sensitivity into current evidence-based treatment protocols, and creating new culturally sensitive protocols that may show efficacy, but lack strong research backing. An example of this involves the partnering of Columbia University with clinicians in an effort to research IPT-Group (Interpersonal Therapy-Group) on a global scale (e.g. Lebanon), which will be elaborated on in Chapter 15 of this text.

Conclusion

Practitioners must be able to implement best practices if facilitating groups, teaching, or conducting research, and to create socially just systems that are trauma-informed, if working as an administrator in an organization. Often, practitioners are most aware of issues where they hold marginalization status (woman, LGB, etc.) and are less conscious to their more dominant statuses (such as being White, Christian, U.S. born, etc.). Our work as practitioners is to stay engaged in learning about systems of oppression and how domination plays out in the social identities where we hold privilege. This awareness and engagement can be done through regular professional development and ongoing consultation.

Intersectionality regarding diverse social identities creates complexity across multiple domains. *Intra*-personally, intersectionality can occur within the leader and members without mention to the group as a whole. *Inter*-personally, intersectionality can also occur when members share some of their salient identities with other members and the group is able to understand how they have either inhibited their well-being or something they are still trying to understand. How the therapist successfully navigates social identities in the group can foster trust in members and create an opportunity to heal from oppressive experiences outside of group. However, if left unexplored, socially marginalized or dominant identities can also cultivate destructive dynamics in the form of microaggressions that parallel larger sociopolitical events.

Group therapists need to do the work of exploring their own identities while understanding the importance of shedding their familiar role and subsequent comfort for a role that ventures into a riskier zone, where the leader feels less acquainted. Bringing to light issues of intersecting identities, and the impact they may have on members in the group (as well as on the leader) is an essential role of the group leader. The imperative is to understand that taking this risk may not always be neat and clean but it will demonstrate the value in recognizing that these issues exist, and that the group is a place for all marginalized voices to be heard and honored.

Appendix A: Guidelines for Creating Affirming Group Experiences at AGPA Connect and Beyond

(Permission to use this work was generously provided by the American Group Psychotherapy Association (AGPA) and the AGPA Diversity, Equity and Inclusion Task Force.)

The aim of this document is to broaden the awareness of AGPA members as we work to become a more inclusive organization. The following guidelines, while not exhausted or fixed, have been written to provide strategies for effectively addressing microaggressions and potentially oppressive dialogues and behaviors in groups. As with any change process, AGPA's efforts towards increased inclusivity is a complex, challenging process that requires patience and compassion.

Intersectionality and Increasing Awareness of Power and Privilege

Intersectionality, a term coined by Dr. Kimberlé Crenshaw, takes into account individuals overlapping identities and experiences in order to understand the complexity of the advantages and disadvantages they face. Intersectionality is a framework for conceptualizing diversity, specifically social identities, as operating within systems of power, privilege, and oppression. We all have multiple facets of identities: some identities give us privileges and other aspects lead us to being marginalized or disadvantaged. Intersectionality takes into account individuals' overlapping identities and experiences in order to understand the complexity of the advantages and disadvantages they face.

It is important to explore and be aware of your own power and privileges based on your identities and how these may lead you to inadvertently cause further harm in your approach and interventions.

- There are numerous identities that, depending on context, hold more privilege than others. Some examples in mainstream U.S. society: being White, Heterosexual, Cis-gender (identifying with the gender assigned to you at birth), Male, Christian, Able-bodied, a United States citizen, English-speaking, etc. With privilege comes unearned benefits, including power.

Intersecting Axes of Privilege, Domination, and Oppression

As a group facilitator you need to be aware of your positionalities in order to not abuse your power and reify oppression that already occurs in society at large.

- If individuals are discussing their marginalized identity or identities, notice your responses (emotional, physiological, cognitive) that indicate you are becoming defensive a   Focus on their experience and avoid bringing up your own feelings of marginalization; this can be invalidating to the person speaking

- If a group member has a certain identity, do not expect them to speak for all people who share that identity or to educate the group about their identity
- Be aware of who is speaking in your groups

    a   Are members with privileged identities taking up more of the space in the group?
    b   Is the group dialogue oriented toward a privileged perspective?
    c   Be diligent about making space for other voices.

- Be attentive to cultural assumptions, and open to discussion of and feedback about assumed norms, values, expectations, etc. For example, the assumption that adult members who live with their parents are doing so because of some shortcoming, rather than following cultural norms.

Microaggressions and How to Intervene (Microinterventions)

Microaggressions are everyday verbal, nonverbal, and environmental slights, snubs, or insults, intentional or unintentional, which communicate hostile, derogatory, or hurtful messages to someone based only on that person's membership in a marginalized group.

As a response, **microinterventions** are the everyday words or deeds, whether intentional or unintentional, that communicates to targets of microaggressions (a) validation of their experiential reality, (b) value as a person, (c) affirmation of their racial or group identity, (d) support and encouragement, and (e) reassurance that they are not alone. These responses incorporate four major strategic goals: (1) make the invisible visible, (2) disarm the microaggression, (3) educate the perpetrator, and (4) seek external reinforcement or support (Sue, Alsaidi, Awad, Glaeser, & Calle, 2019, p. 128).

- If you commit a microaggression:

    a   Notice the urge to defend yourself – recognize that despite your intentions, we need to attend to the impact of our words and actions
    b   If you are able to be sincere, apologize as soon as possible, and invite everyone into the conversation, welcoming constructive feedback about the impact of your microaggression
    c   Express appreciation for being alerted to your mistake
    d   Describe what you think you have learned and recognize that if you expect accolades, recognition or forgiveness, you may inadvertently be creating another microaggression – by asking the target of our original microaggression to validate us

e   Reminder: Despite the benefits of rupture and repair, injured group members do not have to forgive you

Do your research – read and learn more (life-long learning)

- If you witness others making a microaggression:

  a   Consider utilizing strategies of "Opening The Front Door" (Ganote, Cheung, & Souza, 2015):
  b   Observe: Describe clearly and succinctly what you see happening
  c   Think: State what you think about the microaggression
  d   Feel: Express your feelings about the situation
  e   Desire: Assert what you would like to happen

- Be careful not to shame either party, but invite reflection

Gender Identity and Sexual Orientation Considerations

- Don't assume all group members identify on the gender binary, as either men or women
- Some members may identify as genderqueer, genderfluid, non-binary, or transgender
- As a leader, consider sharing your pronouns with the group during your introduction
- Consider asking members to share their pronouns during introductions
- Use "they" versus "he or she" if unsure of someone's pronouns
- Understand that some members may be exploring their gender identity and unclear how they identify. Do not pressure anyone to "choose" a gender identity if they are not comfortable doing so
- Expect diverse sexual orientations will be present among members of your group
- Use the term "partner" instead of wife, husband, boyfriend or girlfriend, unless/until a member addresses their romantic partner or partners using a specific term.

Use a Universal Design model when shaping norms and rules of the group

- At the start of your workshop or institute, explain that you want the environment to be as accessible as possible and encourage participants to let you know if there is anything you or the group can do to facilitate their access or comfort
- Be aware of factors such as physical access or other ability issues. This may include, but not be limited to, being aware of the location of the nearest bathroom and elevators

- Health and medical issues may trump attendance or punctuality. It can be helpful to be flexible and to avoid pathologizing
- Be aware that not all group members have English as their primary language and some members may have a hearing impairment
- Be ready to ask members to slow down if talking too quickly, to articulate as clearly as possible, and to repeat themselves if necessary so all members can understand the group discussion

Communicating with Members who have Low Vision

- Speak to the individual when you approach them
- State clearly who you are – speak in a normal tone of voice, being careful not talk louder or slower than you normally would
- When conversing in a group, remember to identify yourself and the person to whom you are speaking. It will also help to ask group members to do the same
- Tell the individual when you are leaving their side or the room
- Offer assistance but do not insist on helping
- If you are offering a seat, ask the individual for permission to place their hand on the back or arm of the chair so that the person can locate the seat

Communicating with Members who are Hard of Hearing

- Ask the person if they are able to hear you and ask about the best way to communicate
- Look directly at the individual, face the light, speak clearly, in a normal tone of voice, and keep your hands away from your face
- Rephrase rather than repeat statements
- Short sentences tend to be understood better
- If the person did not understand you, then try using different words to express your ideas
- If there is an interpreter present, speak directly to the member and not the interpreter

Communicating with Members with Mobility Disabilities

- If possible, put yourself at the wheelchair user's eye level, or take a few steps backward so the other person does not have to "look up" at you
- Do not lean on a wheelchair or any other assistive device
- Do not assume the individual wants to be pushed; ask first and respect their response
- Offer assistance if the individual appears to be having difficulty opening a door but wait for the response and respect their answer

Communicating with Members with Speech Disabilities

- If you do not understand something the individual says, do not pretend that you do; ask the individual to repeat what they said and then repeat it back to confirm your understanding
- Be patient. Take as much time as necessary
- Never assume a person has a cognitive or intellectual disability when they have difficulty with speech
- Do not speak for the individual or attempt to finish their sentences
- If you are having difficulty understanding the individual, consider writing as an alternative means of communicating, but first ask

Best Practices For Facilitating Difficult Dialogues

In Sue, Lin, Torino, Capodilupo, & Rivera's (2009, p. 188) important article, they identified the following best practices for facilitating difficult dialogues that can assist us all in our group work:

- Support members who take risks to share their experiences of oppression and marginalization
- Validate the experiences of People of Color (PoC)
- Leaders of Dialogues on Race need to assess their own comfort level and where they may feel triggered in these dialogues
- Discussions regarding race are necessary
- White-identified Leaders and Members need to be willing to accept a different racial reality from People of Color
- Using a direct approach in managing and discussing racial dialogues is helpful

Acknowledgments

These guidelines were developed by the AGPA Diversity, Equity and Inclusion Task Force chaired by Sophia Aguirre. The mission of this Task Force is to promote the values of diversity, equity and inclusion throughout the organization in the areas of leadership, training, policy, research, and practice.

Diversity, Equity & Inclusion Task Force Members: M. Sophia Aguirre, PhD, CGP (Chair), Eri Bentley, PhD, CGP, Li Brookens, LCSW, Karen Cone-Uemura, PhD, CGP, Wendy Freedman, PhD, CGP, Paul Gitterman, LICSW, MSC, CGP, Craig Haen, PhD, RDT, LCAT, CGP, FAGPA, Phillip Horner, LCSW, CGP, Michele Ribeiro, EdD, CGP, FAGPA, and Ann Steiner, PhD, MFT, CGP, FAGPA.

References

Adams, M., Blumenfeld, W. J., et al. (eds). (2000). *Readings for diversity and social justice: An anthology on racism, antisemitism, sexism, heterosexism, ableism, and classism*. New York, NY: Routledge.

American Group Psychotherapy Association. (2019). Guidelines for Creating Affirming Group Experiences at AGPA Connect and Beyond, compiled by Diversity, Equity, and Inclusion Task Force. New York, NY: AGPA.

American Psychological Association. (2017). Multicultural Guidelines: An Ecological Approach to Context, Identity, and Intersectionality. Retrieved from: http://www.apa.org/about/policy/multicultral-guidelines.pdf.

Andersen, M. L., & Collins, P. H. (2007). Why race, class, and gender still matter. In M. L. Andersen, & P. H. Collins (eds.). *Race, class, and gender: An anthology* (1–16). Belmont, CA: Wadsworth.

Awad, G. H., Kia-Keating, M., & Amer, M. M. (2019). A model of cumulative racial-ethnic trauma among Americans of Middle Eastern and North African (MENA) descent. *American Psychologist*, 74(1), 76–87.

Bateman, A., & Fonagy, P. (2006). *Mentalization-based treatment for personality disorder: A practical guide*. Oxford: Oxford University Press.

Bonilla-Silva, E. (2012). The invisible weight of Whiteness: The racial grammar of everyday life of in contemporary America. *Ethnic and Racial Studies*, 35, 173–194.

Chavez-Duenas, N. Y., Adames, H. Y., Perez-Chavez, J. G., & Salas, S. P. (2019). Healing ethno-racial trauma in Latinx immigrant communities: Cultivating hope, resistance, and action. *American Psychologist*, 74(1), 49–62.

Collins, P. H. (1990). *Black feminist thought: Knowledge, consciousness, and the politics of empowerment*. Boston, MA: Unwin Hyman.

Comas-Diaz, L. (2007). Ethnopolitical psychology: Healing and transformation. In E. Aldarondo (ed.). *Advancing social justice through clinical practice* (91–118). Mahwah, NJ: Lawrence Erlbaum.

Cone-Uemura, K., & Bentley, E. S. (2018). Multicultural/diversity issues in groups. In M. D. Ribeiro, J. M. Gross, & M. M. Turner (eds). *The college counselor's guide to group psychotherapy* (21–35). New York: Routledge.

Crenshaw, K. (1989). Demarginalizing the intersection of race and sex: A Black feminist critique of antidiscrimination doctrine, feminist theory and antiracist politics, *University of Chicago Legal Forum*, 139–168. Article 8. Retrieved from: https://chicagounbound.uchicago.edu/uclf/vol1989/iss1/8.

Crenshaw, K. (2015). Why intersectionality can't wait. *The Washington Post*, September 24. Retrieved from: https://www.washingtonpost.com/news/in-theory/wp/2015/09/24/why-intersectionality-cant-wait/?noredirect=on&utm_term=.95c6ae431844. Accessed July 28, 2019.

Descilo, T., Vedamurtachar, A., Gerbarg, P. L., et al. (2010). Effects of a yoga breath intervention alone and in combination with an exposure therapy for post-traumatic stress disorder and depression in survivors of the 2004 South-East Asian tsunami. *Acta Psychiatrica Scandinavica*, 121(4), 289–300.

DiAngelo, R. (2011). White fragility. *The International Journal of White Pedagogy*, 3 (3), 54–70.

Ganote, C., Cheung, F., & Souza, T. (2015). Don't remain silent!: Strategies for supporting yourself and your colleagues via microresistances and ally development. In P. Roy, A. Harrell, J. Milano, & L. Bernhagen (eds). *POD Diversity*

Committee White Paper at the 40th Annual POD Conference (3–4). San Francisco, CA.

Hartmann, W. E., Wendt, D. C., Burrage, R. L., Pomerville, A., & Gone, J. P. (2019). American Indian historical trauma: Anticolonial prescriptions for healing, resilience, and survivance. *American Psychologist*, 74(1), 6–19.

Helms, J. (1990). *Black and White racial identity: Theory, research & practice*. New York, NY: Greenwood.

Hook, J. N., Davis, D. E., Owen, J., Worthington Jr, E. L., & Utsey, S. O. (2013). Cultural humility: Measuring openness to culturally diverse clients. *Journal of Counseling Psychology*, 60(3), 353–366.

Kaklauskas, F., & Nettles, R. (2019). Towards multicultural and diversity proficiency as a group psychotherapist. In F. J. Kaklauskas, & L. R. Greene (eds). *Core principles of group psychotherapy: A theory-, practice-, and research-based training manual* (25–45). New York, NY: Routledge.

Liu, W. M., Liu, R. Z., Garrison, Y. L., Kim, J. Y. C., Chan, L., Ho, Y. C. S., & Yeung, C. W. (2019). Racial trauma, microaggressions, and becoming racially innocuous: The role of acculturation and White supremacist ideology. *American Psychologist*, 74(1), 143–155.

Marmarosh, C. L., Markin, R. D., & Spiegel, E. B. (2013). *Attachment in group psychotherapy*. Washington, DC: American Psychological Association.

McRae, M. (1994). Interracial group dynamics: A new perspective. *The Journal for Specialists in Group Work*, 19(3), 168–174, doi:10.1080/0193392940814361.

Mock, M. R. (2008). Visioning social justice: Narrative of diversity, social location, and personal compassion. In M. McGoldrick, & K. V. Hardy (eds). *Revisioning family therapy* (425–441). New York, NY: Guilford.

Nagata, D. K., Kim, J. H. J., & Wu, K. (2019). The Japanese American wartime incarceration: Examining the scope of racial trauma. *American Psychologist*, 74(1), 36–48.

Owen, J., Drinane, J. M., Tao, K., Adelson, J., Hook, J., Davis, D., et al. (2017). Racial-ethnic disparities in client unilateral termination. The role of therapists' cultural comfort. *Psychological Research*, 27, 102–111, doi:10.1080/10503307.2015.1078517.

Owen, J., Drianne, J. M., Tao, K. W., DasGupta, D. R., Zhang, Y. S. D., & Adelson, J. (2018). An experimental test of microaggression detection in psychotherapy: Therapist multicultural orientation. *Journal of Professional Psychology: Research and Practice*, 49(1), 9–21, doi:10.1037/pro0000152.

Petty John, M. E., Tseng, C., & Blow, A. J. (2019). Therapeutic utility of discussing therapist/client intersectionality in treatment: When and how? *Family Process*, doi:10.1111/famp.12471.

Ribeiro, M. R., & Turner, M. M. (2018). Racial and social justice implications on the practice of group psychotherapy. In M. D. Ribeiro, J. M. Gross, & M. M. Turner (eds). *The college counselor's guide to group psychotherapy* (36–56). New York, NY: Routledge.

Schneider, F. W., Gruman, J. A., & Coutts, L. M. (eds) (2016). *Applied social psychology: Understanding and addressing social and practical problems*. Thousand Oaks, CA: Sage Publications.

Shin, R. Q. (2014). The application of critical consciousness and intersectionality as tools for decolonizing racial/ethnic identity development models in the fields of counseling and psychology. In R. D. Goodman, & P. C. Gorski (eds).

Decolonizing "multicultural" counseling through social justice (11–22). New York, NY: Springer.

Sue, D. W., Alsaidi, S., Awad, M. N., Glaeser, E., & Calle, C. Z. (2019). Disarming racial microaggressions: Microintervention strategies for targets, White allies, and bystanders. *American Psychologist*, 74(1), 128–142.

Sue, D. W., Lin, A. I., Torino, G. C., Capodilupo, C. M., & Rivera, D. P. (2009). Racial microaggresions and difficult dialogues on race in the classroom. *American Psychologist*, 15(2), 183–190.

Tajfel, H. (1978). Social categorization, social identity, and social comparison. In H. Tajfel (ed.). *Differentiation between social groups: Studies in the social psychology of intergroup relations* (61–76). London: Academic Press.

Telles, S., Naveen, K. V., & Dash, M. (2007). Yoga reduces symptoms of distress in tsunami survivors in the Andaman Islands. *Evidence-Based Complementary and Alternative Medicine*, 4(4), 503–509.

Tervalon, M., & Murray-Garcia, J. (1998). Cultural humility versus cultural competence: A critical distinction in defining physician training outcomes in multicultural education. *Journal of health care for the poor and underserved*, 9(2), 117–125.

Van Dick, R. (2001). Identification in organizational contexts: Linking theory and research from social and organizational psychology. *International Journal of Management Reviews*, 3, 265–283.

Yalom, I. D., & Leszcz, M. (2005). *The theory and practice of group psychotherapy.* New York, NY: Basic Books.

2 The Shadows of Liberty

Compassion Practice as a Shared Responsibility

Gaea Logan

> Give me your tired, your poor,
> Your huddled masses yearning to breathe free.
> The wretched refuse of your teeming shore.
> Send these, the homeless, tempest-tost to me.
> I lift my lamp beside the golden door.
>
> The Statue of Liberty, 1886

In 1886, President Grover Cleveland dedicated the Statue of Liberty, a gift from France, overseeing its installation in New York Harbor. The gift, "Liberty Enlightening the World," was inspired by Édouard René de Laboulaye, a French consultant to the U.S. Constitution. Liberty symbolized democracy and the abolition of slavery in the aftermath of the Civil War. She lifts her torch high, illuminating a pathway to freedom; broken shackles at her feet. She offers safe harbor to the tempest-tossed. She is the mother icon of the American experiment. Her call to action is compassion.

Yet, like all of us, Liberty has her shadow. Discrepancies remain between Liberty's romantic identity as inclusive versus the reality of history. Liberty is blind to our oppressive violence: the genocide of Indigenous peoples, 250 years of Black slavery, the abject privileging of White males. Hundreds of years of culturally condoned hate crimes and the annihilating impact of institutionalized racism towards Black Americans did not end with the Civil War or Liberty's arrival. Her presence did not convey women's right to vote. Yet, for generations of immigrants, Liberty has stood for the "dream of refuge"; the dream that still holds a promise of safety from persecution and poverty; the possibility of belonging; the hope for a better future. We are a "nation of immigrants." Many of us carry family stories of being "tempest tossed," seeking refuge and holding hope for freedom.

Myth, Migration, and Tribalism

Migration is central to evolutionary biology. Over millions of years, we evolved larger brains to navigate the complex and diverse environments we encountered, imagining and re-imagining ourselves in possible futures beyond each horizon. We developed the capacity to self-reference and evolved complex representational systems and language. We became storytellers and myth-makers, integrating left and right brain hemispheric functioning. Our oral traditions, encoded in migration myths, identified our origins and consolidated our cultural identities. Diasporas of human movement have always captured our imagination. Joseph Campbell, American mythologist, referred to the hero's journey as a representation of the arduous psychological, physical, and spiritual aspects of human movement (Campbell, 1949).

Rooted in our evolutionary biology is the basic need for belonging, on par with food, water, and shelter (de Waal, 2013). From infancy, we are hardwired to attach. Secure attachment enables embodied belonging which in turn regulates and calms the limbic system. Neuro-cognitive processes associated with self-identity are connected to belongingness, a kind of "in group love" that evokes empathy, altruism, and pro-social behavior (Mathur, Harada, Lipke, & Chiao, 2010). We exhibit an empathy bias and ease towards "our own people." This identification and felt sense of belonging extend to other group affiliations beyond family, kinship, and race, and can be transferred to identities that include political parties, religious communities, national identities, and even sports teams. Embodied belonging, so essential to the stabilization of the nervous system, is activated by these self-identities. Deep within the default mode network of our brains, racial identity connects to self-identity, harnessing different neuro-cognitive processes to understand others within and outside of racial in-groups. From our earliest traces of memory, we have been organized around implicit "tribal recognition." We "other" the out-group, the stranger. We war against them. We steal their land, their water. We rape their women and steal their children. We desecrate the bodies of our enemies. We vow reprisal. We are both "us" and "them."

Primate research suggests that groups less identified with hierarchical structure are more able to show altruism towards those outside their in-group (Mathur, Harada, & Chiao, 2012). Many of our wisdom traditions invite us to go beyond tribalism and hierarchy. Siddhartha Gautama, once a privileged young prince, disavowed his identification with caste hierarchy through an awakening to the shared suffering inherent in all human life. As the awakened Buddha, he preached compassion towards the out group – the untouchables, the Dalit caste of India. There was no difference between the Dalit and the Brahmin. A biblical story depicts a traveler on the road to Jerusalem attacked, beaten, and left to die. A priest and a Levite walked past, avoiding contact. Another traveler found him, bound his wounds, brought him to shelter and paid his expenses. The man was a Samaritan, a hated out-group tribe. His capacity to offer compassionate care for someone outside of his tribe, while those within the tribe did not act, represents an important teaching; one that seems to be losing ground in today's climate.

To Other or Not to Other – That is the Question

Othering is a word derived from the Old English ôther. It emphasizes difference rather than similarity. It assigns subordinate social status. The othered are placed at the margins of society where social norms, protections, rights, decency, and civility need not apply. Muslims can be banned. Jews can be exterminated. Women can be sexually assaulted. Black men can be stopped, arrested, and murdered. Brown migrant children can be separated from their parents and placed in cages for indefinite periods of time without a clear legal pathway for reunification regardless of the long-term psychological harm caused.

Rooted in colonialism, othering defines who has or "should have" power over resources and who has the right to remain in power and in control of resources. It is based on the conscious or unconscious assumption that a certain identified group poses a threat to the favored or dominant group (Zur, 1991). Electronic media has a unique power to tribalize by transmitting fear and consensus paranoia. The fear reinforces the need for the safety of the tribe which quickly differentiates enemy from ally (McLuhan & Moos, 2014; Zur, 1991). By trading in stereotypes and enemy images (Rosenberg, 2015) the narrative shifts to the management of "enemies" through the justification of discrimination, punishment, and/or violence.

The practice of othering injures. It creates deep psychological wounding to one's social identity and leaves profound feelings of invisibility. These injuries are cumulative and can extend multi-generationally. To be othered is to be assaulted. It registers as a threat to the nervous system – individually, relationally, and collectively.

There is a growing political divide between globalism and nationalism (Harari, 2017). We are witnessing a time of increasing ethno-nationalism and anti-immigration sentiment in Europe and the U.S. We see a significant shift to the right amidst economic instability coinciding with the largest refugee crisis in human history. An unprecedented 70.8 million people have been forced from their homes (UNHCR, 2019). Collapsing economies, armed conflict, ethnic persecution, drought, food insecurity, and disaster related to climate change create powerful movement across and within national boundaries.

According to the Anti-Defamation League (2019) we are witnessing the internationalization of the White supremacist movement in the U.S. Racist hate is linked to surging violence in the United States, Europe, and beyond. The ADL reports a dramatic increase in the distribution of White supremacist propaganda and a significant increase on the number of rallies and demonstrations by White supremacy groups worldwide. The Center for Strategic and International Studies (2018) shows that terrorist attacks by far-right groups quadrupled in the U.S. between 2016 and 2017. Far-right attacks in Europe have risen 43 percent over the same period. We have seen a 60 percent rise in anti-Semitic incidents. In 2018, a White man was charged with killing 11 worshipers at a synagogue in Pittsburgh. In his social media posts, he accused a Jewish organization that helps resettle migrants of bringing "invaders" to "kill our people."

Othering is at the center of both contemporary and historic socio-cultural trauma. How can we work most skillfully as it emerges in the clinical setting?

First, Do No Harm

To work skillfully with the wounds of othering requires the willingness to be reflective, courageous, and uncomfortable. Training in the areas of diversity, implicit bias, social justice, institutionalized racism, and multi-culturalism are necessary and readily available in conference settings and online continuing education offerings. We must remember the Hippo-cratic oath, "First, do no harm."

Rooted in the neurobiological and social unconscious (Doran, 2017), implicit bias exists and is conveyed linguistically, symbolically, and non-verbally in groups. No one is exempt. As we track increased levels of sociocultural trauma at the macro level, we see its emergence at the micro level, in the treatment room. Therapist and patient alike are impacted by the current heightened social climate. The risk of re-traumatization is always present.

How do we create an atmosphere of safety and inclusivity? How do we pause, reflect, and continue to breathe when critical moments emerge in our clinical work? Can we cultivate humility about our capacity to unconsciously other in subtle and glaring ways? Are we brave enough to "out" ourselves? Can we be non-defensive, secure enough to stand in the spaces (Bromberg, 1996)? Can we be open to the lived experience of the other without dominating the space with privilege? New skills, both per-sonal and clinical, based in cultural humility and compassion, can be learned. But it is through staying curious and welcoming discomfort that we create healthy group dynamics in which change is possible.

Therapeutic Action in the Treatment Room

A recent panel discussion at a professional training included three psy-chologists addressing sociocultural trauma in group psychotherapy. All panelists were White, English-speaking, and worked in private practice. This, in and of itself, could be perceived to be problematic from the outset. Audience members were invited to join a demonstration group led by Dr T, one of the psychologists co-leading the training. The eight volunteers introduced themselves and were asked to explore thoughts, feelings, and associations.

Rose, a single parent, Woman of Color from an immigrant background, began to speak about the resurgence of the swastika symbol in her community and in the media. It signaled evidence to her of increasing White nationalism. She works exclusively with Clients of Color from minority and immigrant backgrounds. She reported, "If anyone came to my office displaying the swastika like on a tee shirt or tattoo, I would have to turn them away. I would not feel safe."

Another member of the group, John, a divorced White male of Anglo background, responded differently. He focused on how, as a clinician, he might engage with curiosity.

He questioned, "Really? You would turn them away? I would ask about the swastika. If the client returned and was not displaying the symbol, I would ask, 'why not?'"

Rose wondered if John's privilege, which could construct a very different social identity and background, might provide him with more of a sense of safety in the world. Rose perceived the Nazi symbol as an active threat and wanted to understand John's ability to have a different response.

Rose asked, "Do you think your ability to imagine working with a Nazi comes from a sense of privilege?"

John shot back in a dismissive and angry tone, "You are just angry!"

Rose startled then replied quietly, "No ... I am just curious."

John, in an accusatory tone, replied, "I'm sure you WOULD think that."

Rose lowered her head and looked away. She had initially located fear outside the room; now she experienced it in the room. John's response was immediate and aggressive. His reactivity exposed a surprising fragility. Rose felt dismissed and othered. A critical moment of meeting had occurred between them.

Rose's question had triggered John. He admitted that his reaction was uncharacteristic, his usual demeanor more "measured." Yet, in the "unmeasured" moment that occurred, it was difficult to understand his communication; whether intended or unintended, conscious or unconscious. Several observers perceived John's comments as aggressive and demeaning microaggressions unconsciously reinforcing the stereotype of the angry minority woman. Some observers perceived Rose's question as aggressive.

Within the first few minutes of the group, an enactment had occurred reflecting the larger systemic dynamic. The clinical challenge for the group leader would be to manage the rapid escalation, unpack the underlying assumptions between group members, name the powerful emotions evoked, and facilitate a safe enough environment for the group to move forward.

Dr T.'s credentials suggested she could navigate the storm. The tension was palpable. When the brain's emergency circuitry gets activated, the instinctive reaction of fight, flight, or freeze precedes cognition or emotion. John's immediate response was to manage his physiological arousal through the fight instinct. His words were fighting words. In contrast, Rose had shut down, withdrawing into a freeze response. Dr T. became increasingly distressed. Ill at ease, several group members tried to divert attention away from Rose and John, while others acted like bystanders at a train wreck, in shock. The group was not prepared to metabolize the powerful interaction between Rose and John. The image of the swastika was in command of the group unconscious.

Dr T. had roughly 50 minutes to unravel the question of privilege; explore reactions to the swastika symbol; support the vulnerability of each group member; and create a safe enough container to engage in courageous conversations in real time. However, the heat of the conflict had de-skilled Dr T., rendering her unable to effectively intervene.

At the close, she became more engaged, displaying warmth towards Rose yet seemed anxious and apologetic. Rose left the group feeling stereotyped, alone, and re-traumatized.

The dynamics of racism, implicit bias, and the impact of the therapist's unconscious relationship to their own power and privilege are destructive to group dynamics and the therapeutic alliance. Even those who identify as politically liberal and are deeply empathic by nature are not necessarily equipped in today's climate. Most social justice trainers do not have group psychotherapy skills. Psychotherapists who have not undergone formalized inquiry into the questions of othering may, in fact, be working outside of their scope of practice. Psychotherapists married to theoretical orientations or cultural identities are easily de-skilled by the power of emerging material. Group members, like John, who become defensive if given feedback or questioned about privilege, are not helped by group leaders who have not examined their own power and privilege.

None of us are exempt from blind spots. Empathic failure is inevitable in the work of psychotherapy, but what happens *next*, is what's crucial to the healing process. We must be willing to be uncomfortable if we are to step into this territory and also know that we will make mistakes. When systemic dynamics are enacted in group, we must hold in mind the risk of re-traumatization for patients who have already been wounded and made to feel invisible by othering. The symbols, thoughts, feelings, and interactions that emerge require an active therapeutic stance. The urgent need in our larger society for leadership to call out degradation, oppression, and the violation of basic human rights is reflected in the treatment room. In today's climate of rising nationalism and resurgent racism, the skillful group psychotherapist must listen for parallel processes. The group leader, or conductor, as is referred to in European group psychotherapy communities, works to create a holding environment that enables each group member to find their voices and to risk uncomfortable exploration. If we can rewind, repair, and adopt a reflective bi-directional learning stance, healing is possible.

Rose expressed fear about the swastika, a potent symbol of annihilation, White nationalism, and the silencing of opposition. John seemed cavalier, in denial, or insensitive to the dangers associated with the symbol. Rose raised the question of privilege, a question that belongs in any group, and is all the more relevant for a group tasked to explore issues of socio-cultural trauma. Yet, in this example the questioner was maligned and stereotyped for asking the question. No intervention occurred. Dr T. became paralyzed, not unlike many good Germans during the Second World War. Silence on the part of group members reinforced complicit consent.

Elie Wiesel, in his Nobel Prize acceptance speech, reminds us:

> The world did know and remained silent. And that is why I swore never to be silent whenever and wherever human beings endure suffering and humiliation ... Sometimes we must interfere ... Wherever men or women are persecuted because of their race, religion, or political views, that place must – at that moment – become the center of the universe.
>
> (Wiesel, 1986)

Somatic Anchors – *Putting our Oxygen Masks on First*

In 1890 William James advocated that the greatest task in education is to make our nervous system our ally and not our enemy. Having an understanding of the neurobiology of trauma and using practices that help strengthen self-regulation help the psychotherapist tolerate intense affect and dysregulation. The therapist must be able to reliably re-regulate in order to support group members to return to a more reflective rather than reactive stance. When the group therapist can put their oxygen mask on first, it is possible to formulate more attuned interventions which strengthen the driving forces rather than restrain forces of the group.

First the therapist checks her arousal level on a scale from 1–10. Anything over a 3 would warrant the use of calming skills. She lengthens her exhale, breathing out tension, breathing in self-compassion. She might take a moment to feel her feet firmly planted on the ground, or her sitz bones in the seat. By using somatic anchors like the breath, feet, and seat, she uses her sensory experience to stabilize arousal and attention. She is in charge of her own psychological system. From there she can explore what is happening in the group.

Example 1 – Somatic Anchors – Group Intervention

THERAPIST: "Since the interaction between Rose and John, the group seems to have shut down. What sensations do we notice in our bodies? What do we notice with the breath?"

Example 2 – Somatic Anchors – Interpersonal Intervention

THERAPIST: "Rose and John, you both started out feeling safe to explore, but then something happened. What do you notice in your bodies right now? Do you have words for the sensations?"

Example 3 – Somatic Anchors – Intra-psychic Intervention

THERAPIST: "Rose, after John's remarks you seemed to shut down. You mentioned not feeling safe in your community. I wonder if you feel safe here? When we don't feel safe, we often stop breathing. I wonder if you notice anything about your breathing right now ..."

Being able to describe moment-to-moment sensory experience when thoughts or affects are difficult to name is calming or down-regulation. The psychotherapist is tasked to put their oxygen mask on first.

The Language of Rewind: *Strengthening the Reflective Function*

Mentalization is a technique known by different names across a variety of therapeutic orientations. It can be thought of as *meta-communication*. It focuses on strengthening the reflective function by utilizing our imaginal capacity to understand the mental states that underlie behavior in ourselves and others (Bateman & Fonagy, 2006). Mentalization is a way of thinking about thinking. Under the influence of intense affect dysregulation, the capacity to mentalize is greatly diminished. John rapidly escalated, losing his capacity for self-regulation, and in turn self-reflection. When people are othering, no mentalization is going on. Rose's escalation was internal and presented as withdrawal. It is likely that she, too, was unable to mentalize her experience. In the group process, there seemed to be "no going back." Rewinding is essential for mentalization.

Example 1 – Rewind – Intrapsychic Intervention

THERAPIST: "John, let's rewind ... You say you are usually more measured. Yet, it seems some strong feelings arose in the conflict with Rose. I'm wondering if you have some feelings or thoughts you haven't been able to put into words."

Example 2 – Rewind – Intrapsychic Intervention

THERAPIST: "Rose, let's rewind. You were the first to engage and then you shut down. I imagine you feel less safe now. What happened? Can you help us understand by putting your experience in words?"

The group was unable to go back and make sense of the intensity. The group dissociated, avoiding the discomfort of the affect, without confidence that the interactions could be metabolized. Rewinding could help John learn more about his uncharacteristic response and help Rose to re-engage. Most importantly, both Rose and John could have felt validated, not left alone with intense feelings, nor at risk of feeling othered.

Tapping the Group Mind – *Group-as-a-Whole Interventions*

When the therapist offers a *meta-communication*, they engage the reflective capacity of the group mind. Meta-communication can help group members and the group leader unhook from a specific interpersonal conflict and redirect towards the developmental task of the group.

Example 1 – A Developmental Lens – Group Mind

THERAPIST: "We are just beginning to know one another, our similarities and our differences. We can easily misunderstand one another and become reactive. I'm wondering if that what is happening here."

Example 2 – Reflecting the Larger Sociocultural Trauma – Group Mind

THERAPIST: "Perhaps the group is struggling with the emergence of a larger systemic conflict. It is a challenge to explore our vulnerability around oppression, or to look at what we are spared or how we benefit from privilege. This conversation requires courage for each of us. We may not be ready, as a group, to go there. What thoughts and feelings are emerging?"

Taking the Heat – *Owning Responsibility, Absorbing the Blame*

In Tibetan Buddhist training there is a pragmatic fifteenth-century text known as the *Lojong*, or *Mind Training* (Jinpa, 2006). One of the more radical practices is the suggestion to "Drive all Blames into the One." It involves taking full responsibility for whatever occurs in the spirit of reflection without directing blame towards anyone else. In the early phases of group development, members are anxious around the issues of safety and belonging. In commenting on the image of the swastika and her own fears of safety, Rose may have been expressing concern over whether she could feel safe in the group. John dismissed fears around the swastika but demonstrated vulnerability in response to Rose's question. If the leader had turned towards the emerging conflict and drawn the "heat" to herself, she may have established a stronger sense of safety for group members. In demonstrating humility and ultimate responsibility for the culture of the group, she also helps prevent scapegoating.

Example 1 – Owning Responsibility: Group Intervention

THERAPIST: "I think I made a mistake by remaining quiet. I was not helpful to Rose, John, or the group. You needed more from me. You might feel unsafe, let down or angry. I am wondering if there are any thoughts or feelings towards me?"

Example 2 – Owning Responsibility: Interpersonal Intervention

THERAPIST: "Rose, I wonder if you worry that I may be unaware of how my power or privilege might impact the group."

When the leader owns that she may have something to do with the difficulty, can tolerate bringing out unexpressed negative transferences, and seeks to *repair*, a shared reflective space becomes possible. The group leader's decision to address or avoid creates the culture of the group. The leader's bold engagement around systemic enactment within the group is essential to the process.

Functional Subgrouping – *Naming Subgroups, Framing Group Conflict*

System Centered Therapy (Agazarian, 2018) explores ways of formulating group dynamics and intervention from a systems perspective. Group members must first join around their similarities before they can tackle differences, otherwise a group is vulnerable to stereotyping or making one member the "identified patient" for the group. To build "functional subgrouping" the group leader looks for the similarities of affect and/or sensation, enabling group members to join one another despite differences in the details of their narratives. This helps focus the group on its developmental task, to create a space of belonging, by first discovering similarity.

Example 1 – Naming the Subgroup

THERAPIST: "Perhaps both Rose and John feel 'othered' rather than understood. I wonder if anyone else fears they could be 'othered' for any reason in this group?"

The therapist might frame the group conflict:

Example 2 – Framing the Group Conflict

THERAPIST: "I wonder if some group members are struggling with wanting to push away (others or parts of ourselves) while others fear being pushed away, or othered. Who is in the subgroup that fears being pushed away? What do you notice? Who wants to push away? What do you notice?"

Example 3 – Returning to the Group as a Whole

After exploring functional subgrouping, the therapist can skillfully bring the group back to a group-as-a-whole question.

Therapist: "How can we create a group in which differences can be celebrated and unexpected similarities experienced?"

Turning Towards – *Prompting Engagement*

When members can stay turned towards each other in conflict and states of high arousal, productive work can occur. When group members feel held by the leader, they can more readily turn towards and hold each other.

But in a new group struggling with an unformulated dynamic, member-to-member interaction can easily shut down. Skillful intervention requires the therapist to "turn towards," to track nonverbal cues of fight/flight/freeze and to prompt member-to-member engagement. One group member looks connected but remains silent, while another member seems frozen, a bystander to the incident. The therapist turns towards the silent members to prompt interaction and expression:

Example 1 – Naming the Silence

THERAPIST: "Marty, I notice you have been quiet. Perhaps you are wondering how to bring your voice in. What are you feeling about where the group is right now?"

Example 2 – Thawing the Freeze

THERAPIST: "Fred, you look like you want to say something to John. I'm wondering if you feel held back or frozen. Does anyone else feel shut down?"

Prompting member-to-member interaction intervenes on the disconnection that can occur when members feel overwhelmed, unsafe, or powerless to act. Freeze responses occur from a heightened state of activation. Member-to-member interaction helps dismantle the hierarchical structure of leader–member interaction.

Compassion Practice as a Shared Responsibility

The Center for Compassion and Altruism Education and Research (CCARE) at Stanford Medical School brings together scholars, clinicians, researchers, and students to develop curricula and conduct neuroscience research on the effects of compassion on brain and behavior.

Tania Singer's research at the Max Plank Institute (Singer & Klimeck, 2014) suggests that compassion rather than empathy activates neural circuitry that enables us to remain more resilient in working with trauma. Through fMRI studies of the activation of empathy versus compassion, the data suggests that empathy, a right brain activation process, results in withdrawal and burnout for clinicians and caregivers working with trauma. However, the left brain activation of daily compassion seems to strengthen protective factors against burnout by the increase in positive affects, self-compassion, the capacity to remain pro-social, or turned towards. Compassion training also increases more accurate empathy.

The compassion practice used in the study begins with self-compassion and expands to increasingly challenging subjects. Derived from secularized Buddhist meditation, participants extend compassionate wishes towards the loved one, the stranger, the difficult other, the enemy, to wounded community and beyond, to all life.

Central to the structure of compassion practice, whether directed to a loved one or an enemy, is the internal recognition and repetition of these words:

> Just like me, you want to be free from suffering.
> Just like me, you want to live with greater ease in the challenges you face.
> Just like me, you want to come to know peace.
>
> (Jinpa, 2015)

By cultivating our muscle for compassion, we deepen our capacity for skillful therapeutic intervention. It strengthens the ability to engage in, rather than withdraw from, the courageous conversations needed to help heal the wounds of othering in the groups we lead. Compassion practice helps enable us to better mentalize our own states of mind and that of the "other." Increased self-compassion supports us in owning responsibility for negative group dynamics. The practice enables us to find the similarities in the differences, to find the *just like me* in the other, someone who wants to be free from suffering.

Conclusion

We began this chapter with the image of the Statue of Liberty, a symbol of American and European democratic ideals. Liberty is the mother icon of a so-called "nation of immigrants." The words etched in bronze at her feet reflect a stance of profound compassion yet when we take a deeper look, we see the shadow, implicit bias, evidenced in subtle and glaring ways, within each of us. As humanity faces the largest refugee crisis in human history, ethno-nationalism is on the rise, resulting in dramatic increases in hate crimes and anti-immigrant sentiment. Tribalism, deeply rooted in evolutionary biology, is central to implicit bias, the social unconscious, and the systemic institutionalization of othering and racism. In-group belongingness, crucial to survival, simultaneously sets the stage for diminished empathy and compassion towards the out-group, justifying and promoting dismissive and/or violent actions, resulting in multi-generational sociocultural trauma. These destructive systemic group dynamics, as part of the social unconscious, emerge as parallel processes in the treatment room, increasing the risk of re-traumatization. In order to be effective and do no harm, clinicians must learn new skills that reflect compassionate awareness of social justice, inequality, privilege, and implicit bias around race, gender, and class. The willingness to remain curious and to be uncomfortable is essential.

Compassion practice is a shared responsibility. Empathy is not enough. Skillful intervention requires a keen awareness of the larger social context, and a fierce commitment to active group engagement in our roles as either members or leaders. We have a shared responsibility to soften the grip of our unavoidable tribalism, to practice compassion beyond the in-group, and to embrace a larger "us." As His Holiness the Dalai Lama suggests, compassion is a necessity for human survival. If we follow the call to action, we circle back to Liberty, holding the lantern to illuminate a path and bring light to the darkness. And through self-compassion, we can begin to see the outlines of our own shadows.

References

Agazarian, Y. (2018). *Systems-centered theory and practice: The contributions of Yvonne Agazarian*. New York, NY: Routledge.

Anti-Defamation League. (2019). Hate beyond borders: The internationalization of White supremacy. Retrieved from: https://www.adl.org/resources/reports/hate-beyond-borders-the-internationalization-of- white-supremacy.

Bateman, A., & Fonagy, P. (2006). *Mentalization-based treatment for personality disorder: A practical guide*. Oxford: Oxford University Press.

Bromberg, P. M. (1996). Standing in the spaces: The multiplicity of self and the psychoanalytic relationship. *Contemporary Psychoanalysis*, 32(4), 509–535.

Campbell, J. (1949). *The hero with a thousand faces, Bollingen Series XVII*. New York, NY: Pantheon Books.

de Waal, F. (2013). *The Bonobo and the Atheist: In search of humanism among the primates* (1st ed.). New York, NY: W. W. Norton & Company.

Doran, Y. (2017). The Social Unconscious. *Group Analytic Society International.* https://groupanalyticsociety.co.uk/the-social-unconscious/.

Harari, N. (2017). Nationalism vs. globalism: the new political divide. *YouTube.* https://www.youtube.com/watch?v=szt7f5NmE9E.

Jinpa, T. (2015). *A fearless heart: How the courage to be compassionate can transform our lives.* New York, NY: Hudson Street Press.

Jinpa, T. (2006). *Mind training: The great collection: The institute of Tibetan classics.* Somerville, MA: Wisdom Publications.

Mathur, V. A., Harada, T., & Chiao, J. Y. (2012). Racial identification modulates default network activity for same and other races. *Human Brain Mapping*, 33, 1883–1893. https://www.ncbi.nlm.nih.gov/pubmed/21618667.

Mathur, V. A., Harada, T., Lipke, T., & Chiao, J. Y. (2010). Neural basis of extraordinary empathy and altruistic motivation. *NeuroImage*, 51, 1468–1475.

McLuhan, M., & Moos, M. (2014). *Media research: Technology, art and communication.* New York, NY: Routledge.

Rosenberg, M. (2015). Transforming enemy images. Retrieved from: https://www.nonviolentcommunication.com/freeresources/article_archive/enemy_images_m rosenberg.htm.

Singer, T., & Klimeck, O. (2014). Empathy and compassion. *Current Biology*, 24 (18), R875–878. http://dx.doi.org/10.1016/j.cub2014/06.054.

The Center for Strategic and International Studies. (2018). Retrieved from: https://www.csis.org/.

UNHCR. (2019). Figures at a glance. Retrieved from: https://www.unhcr.org/fig ures-at-a-glance.html.

Wiesel, E. (1986). Elie Wiesel – acceptance speech. *The Nobel Prize.* Retrieved from: https://www.nobelprize.org/prizes/peace/1986/wiesel/26054-elie-wiesel-a cceptance-speech-1986/.

Zur, O. (1991) The love of hating: The psychology of enmity. *History of European Ideas*, 13(4), 345–369.

Section II

Social Identities in Group Psychotherapy

3 Gender Identity in Group

Sydney M. LeFay

Introduction

While discussion of gender identity has recently been popularized in modern media, transgender and gender-nonconforming identities (see Table 3.1 for definitions) have been long overlooked and oppressed, both in psychotherapeutic settings and in the culture at large. The prevalence of trans* and gender-nonconforming adults is of some debate, with a variety of studies across the world finding rates of 1:11,900–1:45,000 individuals identifying as trans female, and 1:30,400–1:200,000 people identifying as trans male (Coleman et al., 2012). These numbers are often considered a minimum estimate rather than a genuine representation of the trans* demographic, as the majority of these studies drew from populations seeking care for gender dysphoria, and identities outside of strictly transmale or transfemale (such as genderqueer, nonbinary, agender, etc.) are frequently excluded entirely (Coleman et al., 2012). A 2009 study from the UK found that individuals identifying as trans* in health care settings has increased by 15 percent per year since those surveyed in 1998 (Reed, Rhodes, Schofield, & Wiley, 2009). This increase in individuals openly identifying as transgender or gender-nonconforming highlights the importance of educating professionals on gender-affirming practices, particularly those intersecting with the realm of mental health.

The historical lack of acknowledgment of trans* identities in therapeutic training, combined with ever-evolving contemporary language around gender, sets the stage for conscious and unconscious bias and relationship ruptures (Benson, 2013). Although the judicious use of language and conscious inclusion of a range of gender expression may appear to be a "minor" consideration on the surface, everyday erasure of transgender and gender-nonconforming identities contributes to cumulative psychological distress (Grant, Mottet, & Tanis, 2013; Nadal, Skolnik, & Wong, 2012). Unfortunately, rates of mental health diagnoses and suicide attempts/completions among trans* individuals remain high. The U.S. National Transgender Discrimination Survey found that of their sample of 6,436 trans-identifying individuals (including gender-nonconforming identities), 41 percent had

Table 3.1 Terminology

Terminology	
Gender Identity	An individual's internal sense of their gender identity
Gender Expression	External presentation of gender (clothing, behavior, voice, hair styling, etc.)
Sexual Orientation	Pattern of sexual/emotional/romantic attraction, occurring independent of gender identity
Cisgender	Individuals whose sex assigned at birth is congruent with their gender identity
Transgender	Individuals whose sex assigned at birth differs from their gender identity
Gender binary	Defining gender as confined to two gender identities, male and female
Trans*	Term inclusive of a variety of gender experiences outside of traditional binary gender definitions (agender, nonbinary, transwomen, transmen, genderqueer, genderfluid, etc.)
Nonbinary	Individuals whose gender identity is not confined to the binary (male/female) definition of gender
Genderqueer	Sometimes equated with nonbinary, similarly, describes individuals not exclusively within a binary gender identification
Genderfluid	Gender identity which may fluctuate between gender identities/expressions
Agender	Without gender or sometimes described as gender-neutral
Intersex	Individuals who are born with physiologic elements of both male and female reproductive anatomy

attempted suicide, compared to the rate of 1.6 percent in the general U.S. population (Grant, Mottet, & Tanis, 2013). In that same sample, 75 percent of respondents sought counseling regarding their gender identity, with an additional 14 percent who wished to seek counseling someday. Fifty percent had to "educate" their medical professionals about transgender care, with comments stating that some trans* individuals had been turned away by providers who felt they did not understand enough about trans* identities to be helpful. This perception of lack of knowledge on the part of mental health professionals is pervasive, and backed by research showing that a majority of mental health professionals have very limited formal training on issues of gender identity (Benson, 2013).

In group psychotherapy the group leader must contend with a variety of identities, life experiences, and personal transference issues. Although issues of gender may be more clearly acknowledged by individuals who self-identify as transgender or gender-nonconforming, all of the clients in a group setting have a gender identity unique to them, which may or may not share similarities with the leader. In this chapter we seek to provide a context for approaching the trans* client in group psychotherapy (noting that for the purposes of this chapter, "trans*" will refer to all individuals identifying outside of the *cis*-gender experience), while also exploring ways in which gender identity impacts human beings everywhere along the gender spectrum.

Gender Identity and Language

Of fundamental importance to the discussion of gender identity is the separation of gender identity from gender expression, sexual orientation, and anatomical sex. In practical terms, the separation of these concepts reminds us to remain vigilant in our presumptive use of language, as a person's outward appearance (gender expression) may or may not match their internal experience (gender identity), all of which is separate from their anatomical sex (reproductive organs at birth). Similarly, just as cis-gendered people may be heterosexual, homosexual, or some other sexual identity (such as bisexual, pansexual, or asexual), trans* individuals also exhibit a range of sexual attraction. The relative invisibility of many of these identities in a heavily heteronormative culture creates an environment rife with mis-identifications and empathic failures, particularly when group leaders themselves may lack the vocabulary to articulate these concepts (Benson, 2013; Sennott & Smith, 2011).

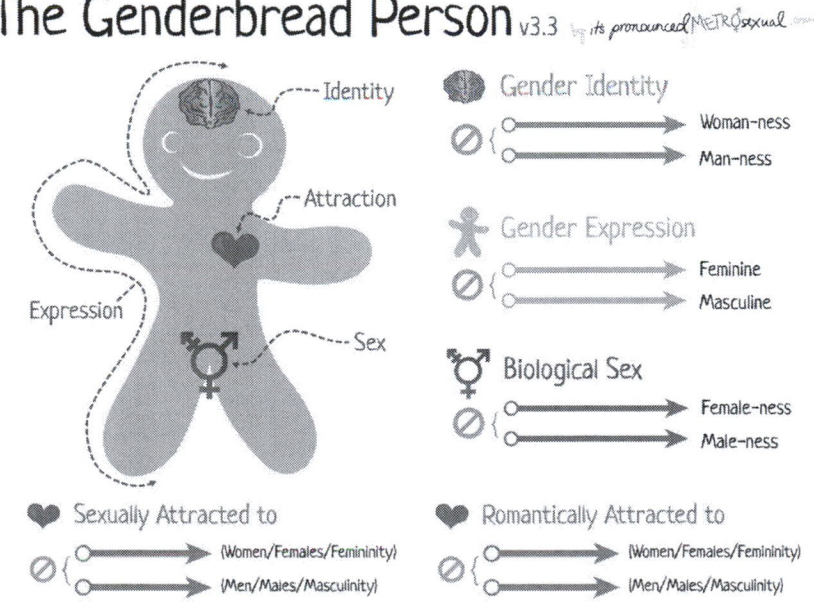

Figure 3.1 The Genderbread Person

> **Vignette 1: All the ways we assume**
>
> Jerry A is a 32-year-old African American client who presents for a pre-group screening. Jerry is called to the desk by the waiting room receptionist as "Mr A." Jerry has a goatee and wears jeans with a plain T-shirt. Notes in the chart use the pronouns he/him. Even though Jerry's gender expression would be presumed male, during the screening the interviewer asks Jerry about preferred name and appropriate pronouns. Jerry opens up and describes identifying with pronouns she/her, as she has never felt "right" as a man even though she was born with male anatomy. She sometimes experiments with more feminine clothing when traveling for work and feels much better with a feminine presentation. Jerry is anxious about making any changes, as her partner and young daughter are not aware of Jerry's female gender identity. She mentions in passing that she considers herself bisexual as she experiences attraction to both males and females, though she is currently in a committed monogamous relationship with a male.

In this example, Jerry's gender expression is masculine or male, while her gender identity is female. Her anatomical sex is male. Her sexual orientation is bisexual, which might not be apparent if one only asked about her current partner. In Jerry's case, it would be important to establish how she would like the leader to address her in the group setting.

Gender-related language is currently in a period of rapid evolution, such that some of the terminology in this text is likely to change in the coming years (Jacobson & Donatone, 2009). For example, while terms like "gender reassignment surgery," "gender identity disorder," "transsexual," and "hermaphrodite" are sometimes still used, many are viewed as antiquated or even offensive, replaced by revised contemporary language ("gender affirming surgery," "gender dysphoria," "transgender," and "intersex," respectively; see Table 3.1). The dynamic nature of gender definitions in society presents a challenge for group leaders working with a diverse range of clients, and may initially overwhelm leaders with limited experience working with the trans* demographic, creating fears that they may misuse pronouns or focus so much on gender-affirming language that they find themselves unable to be present in the moment with clients (Hund & Thomas, 2015; Sennott & Smith, 2011).

As with many content-related dilemmas, attention towards a client's underlying process and curiosity about their unique experience provides greater understanding in the moment than rote memorization of specific terms. Self-education is of course important, and leaders should make a point to educate themselves rather than place that burden on their clients; however, clients themselves offer the best explanations for what *they* mean when they describe their identity (Sennott & Smith, 2011). Assigning pronouns without asking, for example, can lead to an empathic rupture with a client who may feel deeply invisible or misunderstood. The solution to this dilemma need not be complex, and is merely the habit of asking for a person's name and pronouns regardless of presumed gender based on expression or prior documentation, and making efforts to use them appropriately. A variety of pronouns are currently in use, the most common being she/her/hers, he/him/his, and they/them/theirs, though other pronouns may be used particularly by nonbinary/genderqueer people (ze/hir/hirs, ze/zir/zirs, xe/xem/xyr). Even well-intentioned leaders may make mistakes in the use of pronouns, and politely self-amending them in the moment where possible is considered good practice. A leader should not belabor an error through displays of guilt, which may place the client in a position to feel they must "take care" of the leader (Sennott & Smith, 2011). Appropriate exchanges provide good role-modeling of relationship repairs both for the client and other members of the group.

Individual interventions to explore and honor a person's preferences is in many ways an exercise in basic therapeutic techniques; to that end, a study of helpful versus unhelpful therapeutic interactions for trans* individuals found fundamental therapeutic techniques including warmth, ability to listen, and appropriateness of interventions to be of greatest importance (Israel, Gorcheva, Burnes, & Walther, 2008). What may be less apparent, and potentially more challenging, are the ways everyday language and practice subtly enforces the gender binary and leads to trans* erasure. Forms with only two options for gender, gender-exclusive bathrooms, assumptive use of *ma'am/sir* or *Mr/Mrs*, phrases like *ladies and gentlemen* or *boys and girls*, all subtly exclude or may blatantly mis-identify trans* people. In the therapeutic setting it is important to make note of these issues and correct them where possible.

Unconscious Bias and Group Dynamics

Trans* bias or internalized transphobia may be present even in well-intentioned individuals and is most problematic when left unexamined. As group leaders we are faced with a host of transference and counter-transference dilemmas during each session, and those related to gender may be particularly sensitive. Our level of comfort with nonconformity intersects with our various cultural identities, just as it does with our clients. Socioeconomic status, race, family dynamics, and religion may all influence how a given person experiences gender-nonconformity in themselves and in others (American Psychological Association, 2015). Even cisgendered people have a gender identity unto themselves, regardless of whether they have had to confront issues with their identity on a conscious level. In this way, the question of identity for trans* individuals is not so different as the identity of anyone else; we all have ways that we conform or rebel against traditional gender roles (Sennott & Smith, 2011). That said, for many trans* people, struggles with that identity have been observable by others, and are often complicated by intensified anxiety, shame, and sometimes a history of trauma or hate crimes (Dickey & Loewy, 2010; Grant, Mottet, & Tanis, 2013). Physical violence and the threat of violence remain highly prevalent in the trans* community, with 19 percent of all trans* people experiencing a history of domestic violence, which is higher in Native American (45 percent), Asian (36 percent), Black (35 percent), and Latinx (35 percent) trans* communities (Grant, Mottet, & Tanis, 2013). Homelessness, loss of relationships, and involvements in the sex industry are all found at higher rates in the trans* demographic, often as a result of transphobia and discrimination (Grant, Mottet, & Tanis, 2013; Nadal et al., 2012). Cisgender leaders should remain aware of their own cisgender privilege, which manifests in a multitude of ways, including existence in a primarily binary culture which supports, affirms, and prioritizes individuals whose sex assigned at birth is congruent with their gender identity (Hund & Thomas, 2015). Importantly, guidelines are being developed by a variety of organizations on therapeutic competencies for working with trans* people, including the American Psychological Association Guidelines listed in Table 3.2 (2015).

Member-to-member trans* bias additionally presents a challenge, much like any situation in which one member (or subgroup) comes into conflict with another. The risk of the leader being perceived as "aligning" with one side over the other can create turmoil in the group; resolving such conflicts may be interpreted as taking a moral stance as opposed to a therapeutic one. Additionally, group leaders should carefully consider their own feelings about gender identity and transition, to work towards reducing any of their own trans* bias. Common misperceptions and non-affirming language which may come up in groups include persistent misgendering of trans* individuals, insinuations that transmen and transwomen are not "real" men and women, and use of language now clearly experienced as offensive (words such as "tranny," "she-man," and pejorative uses of "gay"). Challenging of a trans* individual's identity, including questions related to why they can't "just" be the sex they were assigned at birth, a heteronormative focus on the trans* individual "passing" as their intended gender expression, and asking intrusive questions about surgical and hormonal interventions when not explicitly brought up for discussion by the trans* person in question, all represent painful microaggressions frequently experienced by trans* people (Hund & Thomas, 2015; Nadal et al., 2012). Management of these microaggressions in group settings should aim to re-establish safety for all clients involved and provide some measure of a reparative experience. In situations where a repair is not possible, or when conflict has occurred which has inflicted (or poses a risk to inflict) significant psychological damage on a client,

Table 3.2 Guidelines on psychological care of transgender and gender non-conforming people

American Psychological Association Guidelines for Psychological Practice with Transgender and Gender Nonconforming (TGNC) People

1. Understand that gender is a nonbinary construct that allows for a range of gender identities and that a person's gender identity may not align with sex assigned at birth.

2. Understand that gender identity and sexual orientation are distinct but interrelated constructs.

3. Seek to understand how gender identity intersects with other cultural identities of TGNC people.

4. Be aware of how your attitude about and knowledge of gender identity and gender expression may affect the quality of care you provide to TGNC people and their families.

5. Recognize how stigma, prejudice, discrimination, and violence affect the health and well-being of TGNC people.

6. Recognize the influence of institutional barriers on the lives of TGNC people and assist in developing TGNC-affirmative environments.

7. Understand the need to promote social change that reduces the negative effects of stigma on the health and well-being of TGNC people.

8. Those working with gender-questioning and TGNC youth understand the different developmental needs of children and adolescents, and that not all youth will persist in a TGNC identity in adulthood.

9. Strive to understand both the particular challenges that TGNC elders experience and the resilience they develop.

10. Strive to understand how mental health concerns may or may not be related to TGNC person's gender identity and the psychological effects of minority stress.

11. Recognize that TGNC people are more likely to experience positive life outcomes when they receive social support or trans-affirmative care.

12. Strive to understand the effects that changes in gender identity and gender expression have on the romantic and sexual relationships of TGNC people.

13. Seek to understand how parenting and family formation among TGNC people take a variety of forms.

14. Recognize the potential benefits of an interdisciplinary approach when providing care to TGNC people and strive to work collaboratively with other providers.

15. Respect the welfare and rights of TGNC participants in research and strive to represent results accurately and avoid misuse or misrepresentation of the findings.

16. Seek to prepare trainees to work competently with TGNC people.

Source: American Psychological Association (2015).

consideration should be given to removing disruptive and unsafe individuals from the group setting. This is daunting, of course, as the goal of any group is to provide therapeutic support for all members of the group; however, in the case of minority microaggressions and discrimination, maintaining the aggressor's position of power perpetuates an already-discriminatory culture of bias against trans* people.

Creating Space

Creating space for trans* identities in group can begin as early as the pre-group screening, where history-taking should include gathering information about an individual's gender identity. As with any demographic, group leaders should be attentive to the composition of a group during the screening process, and work to create environments which are diverse enough to facilitate necessary conflict but at the same time cohesive enough for individuals to work together (Jacobson & Donatone, 2009). Inclusion of trans* individuals in groups with other queer identities may be helpful in creating safety and cohesion. In several studies, transmen and transwomen found it more beneficial to be in groups with similarly identified individuals, as a means to share experiences unique to them, noting that challenges shared by transwomen may be different than those experienced by transmen (Dickey & Loewy, 2010). While group needs may be different for individuals of various gender identifications, it is important to be inclusive where possible, as to not discriminate against certain identities. In smaller, less-diverse communities, this may require groups where members are selected who demonstrate flexibility in relating to people of gender minorities (for example, the inclusion of a nonbinary member in an otherwise cisgendered group). In group psychotherapy there may be gender-exclusive groups such as women's groups, where leaders need to have a systematic and clear way to address the needs of transwomen and femme clients who may not have been assigned female at birth. In these cases, trans* identity alone should not exclude a person from participation in groups, as this only perpetuates trans* discrimination. Rather, those challenges should be specifically discussed with the individual in question to assess their experiences with bias/discrimination and transphobia, and a determination made as to whether the group would represent a safe and affirming space for the trans* individual. Goals of therapy may also guide the decision to include certain identities in group; while some trans* people may seek group therapy specifically to process issues of identity, others may have broad needs amenable to inclusion in mixed-gender groups (Israel et al., 2008). Giving language and space for these issues early on opens up a dialogue in which it is safe for clients of all genders to bring those concerns up to the leader. Additionally, leaders who are prepared to address issues of gender identity prior to the first group session are poised to maintain a reliable therapeutic frame when these issues arise.

Although conscious inclusion and inquiry around issues of gender identity are helpful in making trans* identities more visible, it is again important to avoid assumptions about what it means to live as a trans* person. The trans* community is highly heterogeneous, comprising a range of individuals with intersecting identities and diverse experiences. As an example, a person who is both Latinx and trans* may have a very different experience of what it means to be masculine, feminine, or androgynous than a person who is trans* and White (American Psychological Association, 2015; Harper et al., 2009). Though the struggles and gender dysphoria that many trans* people experience should be respected, not all trans* people are currently experiencing conflict regarding their identity (Jacobson & Donatone, 2009). They may be at a stage of life and transition where they are comfortable with their gender identity and expression, or may never have experienced their nonconformity as significantly dysphoric. Some may not wish for the group to see them as a trans* person, while others may publicly announce their trans* identity. Trans* individuals may engage in varying levels of transition, from changing how they dress and behave, to hormone use and surgery. Many trans* people will utilize only some medical interventions for gender affirmation (e.g. using only hormones but not surgery, having "top" surgery but not "bottom" surgery, using hormones at some times and not others). If these details are medically or personally relevant to the client they may be worth exploring; however, these medical decisions are considered private in the way any medical condition would be addressed in group, and should only be discussed when useful to the client. The usefulness of involving a person's gender identity in therapy is worth noting, as some leaders may be tempted to implicate gender identity issues as a cause of certain symptoms before considering other contextual issues, which can lead to significant empathic failures between leader and member (Israel et al., 2008). Likewise, the leader must manage assumptions made by other group members who may also misattribute problems as being related to gender identity before considering other factors. In these cases, psychoeducation around the complexity of distress may be indicated (see Vignette 2).

Vignette 2: The gender red herring

Alex is a 27-year-old nonbinary nurse with a history of major depressive disorder who has attended an exploratory psychotherapy group for the past 12 weeks. Alex's sex assigned at birth was male; they use the pronouns they/them and have been open and comfortable describing their gender identity with the group from the first session on. Alex's gender expression fluctuates but most often comes across as androgynous. Alex is the only nonbinary member of a group otherwise comprising of three cisgender female and two cisgender male clients.

ALEX: (they/them) My partner Laura and I have been having a hard time lately. She's stressed with her new boss and I've switched to night shifts. I feel like we don't get to talk at all when we're together, we're so busy dealing with basic stuff like rent and buying groceries. She's been a big support for me and without that my depression has been getting worse, but I don't want her to worry about me. She has enough to worry about.

ANDREA: (she/her) Have you told her what you've been going through at all?

ALEX: Not really. I told her I'm stressed with the new schedule, and she says she gets it. I'm not sure she knows I've been getting down on myself. I feel like I'm not doing anybody much good, at work or at home. I'm just trying to get through the days.

DREW : (he/him) Are people treating you okay at work?

ALEX: Um ... yeah, I guess so. I don't really know the staff on nights yet.

DREW: I bet it's hard, you know, to meet new people. Alex shrugs, but does not reply.

LEADER : (she/her) What were you curious about, Drew?

DREW: I just ... I mean, it's probably hard when you have to tell people about your pronouns and all that. I wondered if it was making Alex feel more depressed, having to deal with it.

BRI : (she/her) That's a good point. I hadn't even thought about that.

ANDREA: I can't even imagine having to deal with that. Alex shrugs again and the group becomes silent.

LEADER: Alex, I noticed you became quiet after Drew asked about your work. What came up for you?

ALEX: I get the question, but it's not really the main issue.

LEADER: Can you say more about that?

ALEX: It can be hard to explain my gender to my coworkers, but I'm more worried about me and Laura. I deal with the pronoun thing every day, not that it's easy. The problems in my relationships are new.

LEADER: I'm hearing that navigating your identity with new people can be challenging, and also that it's only one aspect of challenges you're facing lately. Like for any of us, gender identity can play a role in our lives, and may not be a primary concern in a given situation.

DREW: I didn't mean to get it wrong ...

ALEX: You weren't wrong exactly ... that just wasn't what I was trying to talk about.

LEADER: We can all misattribute things we hear from others. It's also important to recognize that we might have feelings come up when we are mischaracterized. I'd like to make space for that exchange and also acknowledge that Alex felt they had more to say about their current struggles both to Laura and to the group.

In the group itself, simple interventions to create space for trans* identities include setting an example during introductions. The leader can set a precedent by introducing themselves including their preferred pronouns, opening up this line of thought for all identities in the group. Working to use inclusive language, removing binary gender assumptions from forms, and ensuring that the physical space of the group is welcoming to all gender identities provides structure for a container where expression of identity is safe and affirmed. The American Psychological Association (APA) suggests the use of trans-affirming media in waiting rooms and the avoidance of anti-trans items in therapy settings (2015).

Conclusion

Sensitivity to the needs of trans* people in therapeutic settings will continue to evolve over time. Culture around gender is fundamentally influenced by society, including the internet, popular media, and politics. With all this change afoot, it is important that group leaders remain flexible in how they conceptualize gender issues and related group dynamics. Leaders should carefully examine their own gender-related biases and seek to understand how these may manifest in the therapeutic setting. In the end, of greatest importance is the ability to authentically connect with clients, whatever their personal identities may be, and foster those connections in member-to-member interactions.

Leaders can find up-to-date information regarding gender issues through the World Professional Association for Transgender Health (WPATH) including their publicly available Standards of Care document, Trans Student Educational Resources (TSER), and the Center of Excellence for Transgender Health through the University of California – San Francisco.

References

Benson, K. E. (2013). Seeking support: Transgender client experiences with mental health services. *Journal of Feminist Family Therapy*, 25(1), 17–40. https://doi.org/10.1080/08952833.2013.

Coleman, E., Bockting, W., Botzer, M., Cohen-Kettenis, P., DeCuypere, G., Feldman, J., *et al.* (2012). Standards of Care for the Health of Transsexual, Transgender, and Gender-Nonconforming People, Version 7. *International Journal of Transgenderism*, 13(4), 165–232, doi:10.1080/15532739.2011.700873.

Dickey, L. M., & Loewy, M. I. (2010). Group work with transgender clients. *The Journal for Specialists in Group Work*, 35(3), 236–245, doi:10.1080/01933922.2010.492904.

Grant, J. M., Mottet, L. A., & Tanis, J. (2013). Injustice at Every Turn: A Report. Retrieved from: https://www.thetaskforce.org/injustice-every-turn-report-national-transgender-discrimination-survey/. Accessed July 30, 2019.

American Psychological Association (2015). Guidelines for psychological practice with transgender and gender nonconforming people. *The American Psychologist*, 70(9), 832–864, doi:10.1037/a0039906.

Harper, A., Pickering, D. L., Moundas, S., Scofield, T., Maxon, W., Harper, B., et al. (2009). Competencies for counseling with transgender clients. In *Association of lesbian, gay, bisexual, and transgender issues in counseling*. Alexandria, VA: Taylor & Francis.

Hund, A., & Thomas, J. (2015). Cisgender therapists working with transgender clients: Building cultural empathy and clinical competence from an outgroup position. Dennis H. May Conference on Diversity Issues and the Role of Counseling Centers. Champaign, IL.

Israel, T., Gorcheva, R., Burnes, T. R., & Walther, W. A. (2008). Helpful and unhelpful therapy experiences of LGBT clients. *Psychotherapy Research*, 18(3), 294–305. doi:10.1080/10503300701506920.

Jacobson, B., & Donatone, B. (2009). Homoflexibles, omnisexuals, and gender-queers: Group work with queer youth in cyberspace and face-to-face. *Group*, 33 (3), 223–234.

Nadal, K. L., Skolnik, A., & Wong, Y. (2012). Interpersonal and systemic micro-aggressions toward transgender people: Implications for counseling. *Journal of LGBT Issues in Counseling*, 6(1), 55–82, doi:10.1080/15538605.2012.648583.

Reed, B., Rhodes, S., Schofield, P., & Wiley, K. (2009). *Gender variance in the UK: Prevalence, incidence and growth and geographic distribution*. Surrey: Gender Identity Research and Education Society (GIRES) UK, 1–36. Retrieved from: https://www.gires.org.uk/wp-content/uploads/2014/10/GenderVarianceUK-report.pdf.

Sennott, S., & Smith, T. (2011). Translating the sex and gender continuums in mental health: A transfeminist approach to client and clinician fears. *Journal of Gay and Lesbian Mental Health*, 15(2), 218–234, doi:10.1080/19359705.2011.553779.

4 Chronic Health Conditions/Ability Issues in Group

Wendy Freedman, Leslie Klein and Katheryne Kopp-Miller

When considering the important facets of diversity in group therapy, it is critical to recognize disability and chronic health concerns as significant and impactful variables affecting group members, therapists, and the group process. Disability can be defined as "an evolving concept including 'physical, mental, intellectual, or sensory impairments that, in the face of various negative attitudes or physical obstacles, may prevent those persons from participating fully in society" (United Nations Enable, 2006). This chapter, focusing on physical and sensory disability, will frame disability as a multicultural experience and diversity variable, and discuss best practices for providing affirming and effective group treatment for this population, including addressing disability-related microaggressions and working through therapists' countertransferential barriers.

The Need for Training in Providing Disability-Affirming Group Treatment

There are members of every identity group, including ethnicity, sexuality, gender, age, socioeconomic status, religious belief, etc., who identify as having a disability or chronic health condition, making the disability community the most prevalent and diverse minority group in the world (World Health Organization & The World Bank, 2011). Across 59 countries surveyed in the World Health Survey in 2004, the average prevalence rate in the adult population aged 18 years and over was 15.6 percent (World Health Organization & The World Bank, 2011). According to data reported by the World Health Survey, the American Community Survey, and the Centers for Disease Control, it is estimated that between 12 to 22 percent of the population of the United States has a disability (Centers for Disease Control and Prevention, 2018; Kraus et al., 2018; Reichard et al., 2011). Almost all people will experience either a temporary or permanent disability, making disability an identity variable that will eventually impact almost all individuals, families, and groups (World Health Organization & The World Bank, 2011). It is, therefore, statistically likely there are individuals with disabilities or chronic health conditions in most therapy groups, making it imperative that group therapists are prepared to work effectively with this population.

Given the prevalence of individuals with disability in our society, it is particularly striking so few mental health practitioners are adequately trained and prepared to work with this population. Less than 2 percent of the American Psychological Association (APA) membership identifies as having disabilities (Olkin, 2002). Clinical and counseling psychologists are rarely trained in working with disability issues (Olkin, 2002) and do not take graduate classes on this topic (Bluestone et al., 1996; Olkin, 2002). Leigh, Powers, Vash, and Nettles (2004) surveyed 481 psychologists about service provision for clients with disabilities, and they identified the barriers to such care as lack of provider knowledge, limited training in disability issues and services, and lack of sensitivity. The authors concluded that additional training for psychologists was needed (Leigh et al., 2004). Additionally, Strike, Skovholt, and Hummel (2004) surveyed 108 mental health professionals about their sense of competence when working with individuals with disabilities. Participants reported having the most competence in awareness of disability, less competence in knowledge about working with disability issues, and the least competence in having specific skill sets for this work. The authors concluded there is a need for mental health professionals to develop disability-affirming attitudes, knowledge, and skills (Strike et al., 2004). Most able-bodied mental health practitioners are conducting "cross-cultural counseling" with clients with disabilities and chronic health conditions without sufficient training, and this increases the risk of poor outcomes, premature termination, and negative perceptions of psychological treatment (Artman & Daniels, 2010; Olkin, 2002).

Conceptualizing Disability as a Multicultural Experience, Minority Identity, and Diversity Variable

As group therapists, it is important to conceptualize disability as a minority identity, multicultural experience, and diversity issue. Individuals with disabilities often have experiences that differ greatly from their able-bodied peers including high needs for support and fear of dependency (Russell, White, & White, 2006; Seligman & Marshak, 2004), disability-related body image concerns and threats to body integrity (Florou et al., 2016; Seligman & Marshak, 2004), internalized stigma and self-esteem issues (Bogart, 2014; Seligman & Marshak, 2004), lack of support from the medical system (Florou et al., 2016), financial struggles due to employment discrimination and exorbitant medical costs (Centers for Disease Control and Prevention, 2018; Kraus et al., 2018), separate but not equal facilities and other environmental barriers (Olkin, 2002), isolation (Oliva, 2004; Olkin, 2002), threats to existing relationships (Seligman & Marshak, 2004), and less access to personal relationships, educational opportunities, and employment opportunities than non-disabled counterparts (Nettles & Balter, 2012).

People with disabilities also face attitudinal barriers that can impact their ability to participate in society fully and equally (World Health Organization & The World Bank, 2011). They experience unique forms of discrimination, different from other groups that are both overt and covert in nature. Ableism is the discrimination experienced by people with disabilities that favors people without disabilities and frames disability as a negative concept, state, and experience. Ableism posits there is a "normal" way of living and being, and people with disabilities are a deviation from this normality (Keller & Galgay, 2010).

For people with disabilities who are also members of other minority groups, the intersection of these identities can greatly impact the experience of marginalization and the advantages or disadvantages experienced (Nettles & Balter, 2012; World Health Organization & The World Bank, 2011). For example, an African American woman with cerebral palsy may face vastly different life challenges than a White male with the same condition. The various race- and gender-based societal barriers might compound the discrimination and marginalization she experiences as an individual with a chronic health condition.

Marginalized communities often buffer themselves from the negative impact of societal prejudice through connection; similarly, people with disabilities have worked to minimize devaluation by developing community and a disability culture (Gill, 1998). The disability culture is rich and vibrant, including history, art, humor, language, beliefs, values, and worldviews (Gill, 1998; Whaley & Davis, 2007). Developing identity and culture is a protective factor for individuals with disabilities. This process empowers the disability community to remain strong, push back against oppression, unify across intersecting identity groups, communicate to each other and to the world, and celebrate their differences from the able-bodied world (Gill, 1998). The benefits of belonging to a wider disability community and culture parallels the benefits that can be obtained from the supportive community and culture of group therapy.

Best Practices in Providing Affirming Group Treatment for People with Disabilities

Group therapy is an ideal modality for people with disabilities and chronic health conditions to be affirmed and empowered. The therapeutic factors and mechanisms that enable effective group treatment and client growth (i.e. universality, reduced isolation, cohesion, self-understanding, imparting information, catharsis and existential learning, etc.) are highly useful in addressing this population's unique needs and common concerns (American Group Psychotherapy Association, 2007; Yalom & Leszcz, 2005). Therapists can work with people with disabilities in group skillfully and therapeutically through utilizing Disability-Affirmative Therapy (Olkin, 1999b, 2002, 2017) and universal design principles, addressing microaggressions as they arise, and working through disability-related countertransference.

Disability-Affirmative Therapy

Disability-Affirmative Therapy (D-AT), developed by clinical psychologist Rhoda Olkin, is an effective model to work ethically with this population. Disability-Affirmative Therapy is not a theory of psychotherapy, but rather a comprehensive model to frame work with clients with disabilities and chronic health conditions (Olkin, 2017). It is meant to overlay any theoretical approach to running groups and to foster the integration of disability-related skill, knowledge, and affirming attitudes (Cornish et al., 2008).

One key component of D-AT is placing the disability in proper focus. It is a common therapeutic mistake either to over-inflate or underestimate the role disability plays in a client's presenting concern (American Psychological Association, 2012b; Keller & Galgay, 2010; Olkin, 2002). To avoid this, it is essential to separate the disability from the client's mental health issues and refrain from assuming the disability is central (Gerke, 2017). Learning how to ask about disability directly and explore the topic comfortably during group screening and beyond is an important skill to develop. Given many disabilities are invisible, routinely assessing disability just as one would other diversity variables demonstrates awareness and interest (Olkin, 2017). If a client does not mention a disability in the group screen, a therapist can open a dialogue and ask whether disability plays a role in the presenting concern (Olkin, 1999b). When the group leader views the client as the expert of their condition and avoids the traditional dynamic of the disabled person needing "help," there is a decrease in client dependency, an increase in client independence, and more joint-ownership of the therapeutic work (Gerke, 2017; Schofield, 2014).

Another primary component of D-AT is the therapist mindset or "stance." It is essential for group leaders to adopt and promote the social model of disability in which disability is viewed as a social construct. In applying this model, the group therapist views the "problem" as the greater physical and social environment that is not accessible to the client, rather than residing within the client him or herself (Olkin, 2002). It is important to hold this viewpoint regardless of the client's perception of disability (see American Psychological Association, 2012b; and Olkin, 2017 for more information about the models of disability). Learning how to utilize the social model of disability to facilitate positive disability identity, self-advocacy skills, and a voice in decision making within group are essential components of D-AT. Further applying D-AT, the group leader adopts a social justice orientation and an understanding of the environmental barriers and social marginalization faced by people with disabilities.

Effective therapists strive to learn disability-related knowledge to prevent clients from being placed unfairly in the role of educating fellow group members and the group therapist. Understanding of the heterogeneity of disability and chronic health concerns, disability-related social justice issues, the legal rights of people with disabilities (i.e. the Americans with Disabilities Act, Individuals with Disabilities Education Act, Section 503–504 of the Rehabilitation Act) (American Psychological Association, 2012b), the importance of accessibility and obstacles to attending group, and developmental issues around dating and relationships, facilitates culturally competent practice and increased ease (see American Psychological Association, 2012a, 2012b; and Cornish et al., 2008 for comprehensive lists of target knowledge to attain). Training, consultation, and supervision will aid this process.

Beyond attaining disability-related knowledge, skill, and a social justice stance, inclusive therapists implement universal design principles in their groups to maximize access for all (American Psychological Association, 2012b). Universal design is a concept which aims to create environments to be usable by all people, to the greatest extent possible, without adaptation or specialized design (Burgstahler, 2008). For example, maintaining low-level lighting for a group member with light allergy or chronic migraines, providing chairs that can accommodate larger body sizes, and securing a group room in an area with reduced noises for people with autism spectrum disorder are all examples of applying universal design. Utilizing the universal design model to shape the norms and rules of the group allows the group to meet the needs of all participants and not shame anyone for taking care of oneself. Group leaders should inform group members of their intention to make the group experience as accessible and successful as possible, and invite members to request any modifications or accommodations needed to improve the experience (Artman & Daniels, 2010). When setting the group therapy frame, the therapist can consider disability issues around attendance and punctuality, regularly check in with the group on the accessibility of the group environment, and flexibly respond as needed. Further, universal design principles can be considered around the accessibility of a workplace's website (i.e. low vision access), forms or handouts (i.e. large print, electronic, or willingness to read aloud to assist a blind client or write for those who need assistance), and appointment scheduling (i.e. via email or text for Deaf or hard of hearing clients) (Artman & Daniels, 2010).

The issue of how and whether to talk about therapist (disability) identity is another area to consider. If a group leader has a visible disability, disclosure is automatic; however, if a leader has an invisible disability or medical issue, the question of whether to disclose is raised. While this choice is highly personal and likely influenced by theoretical orientation and style, it is recommended the therapist work with the group's fantasies and assumptions that come into the room around the therapist's disability/health status. Validate the group's curiosity and explore what the function of their curiosity may be (e.g. "If you have the same issue as me, you will understand me or if you don't you, you won't"). When a therapist has a disability or medical condition the group knows about, it is helpful to model self-care and expression of needs in group (e.g.. standing when necessary for optimal comfort).

Addressing Ableist Microaggressions

To be an effective group therapist when working with individuals with disabilities, one must become aware of and attend to the impact of microaggressions on their clients and therapy groups. The term micro-aggression was first created to address racial devaluations through micro-interactions and has since been expanded and studied in most margin-alized social groups, including people with disabilities (Sue, 2010). According to Kattari (2017), ableism is sustained not only through macro-level discrimination, but also at the micro level through interpersonal interactions and microaggressions.

The existence of "ableist microaggressions" or "disability microaggres-sions" that denigrate, oppress, and marginalize members of this popula-tion has been validated by a growing number of research studies (Bell, 2013; Kattari, 2017; Keller & Galgay, 2010; Robb, 2015). Well-intentioned people may have distorted attitudes towards people with disabilities, often outside of their awareness, that can lead to microaggressions (Keller & Galgay, 2010). As examples, group members may ask intrusive health questions to the person with disabilities, such as "can you have sex?" or "what happened to your arm?" They may also inadvertently minimize the severity of the person's symptoms by making comments such as, "I understand, I get tired too," when discussing the debilitating fatigue that can accompany chronic illness. Statements such as "you don't look like you are in pain" may invalidate or deny the person's experience and dis-ability identity. Finally, out of a desire to help, group members may be patronizing and assume the helplessness of the person with a disability by saying, "I'll do that for you." There are additional resources about common ableist microaggressions available as well (Bell, 2013; Clemency Cordes, Cameron, Mona, Syme, & Coble-Temple, 2016; Kattari, 2017; Keller & Galgay, 2010; Robb, 2015).

Study findings have indicated microaggressions harmfully impact the mental and physical health of people with disabilities (Bell, 2013; Keller & Galgay, 2010; Sue, 2010). The more ableist microaggressions experi-enced by people with disabilities, the greater the negative mental health outcomes (Kattari, 2017). Beyond the exhaustion that may occur from living with a disability, people with disabilities also have to live with the psychological wear and tear of dealing with regular microaggressions (Keller & Galgay, 2010; Schaff, 2016). Targets of microaggressions have reported reactions of frustration, anger, rage, embarrassment, insult, and invalidation from the continuous stream of microaggressions that they experience from family, friends, acquaintances, and strangers. Many commented that they felt unimportant, invisible, and misunderstood (Keller & Galgay, 2010).

As group therapists, paying careful attention to the ways group members with disabilities are expending energy and struggling with microaggressions can inform helpful group interventions. Therapists may notice members with disabilities engaging in impression management, trying to pass as able-bodied, or hiding their disability in the attempt to blend in and avoid the negative reactions they often receive (Robb, 2015). For example, a group member may remain sitting instead of standing, even if chronic back pain interferes with their ability to focus on the group process, to avoid highlighting their disability. Group members with disabilities also may feel pressure to be "inspirational" and to be positive representations of disability and a source of education for others (Robb, 2015). This pressure can create tremendous internal self-expectations and be a barrier to the group member receiving the care and support they need. When members do experience microaggressions, they may experience internalized ableism and related shame, adding to their own negative self-esteem (Robb, 2015). As an example, a group member with chronic fatigue syndrome relayed the microaggressions they experienced related to their reduced capacity to be highly efficient in their work. They discussed self-critical thoughts related to why they could not "get things done" at the same rate as their non-disabled peers and the shame and anxiety they experienced as a result. Members with invisible disabilities may also find their struggles minimized, overlooked, or forgotten. When any of these experiences are recognized by the therapist as playing out in the group context, bringing attention to the concern in a non-shaming manner is imperative. The facilitator can hold the group and self accountable in taking responsibility for any microaggressions or perpetuation of discrimination through a learning, not blaming intervention.

When we affirm experiences with ableism and microaggressions, we can help clients work through and promote disability identity and simultaneously build group cohesion. Validating ableist microaggressions rather than minimizing their impact can help clients with meaning making and resiliency, which is associated with improved quality of life (Kattari, 2017; Russell et al., 2006; Schaff, 2016). The discussion of common experiences such as microaggressions can help bring members together to further support the development and integration of their disability identity (Forber-Pratt, Lyew, Mueller, & Samples, 2017; Keller & Galgay, 2010; Yalom & Leszcz, 2005). For example, after being chastised for being "dramatic" by a family member, a group member in an autism spectrum group bonded with fellow group members over their shared tactic of going to the grocery store when it was less busy and stimulating.

Members expressed surprise and levity that they were not the only ones overwhelmed by that environment and reassurance that others were strategizing in a similar way.

Addressing microaggressions within the group contributes to a disability-affirming therapeutic experience. Providing education on microaggressions and assessing individual experiences both within and outside of group can give members the language and context to better express, explore, and validate their experiences. For example, in a group for students with cerebral palsy, one member discussed how although he had obvious cerebral palsy symptoms, it was not "as bad or obvious" as another group member. The group leaders processed with the group the emotional impact of this comment, and expressed curiosity around the comment potentially being a microaggression. This intervention led to a rich group discussion around microaggressions and their emotional impact.

Additionally, group therapists grow up in an oppressive, ableist culture, and thus are at risk of microaggressing during group. When this happens, the therapist should acknowledge the mistake to the group, apologize for the misstep, state what was learned by the therapist from this experience, and tend to one's own feelings and reactions independently, without placing the burden on the client. Microaggressions happen and are an opportunity to examine one's own biases related to disability.

Working through Countertransference

Countertransference reactions can impact therapists' sense of competence and willingness to work with group members with disabilities. Although some therapists may have positive countertransferential responses to working with clients with disabilities, others may experience fear, hopelessness, helplessness, death anxiety, loss of control, and pity (Hummel, 2013; Olkin, 1999a; Schofield, 2014; Watermeyer, 2012). Countertransferential reactions can occur regardless of whether the therapist has a disability themselves, and these reactions may significantly impact the way the group therapist facilitates and responds to the group process. To be most effective, countertransferential responses must be identified and worked through.

Countertransferential reactions sometimes occur around group attendance. People with disabilities may have inconsistent attendance due to medical appointments or feeling too physically unwell. This inconsistent attendance can create anxiety in the therapist around their sense of competence and their effectiveness as a clinician (Schofield, 2014). The therapist's anxiety related to the client's health and well-being, and subsequent worries about the client's dependency on the group therapist may contribute to the therapist's possible over-controlling, silencing, and excluding responses as a way to manage fear (Watermeyer, 2012). These responses reinforce what the client likely experiences in other relationships and in the culture as a whole.

Therapists also might project their own perceptions of what life is like as a person with a disability or chronic health condition on the client. This projection may be influenced by internalized cultural fears of disability (Hummel, 2013), including how "horrific" and "unbearable" living with a disability must be. They may share these biased perceptions in their interventions instead of being open and curious about the client's experience of their life. Working with people with disabilities may uncover the therapist's awareness of their own existential anxiety around mortality, vulnerability, and dependency (Olkin, 1999a). Conversely, feelings of helplessness and guilt at being unable to change the disability or health condition can impact the therapy as well (Hummel, 2013; Schofield, 2014).

To work effectively with group clients with disabilities, therapists benefit from learning about common countertransferential reactions, and self-reflecting to identify such reactions when they arise. By examining one's privilege of being temporarily able-bodied (Cornish et al., 2008) and by exploring the internalization of oppressive beliefs regarding disability, a therapist can gain insight into their conditioned beliefs and emotional reactions toward people with disabilities and health concerns (American Psychological Association, 2012b). Ongoing consultation and personal therapy assists therapists in working to minimize the impact of these reactions on the group. Processing fears of disability, aging, death, and dependency helps the group therapist to work more effectively with clients in integrating and accepting their disability (Florou et al., 2016). Additionally, a therapist's ability to build resilience in tolerating strong emotional and physical pain without working to "fix" the disability-related struggles provides safety and containment for the group when these feelings arise (Gordon, Zaccario, Sachs, Ufberg, & Carlson, 2009). Group therapists cannot remove the illness or disability, but they can support group members' resiliency and growth (Schofield, 2014).

Conclusion

Group therapists "are uniquely positioned to help individuals with disabilities become self-determining citizens of our diverse society" (American Psychological Association, 2012b). Groups have been shown to be highly effective with this population (Bogart, Lund, & Rottenstein, 2018; Gebler & Maercker, 2014; Gudenkauf et al., 2015; Hopps, Pépin, & Boisvert, 2003; Lamb et al., 2012; Linton, Boersma, Jansson, Svärd, & Botvalde, 2005; Mejias, Gill, & Shpigelman, 2014; Naylor & Labbe, 2017; Rejeski et al., 2003), and more groups serving this population are needed. Whether adding more members with disabilities and chronic health conditions to heterogeneous groups, starting a general disability or chronic health-concern group, or creating homogeneous groups based on specific medical issues, group therapists will find that clients will grow in significant and meaningful ways. This much-needed and important work may contribute to outcomes such as reduced powerlessness, isolation, and depression as well as increased support, guidance, encouragement, and selfhood (Seligman & Marshak, 2004). As therapists with a mission to better serve underserved communities, group therapists are encouraged to lean in to any discomfort to gain the knowledge and experience needed to work with this deserving population.

Appendix A: Top Six Recommended Readings to Learn More

1   American Psychological Association (2012). Enhancing your interactions with persons with disabilities. Retrieved from: https://www.apa.org/pi/disability/resources/publications/enhancing-your-interactions.pdf.
2   American Psychological Association (2012). Guidelines for assessment of and intervention with persons with disabilities. *American Psychologist, 67*(1), 43–62.
3   Keller, R. M., & Galgay, C. E. (2010). Microaggressive experiences of people with disabilities. In D. W. Sue (ed.), *Microaggressions and marginality: manifestation, dynamics, and impact* (pp. 241–267). Hoboken, NJ: John Wiley & Sons.
4   Olkin, R. (1999). *What psychotherapists should know about disability.* New York, NY: Guilford Press.
5   Olkin, R. (2017). *Disability-affirmative therapy: A case formulation template for clients with disabilities.* New York, NY: Oxford University Press.
6   Seligman, M., & Marshak, L. (2004). Group approaches for persons with disabilities. In J. L. DeLucia-Waack, D. A. Gerrity, C. R. Kalodner, & M. T. Riva (eds), *Handbook of group counseling and psychotherapy* (pp. 239–252). Thousand Oaks, CA: Sage Publications Ltd.

References

American Group Psychotherapy Association (2007). Practice guidelines for group psychotherapy. New York: American Group Psychotherapy Association.
American Psychological Association (2012a). Enhancing your interactions with persons with disabilities. Retrieved from: https://www.apa.org/pi/disability/resources/publications/enhancing-your-interactions.pdf.
American Psychological Association (2012b). Guidelines for assessment of and intervention with persons with disabilities. *American Psychologist, 67*(1), 43–62.
Artman, L. K., & Daniels, J. A. (ed.). (2010). Disability and psychotherapy practice: Cultural competence and practical tips. *Professional Psychology: Research and Practice,* 41(5), 442–448.
Bell, A. K. (2013). Nothing about us without us: A qualitative investigation of the experiences of being a target of ableist microaggressions (doctoral dissertation). Pleasant Hill, CA: John F. Kennedy University. Retrieved from: http://gradworks.umi.com/36/20/3620204.html.

Bluestone, H. H., Stokes, A., & Kuba, S. A. (1996). Toward an integrated program design: Evaluating the status of diversity training in a graduate school curriculum. *Professional Psychology: Research and Practice*, 27, 394–400.

Bogart, K. R. (2014). The role of disability self-concept in adaptation to congenital or acquired disability. *Rehabilitation Psychology*, 59(1), 107–115.

Bogart, K. R., Lund, E. M., & Rottenstein, A. (2018). Disability pride protects self-esteem through the rejection-identification model. *Rehabilitation Psychology*, 63(1), 155–159.

Burgstahler, S. (2008). Universal design in higher education. In S. Burgstahler, & R. Cory (eds), *Universal design in higher education: From principles to practice* (pp. 3–20). Cambridge, MA: Harvard Education Press.

Clemency Cordes, C., Cameron, R. P., Mona, L. R., Syme, M. L., & Coble-Temple, A. (2016). Perspectives on disability within integrated healthcare. In L. Suzuki, M. Casas, C. Alexander, & M. Jackson (eds), *Handbook of multicultural counseling* (4th ed., pp. 401–410). Thousand Oaks, CA: Sage.

Cornish, J. A. E., Gorgens, K. A., Monson, S. P., Olkin, R., Palombi, B. J., & Abels, A. V. (2008). Perspectives on ethical practice with people who have disabilities. *Professional Psychology: Research and Practice*, 39(5), 488–497.

Centers for Disease Control and Prevention (2018, August 9). Data and statistics for disability and health. Retrieved from: https://www.cdc.gov/ncbddd/disabilityandhealth/data.html.

Florou, A., Widdershoven, M., Giannakopoulos, G., & Christogiorgos, S. (2016). Working through physical disability in psychoanalytic psychotherapy with an adolescent boy. *Psychoanalytic Social Work*, 23(2), 119–129.

Forber-Pratt, A., Lyew, D. A., Mueller, C., & Samples, L. B. (eds). (2017). Disability identity development: A systematic review of the literature. *Rehabilitation Psychology*, 62(2), 198–207.

Gebler, F. A., & Maercker, A. (2014). Effects of including an existential perspective in a cognitive- behavioral group program for chronic pain: A clinical trial with 6 months follow-up. *The Humanistic Psychologist*, 42(2), 155–171.

Gerke, A. C. (2017). A phenomenological examination of disability, microaggressions, and the experiences of deaf adults in mental health services (Order No. AAI10108925). Available from ProQuest Dissertations & Theses Global.

Gill, C. J. (1998). A psychological view of disability culture. *Disability Studies Quarterly*, 15, 16–19.

Gordon, R. M., Zaccario, M., Sachs, D. M., Ufberg, H., & Carlson, J. A. (2009). Psychotherapy with children and adolescents with physical disabilities. *Journal of Infant, Child, and Adolescent Psychotherapy*, 8(2), 113–123.

Gudenkauf, L. M., Antoni, M. H., Stagl, J. M., Lechner, S. C., Jutagir, D. R., Bouchard, L. C., Carver, C. S, *et al.* (2015). Brief cognitive-behavioral and relaxation training interventions for breast cancer: A randomized controlled trial. *Journal of Consulting and Clinical Psychology*, 83(4), 677–688, doi:10.1037/ccp0000020.

Hopps, S. L., Pépin, M., & Boisvert, J. M. (2003). The effectiveness of cognitive-behavioral group therapy for loneliness via inter relaychat among people with physical disabilities. *Psychotherapy: Theory, Research, Practice, Training*, 40(1–2), 136–147, doi:10.1037/0033-3204.40.1-2.136.

Hummel, A. M. (2013). Therapist reactions to a client facing terminal illness: A test of ego and countertransference. *Dissertation Abstracts International: Section B: The Sciences and Engineering*. College Park, MD: University of Maryland.

Kattari, S. K. (2017). Development of the ableist microaggression scale and assessing the relationship between ableist microaggressions and the mental health of disabled adults. *Electronic Theses and Dissertations*. 1283. https://digitalcommons.du.edu/etd/1283.

Keller, R. M., & Galgay, C. E. (2010). Microaggressive experiences of people with disabilities. In D. W. Sue (ed.), *Microaggressions and marginality: Manifestation, dynamics, and impact* (pp. 241–267). Hoboken, NJ: John Wiley & Sons, Inc.

Kraus, L., Lauer, E., Coleman, R., & Houtenville, A. (2018). *2017 disability statistics annual report*. Durham, NH: University of New Hampshire.

Lamb, S. E., Mistry, D. J., Lall, R. R., Hansen, Z., Evans, D., Withers, E. J., & Underwood, M. R. (2012). Group cognitive behavioural interventions for low back pain in primary care: Extended follow-up of the back skills training trial. *Pain*, 153(2), 494–501, doi:10.1016/j.pain.2011.11.016.

Leigh, I. W., Powers, L., Vash, C., & Nettles, R. (2004). Survey of psychological services to clients with disabilities: The need for awareness. *Rehabilitation Psychology*, 49(1), 48–54.

Linton, S. J., Boersma, K., Jansson, M., Svärd, L., & Botvalde, M. (2005). The effects of cognitive-behavioral and physical therapy preventive interventions on pain-related sick leave: A randomized controlled trial. *The Clinical Journal of Pain*, 21(2), 109–119, doi:10.1097/00002508-200503000-00001.

Mejias, N. J., Gill, C. J., & Shpigelman, C. (2014). Influence of a support group for young women with disabilities on sense of belonging. *Journal of Counseling Psychology*, 61(2), 208–220, doi:10.1037/a0035462.

Naylor, P. D., & Labbe, E. E. (2017). Exploring the effects of group therapy for the visually impaired. *The British Journal of Visual Impairment*, 35(1), 18–28.

Nettles, R., & Balter, R. (2012). *Multiple minority identities: Applications for practice, research, and training*. New York, NY: Springer Publishing Co.

Oliva, G. A. (2004). *Alone in the mainstream: A deaf woman remembers public school*. Washington, DC: Gallaudet University Press.

Olkin, R. (1999a). The personal, professional, and political when clients have disabilities. *Women and Therapy*, 22(2), 87–103.

Olkin, R. (1999b). *What psychotherapists should know about disability*. New York, NY: Guilford Press.

Olkin, R. (2002). Could you hold the door for me? Including disability in diversity. *Cultural Diversity and Ethnic Minority Psychology*, 8(2), 130–137.

Olkin, R. (2017). *Disability-affirmative therapy: A case formulation template for clients with disabilities*. New York, NY: Oxford University Press.

Reichard, A., Stolzle, H., & Fox, M. (2011). Health disparities among adults with physical disabilities or cognitive limitations compared to individuals with no disabilities in the United States. *Disability Health Journal*, 4(2), 59–67.

Rejeski, W. J., Brawley, L. R., Ambrosius, W. T., Brubaker, P. H., Focht, B. C., Foy, C. G., Fox, L. D., & Stone, A. A. (eds). (2003). Older adults with chronic disease: Benefits of group-mediated counseling in the promotion of physically active lifestyles. *Health Psychology*, 22(4), 414–423.

Robb, J. L. (2015). Attitudinal ableism: A three-study exploration into attitudinal barriers encountered by people with mental illness, substance use, and physical disabilities (Order No. 3742974). Available from *ProQuest Dissertations & Theses Global*. (1752514705).

Russell, C. S., White, M. B., & White, C. P. (2006). Why me? why now? why multiple sclerosis?: Making meaning and perceived quality of life in a midwestern sample of patients with multiple sclerosis. *Families, Systems, & Health*, 24(1), 65–81.

Schaff, M. (2016). Experiences of microaggressions among women with apparent disabilities: A look at the intersection of gender and disability (Order No. AAI10131719). Available from PsycINFO (1908372866; 2017-01054-044).

Seligman, M., & Marshak, L. (2004). Group approaches for persons with disabilities. In J. L. DeLucia-Waack, D. A. Gerrity, & C. R. Kalodner (eds), *Handbook of group counseling and psychotherapy* (pp. 239–252). Thousand Oaks, CA: Sage Publications Ltd.

Schofield, S. (2014). Group art psychotherapy and countertransference with Parkinson's sufferers. *Group Analysis*, 47(12), 22–32.

Strike, D. L., Skovholt, T. M., & Hummel, T. J. (2004). Mental health professionals' disability competence: Measuring self-awareness, perceived knowledge, and perceived skills. *Rehabilitation Psychology*, 49(4), 321–327.

Sue, D. W. (ed.). (2010). *Microaggressions and marginality: Manifestation, dynamics, and impact*, Chapter xiii, 360 pages. Hoboken, NJ: John Wiley & Sons.

United Nations Enable (2006, December 13). Convention on the rights of persons with disabilities. Retrieved from: http://www.un.org/disabilities/default.asp?id223. Accessed November 12, 2007.

Watermeyer, B. (2012). Disability and countertransference in group psychotherapy: Connecting social oppression with the clinical frame. *International Journal of Group Psychotherapy*, 62(3), 392–417.

Whaley, A. L., & Davis, K. E. (2007). Cultural competence and evidence based practice in mental health services: A complementary perspective. *American Psychologist*, 62(6), 563–574.

World Health Organization, & TheWorld Bank (2011). *World report on disability*. Geneva, Switzerland: World Health Organization.

Yalom, I. D., & Leszcz, M. (2005). *The theory and practice of group Psychotherapy* (5th ed.) New York, NY: Basic Books.

5 Inclusivity of Multiple Identities in Sexual Identity Based Therapy Groups in University and College Counseling Settings

Kristin Bertsch

Introduction

Group counseling in college settings is an effective treatment modality that university and college counseling centers can offer students to manage the increasing demand for services (Kitzrow, 2003; Burlingame, Fuhriman, & Mosier, 2003) as well as have academic benefits (Denton & Hodges, 2018). This can be especially true with students who do not identify as heterosexual due to the invisibility of sexual identity. Further, because sexual minorities have multiple identities, the importance of allowing all identities into the group room is emphasized.

Students holding intersecting minoritized identities due to various isms that exist in different minority communities (e.g. racism within the queer community, heterosexism in Black and Brown communities), have different challenges than their White LGBTQ counterparts (Ghabrial, 2017). Therefore, it is important when forming a Queer Student Group to emphasize that all identities are honored, validated, and welcome. The purpose of this chapter is to provide group facilitators an overview of suggestions on how to run a sexual identity based group and how to incorporate cultural humility within the group context, specifically within a college/university setting. However, this work can also be applied to other settings. This chapter is meant as a starting part and not a conclusive resource in running a sexual identity based group. Finally, because incorporating a cultural humility approach is aspirational in nature, references are provided at the end for further reading and development in this area.

Rationale for the Importance of Therapy Groups with This Population

Accumulating research suggests that lesbian, gay, and bisexual individuals are in particular more vulnerable to mental health issues than their heterosexual counterparts. Meyer (2003) discusses these heightened concerns within the minority stress framework. Specifically, minority stress theory posits that discrimination related to one's minoritized identity/identities produces a stressful social environment for LGB individuals, which then leads to increased levels of psychological distress. Moreover, Meyer argues that external events (e.g. objective events) and internalized discrimination (e.g. subjective perceptions) contribute to the psychological distress of sexual minority individuals. This is especially important to keep in mind on college campuses. Despite strides in our understanding and acceptance of non-heterosexual sexual orientations, some campus environments may still be problematic for many sexual minority students. Research suggests that campus climate may affect sexual minority students' integration into their campus community. For instance, Woodford and Kulick (2015) found that lesbian, gay, and bisexual (LGB) students' perceptions of their ability to be open about their sexual orientation were positively associated with acceptance on campus. Further, those who experienced personal heterosexual harassment were more likely to be academically disengaged, have lower GPAs, and have lower social integration.

Discrimination towards sexual minority students on college campuses keeps students isolated from and invisible to their peers. Welch (1996) describes his experience of creating a therapy group for LGB students. Welch suggests that group therapy may be critical to sexual minority students' ability to cope with their varied experiences related to discrimination with friends, family, religious communities, and the campus community. Yalom and Leszcz's (2005) concept of universality may be an important factor in this type of therapy group. Positive interaction with adults and support from a group of peers with similar identities may decrease fears of rejection, violence, and internal struggle that may arise with coming to terms with having a sexual minority identity.

Experiences of isolation and invisibility may lead sexual minority students to search for a caring and inclusive community (Welch, 1996) and has been supported in later research. For instance, Baams, De Luca, and Brownson (2018) found in their sample of heterosexual, lesbian, gay, bisexual, and questioning (LGBQ) college students that these LGBQ students were more likely to utilize mental health services than their heterosexual counterparts. Specifically, gay and questioning males and LGBQ females were more likely to report that religion reduced their ability to cope when compared with their heterosexual counterparts. Additionally, LGBQ females and bisexual males were less likely to seek support from their families and racial/ethnic minority bisexual females were less likely to turn to a friend or roommate than non-Hispanic White bisexual females. This finding is not surprising given the lack of acceptance of an LGBQ orientation in some communities of color (Ghabrial, 2017). This lack of acceptance may leave these individuals feeling isolated.

Although sexual minorities may be more likely to seek mental health services, these individuals also experience specific barriers to mental health services, such as discomfort discussing sexual identity with therapists, fears of discrimination, and breaches of confidentiality (e.g. being outed) (Schmidt, Miles, & Welsh, 2011). Dunbar et al. (2017) recently found that lesbian, gay, bisexual, questioning, and queer (LGBQQ) students were more likely than their heterosexual counterparts to report psychological distress, high stress, and mental health related impairment. On a college campus these concerns may be exacerbated when sexual minority students experience their university environments as lacking acceptance and affirmation. Dunbar and colleagues suggested that improving campus climate by increasing visible support systems (such as establishing sexual minority students groups) is one way to lessen the negative effects of discrimination for this population.

Cultural Humility Approach to Group Work and Setting the Tone

Sue and Sue's (2012) historical model of multicultural competence that emphasizes the importance of therapists' awareness, knowledge, and skills when working with diverse clients has made monumental gains in meeting and addressing the needs of minoritized mental health clients. More recently, scholars have investigated a multicultural orientation (MCO) framework that underscores the therapist's way of being with diverse clients, rather than specific interventions implemented in treatment (Owen, Tao, Leach, & Rodolfa, 2011). The three pillars that comprise the MCO are cultural humility, cultural opportunities, and cultural comfort. Cultural humility describes a therapist's attitude of openness and willingness to be humble when working with a client's social identities that they identify as most salient. Cultural opportunity represents a therapist's active seeking and attunement to spaces in the therapy in which questions/exploration of a client's identified salient cultural identities may be appropriate. Finally, cultural comfort describes a therapist's comfort level when addressing culture in the therapy room with the client (Hook, Davis, Owen, & DeBlaere, 2017).

Research suggests that therapists who are able to exhibit cultural humility, cultural opportunity, and cultural comfort positively contribute to the therapy process and outcome in individual work (Owen, 2013). Better treatment outcomes and stronger therapeutic alliances are reported from clients who have experienced their therapist as culturally humble (Owen et al., 2016). Until recently, the MCO framework has been investigated and conceptualized in the context of individual therapy. Kivlighan and Chapman (2018), sought to extend the MCO framework to group therapy given the plethora of multicultural aspects to group therapy and the call for group therapists to be multiculturally competent.

Taking into account the MCO framework, it is important to recognize that although students are self-selecting to be in a sexual identity based group, students hold many other identities besides their sexual and/or gender identity. For example, many of the students that have been in this author's Queer Student Group have had other salient identities, such as but not limited to international status, Black and Brown students, first generation, and lower income. Concurrently these same groups have consisted of students with more dominant identities (e.g. gay, White, cisgender man). Therefore, LGBT groups on campuses are not immune to the sociopolitical climate that supports heteronormativity and those with more privileged identities.

Kivlighan, Adams, Drinane, Tao, and Owen's (2019) research suggests that addressing issues of culture with openness, humility, and curiosity within the group context is important. Their findings supported prior assertions (e.g. Merta, 1995) that highlight the importance for members to engage in cultural discussions with cultural humility and that this process may be more effective than not engaging in these topics. Group therapists, then, should strive to create a safe and respectful climate and create a norm of having cultural discussions within the group context. Kivlighan and colleagues suggest starting this process in the pre-group screening to prepare members for the multicultural orientation of group. Further, group therapists can help facilitate this atmosphere by modeling cultural humility and openness, comfort, and opportunities (Kivlighan et al., 2019).

Facilitator Identity Development

According to the Association of Specialists in Group Work (ASGW), social justice in mental health refers to recognizing "the influences of both privilege and oppression that shape the wellbeing of individuals, groups, and communities" (Singh, Merchant, Bogusia, & Ingene, 2012, p. 1). Counselors who are not aware of the unique concerns that sexual minorities face may unintentionally cause harm to their clients. Although homosexuality was removed from the DSM IV in 1973, there continue to be counselors who lack that knowledge, awareness, and skills to work with this population, which can be harmful to the clients and the group process. As group therapists it is important to understand the multifaceted minoritized and/or majority identities that we hold and how this has shaped our lives, our therapy work, and our relationship with group members. Awareness of how our identities influence our cultural lens allows us to honor other cultural perspectives without pathologizing minoritized group members (Cone-Uemura & Bentley, 2018).

Recruitment

Individual Therapy Clients and Member Criteria

The majority of clients who occupy Queer Therapy Groups from this author's counseling center are clients who are being seen in individual therapy. Therefore, it is important that everyone on staff who refers to the group understands that the inclusion criteria for group include having a non-heterosexual identity and/or does not identify with the historical gender binary (e.g. trans, nonbinary). It is important to note that a specific identity in these broad definitions is not required, as many of the more well-known identities (e.g. gay, bisexual, pansexual, queer) are not necessarily labels that resonate with students. This can also be a mix of graduate and undergraduate students. In the group pre-screening process the group facilitators can be more transparent about the potential make-up of the group (e.g. graduate students, first years, seniors).

Referrals from Campus Partners

Students are also recruited by various campus partners. For example, having a strong working relationship with other offices on campus such as an LGBTQ Center, or a Student Center for Diversity and Inclusion, is another way to advertise, via flyer, announcements in community meetings, and word of mouth. Due to the history of mistrust between mental health systems and minoritized communities, it is important to be visible via outreach to campus communities and form close relationships with campus partners. Dunbar et al. (2017) found that the most common barriers to accessing mental health treatment in sexual minority students were uncertainty over how to access services, financial concerns, questions about eligibility for services, and embarrassment. Therefore, collaborative relationships with campus partners who have regular contact with sexual minority students are essential to more effectively disseminate accurate information about college mental health services. Further, advertising by other campus organizations and their endorsement to use counseling services for sexual minority students may normalize seeking mental health treatment and decrease stigma.

Pre-group Screening

Although students who are screened for the group vary in terms of group experience, all group members are provided psychoeducation about group process. Topics for discussion in the pre-group screen meeting include: informed consent, limits of confidentiality (between group therapists and clients and clients with each other), and the interpersonal process structure of the group.

Students are informed that although this is a Queer Therapy Group, students come to group with multiple identities and this is a place where all identities are welcome. Students are invited to share their multiple identities (e.g. race, religion, SES), and how those intersect with their sexual minority identity/identities. Similar to general interpersonal process groups, heterogeneous group membership has the potential to decrease stereotypical thinking and increase understanding and empathy between minority and majority groups (Kivlighan et al., 2019). For example, one member may identify as a gay, cisgender man, international student, while another student identifies as a White, U.S. national, cisgender man. Although both students identify as gay, they come from vastly different racial, cultural, and religious backgrounds, both struggling in different ways and potentially having preconceived notions about one another. Through their experiences in group they are able to dispel certain stereotypes and increase understanding of one another in the group and the current political climate (Kivlighan et al., 2019).

Norms

Norms are established in the first few group sessions. One norm could be asking members to attend the first four sessions consecutively before deciding to act on any initial reactions to leave the group (e.g. fears related to sharing with others, initial awkwardness, self-disclosures around sexual identity). Consistency with attendance, along with confidentiality, lends itself nicely to a safe and cohesive group atmosphere for members to feel comfortable with self-disclosure of their presenting concerns.

Typically in interpersonal process groups, contact outside of the group is discouraged. Yarhouse and Beckstead (2011) suggest that due to the nature of this type of group, and the limited social support sexual minorities on campus may have, outside group contact is normalized and allowed. Further, those group members who are connected with other offices on campus (e.g. LGBTQIA resource center and other identity based organizations) may see each other at community meetings and events which may make contact inevitable. The stipulation that is presented to the students is that if they do have contact with one another outside of the group, it is expected that those who had contact will share this experience with the group in the next session and the group can process any feelings related to the situation. The students are informed that group therapy is an opportunity to increase self-awareness, and awareness in how they relate to others so they can learn effective ways to make social connections and form community. Group members are informed that group therapy is not a place to make social connections or find dating partners. Facilitators can highlight that using it this way could hinder group members from achieving their goals and fully experiencing the benefits of group therapy (Yarhouse & Beckstead, 2011).

Initial Sessions

After orienting clients to group therapy, members are invited to discuss what would make the group feel safe versus unsafe. Examples of safety include students and facilitators expressing empathy, compassion, and curiosity. Attitudes of judgment, monopolizing, and boundary crossings are examples that would make the group unsafe. The group is invited to have a discussion on what is needed for the group to be successful and how they see ways to support one another. Group members are also encouraged to explore how they want to structure the group. For instance, some groups prefer to start with silence until someone asks the group if they can share. Another group may feel more comfortable with a check-in. Check-ins may consist of each group member going around and stating a high and low of the week as well as something they are looking forward to that week or in the near future. The choice of how to start the group can be varied and group members always have the space to negotiate what they want to check in about.

Addressing Microaggressions

Microaggressions are unintentional and/or intentional slights that come in the form of words or behaviors that subtly communicate derogatory messages to the receiver (Sue et al., 2007). This is especially prone to happen in groups that are heterogeneous in nature (e.g. sexual identity based group with group members holding multiple minoritized identities). Cone-Uemura and Bentley (2018) assert that despite group leaders' efforts to increase their own self-awareness and sensitivity to cultural issues, group is a social microcosm, and microaggressions are likely to occur. Similar to individual therapy contexts, group therapists hold most of the power and the structure can be hierarchal in nature. Despite this power deferential (between group leaders and group clients), the identities of the group leaders and members may influence how power plays out and who is the receiver of the microaggressive comment. For example, a group therapist may inherently hold power in the group therapist/group client relationship and may also hold more oppressed social identities than their group client(s), which could make the therapist a potential target for a microaggression. Typically, when a microaggression occurs there will also be awkwardness, discomfort, and most likely noticeable in the other group members. The group leader's role is to identify experiences in the room and create space for discussion and exploration. The developmental stage of the members in the group and the developmental stage of the group are important to consider, however. At times, it may be helpful to make a psychoeducational comment that address the notion that people in the group may say something hurtful and that the group is encouraged to get comfortable being uncomfortable by being able to name and share feelings. As a group leader, it's important to leave space for group members to share their feelings, recognizing that some members may want to speak up immediately, while others need a moment to process before sharing their feelings (Cone-Uemura & Bentley, 2018). Although it is important for the perpetrator of the microaggression to be able to process feelings (e.g. shame, embarrassment), it is also imperative to center the experiences of the receivers of the microaggression.

Group members are not the only individuals susceptible to commit microaggressions. Group leaders inherently hold power by the nature of being the therapist and also the social identities that they hold. Group leaders should acknowledge what happened, use self-disclosure as appropriate, and work to heal any therapeutic ruptures that may have occurred (Cone-Uemura & Bentley, 2018). This may also serve as a model to other group members in terms of how to address microaggressions not only in the group but outside of the group with other peers, as well.

Case Example

Below is a clinical vignette that illustrates a group therapist facilitating cultural exploration informed by a multicultural oriented framework.

JASON : (international student, gay, cisgender man) I figured group would be a good idea. Even though it is scary to talk in front of people I don't know that well, I feel like I need to do something. None of my friends know I'm gay and I can't tell them. The other day we were in the car and one of my friends made a gay joke. Everyone laughed, I just stayed quiet. Back home (country of origin), it's illegal to be gay, you could get arrested, beaten up, or worse. I wouldn't want to tell my friends in case they told anyone back home. I went to some of the LGBT organizations on campus but I don't feel like I belong there either.

GROUP THERAPIST : (GT) (U.S. born, queer, fem presenting, White, cisgender woman) I appreciate your willingness to share that with the group and I hear that it can be difficult to share with people you don't know that well. It also seems that you may not feel safe to share this information with people in your life right now (people outside of group). I'm wondering if anyone else in group feels that way – I see others nodding their heads.

MICHAEL : (U.S. born, White, gay, cisgender man) Oh dude I know *exactly* how you feel. I don't fit in anywhere. My fraternity brothers make jokes all of the time about people who are gay. Only a few people know – I don't know if I could ever tell all of them. I have gone to some of the LGBT organizations, though – they are pretty cool. Are you sure you gave them a shot? (He looks at Jason.)(A few other group members roll their eyes.)

GROUP THERAPIST: It seems like some of you had a reaction to what Michael said, I'm wondering if anyone would like to put language to their facial expressions.

STEVEN : (U.S. born, African American, gay, cisgender man)Michael, you don't *exactly* know how it feels but like, you know, neither could I …

even though Jason and I are both Black, he's from Jamaica, I'm from New York – I can relate to us both being Black, gay men but I don't know what it's like to possibly be arrested for being gay. It is obviously not illegal to be gay in New York. You fit the type that these LGBT school groups are looking for – a skinny, gay, White, cis man. You're the "right" kind of gay. Even at those clubs – if you're not White, lean, tall, and athletic – it's not the scene for you.

JASON: It's … it's okay – I know you're only trying to help, Michael (looks at Michael and then toward the floor). It's just different for me than it is for you. It's like, I have to be a different person at different times; at school, in group, talking to my family. And I'm always worried about my safety and stuff.

GT: Jason, that sounds really stressful and exhausting to have to change who you are based on who you are around and to always be thinking about your safety. Michael, I'm wondering what it was like for you to get this feedback from Jason and Steven.

MICHAEL: (Takes a minute, looks down, and then looks at the group.) My first reaction is to say that I didn't mean to offend anyone but I think that's just me feeling defensive. The truth is, what I heard Jason share was feeling like he doesn't fit in anywhere and I immediately was like "yes, I totally relate to that." But the more I think about it, after Steven shared and Jason said a little more, although I still feel like we can all know a similar feeling, I totally missed hearing where Jason said his feelings come from – (says to Jason) I can't believe how unsafe it is to be gay in Jamaica. I know we can have similar feelings but it's important to recognize how different they might be too. For me, I still feel uncomfortable in my own skin. And when I really think about it … you're right. I mean, the organizations on campus are really White dominated and the same with the clubs.

GT: Michael, it sounds like you are recognizing that you have both oppressed (gay) and privileged identities (White, cis man).

GT: I want to take a moment to process what this exchange was like for everyone. It sounds like everyone has really struggled in some ways with their sexual identity but in really different ways. Michael, it seems like you may have made some assumptions about your fellow group members, believing that it was just as easy for them to integrate into the LGBT community. Jason and Steven, you both have had different and similar experiences in your communities and find it difficult to fit in here at school due to the dominant White, cisgender, presence in the LGBT organizations. In our first session (a few sessions ago) and in our group screening I encouraged all of you to be open and consider everyone's multiple identities and this is an example of that. I really appreciate everyone's authenticity in sharing today and being open to learning more about each other.

The clinical vignette above demonstrates an example of a group therapist's cultural comfort when utilizing cultural opportunities to help the group members increase their own self-awareness and awareness about other cultures and experiences. Although everyone is a member of this group based on sexual identity, they each have many other intersecting identities. It is critical for group leaders to acknowledge with cultural humility the problematic comments initially made by Michael. Michael appears to be listening to respond, which inadvertently minimized Jason's self-disclosure. Michael displayed effects of White privilege in his lack of awareness for the complicated experiences of his fellow group members. It is important, however, to avoid focusing solely on Michael as this will shift focus from Jason (the member whose experience was minimized). This is understandable given that the group is a microcosm of a larger societal system of power and privilege. However, it is important to keep the focus on the potential effects that Michael's comment may have had on Jason and other members of the group.

Conclusion

The purpose of this chapter is to provide group therapists with an overview of suggestions on how to incorporate cultural humility in a sexual identity based group, specifically within a college/university setting. With that said, some of these suggestions may be applied to other outpatient settings as well. Whether a seasoned group therapist or an early practicum student, cultural humility is paramount to providing optimal group services to students. Modeling cultural humility for clients can provide corrective experiences with the dual benefit of teaching clients how to approach each other and other people in their lives.

References

Baams, L., De Luca, S. M., & Brownson, C. (2018). Use of mental health services among college students by sexual orientation. *LGBT Health*, 5(7), 421–430, doi:10.1089/lgbt.2017.0225.

Burlingame, G. M., Fuhriman, A., Mosier, J. (ed.) (2003). The differential effectiveness of group psychotherapy: A meta-analytic perspective. *Group Dynamics: Theory, Research, and Practice*, 7(1), 3–12, doi:10.1037/1089-2699.7.1.3.

Cone-Uemura, K., & Bentley, E. S. (2018). Multicultural/diversity issues in groups. In M. D. Ribeiro, J. M. Gross, & M. M. Turner (eds), *The college counselor's guide to group psychotherapy* (pp. 21–35). New York: Routledge.

Denton, L. K., & Hodges, J. (2018). Research on groups in college counseling centers. In M. D. Ribeiro, J. M. Gross, & M. M. Turner (eds), *The college counselor's guide to group psychotherapy* (pp. 59–68). New York: Routledge.

Dunbar, M. S., Sontag-Padilla, L., Ramchand, R., Seelam, R., & Stein, B. D. (2017). Mental health service utilization among lesbian, gay, bisexual, and questioning or queer college students. *Journal of Adolescent Health*, 61, 294–301, doi:10.1016/j.jadohealth.2017.03.008.

Ghabrial, M. A. (2017). "Trying to figure out where we belong": Narratives of racialized sexual minorities on community, identity, discrimination, and health. *Sexuality Research and Social Policy*, 14(1), 42–55, doi:10.1007/s13178-016-0229-x.

Hook, J. N., Davis, D. D., Owen, J., & DeBlaere, C. (2017). *Cultural humility: Engaging diverse identities in therapy* (1st edn). Washington, DC: American Psychological Association.

Kitzrow, M. A. (2003). The mental health needs of today's college students: Challenges and recommendations. *NASPA Journal*, 41(1), 167–181. doi:10.2202/1949-6605.1310.

Kivlighan, D. M., & Chapman, N. A. (2018). Extending the multicultural orientation (MCO) framework to group psychotherapy: A clinical illustration. *Psychotherapy*, 55(1), 39–44, doi:10.1037//pst0000142.

Kivlighan, D. M., Adams, M. C., Drinane, J. M., Tao, K. W., & Owen, J. (2019). Construction and validation of the multicultural orientation inventory-group version. *Journal of Counseling Psychology*, 66(1), 45–55, doi:10.1037/cou0000294.

Merta, R. (1995). Group work: Multicultural perspectives. In J. G. Ponterotto, J. M. Casas, & L. A. Manuel (eds), *Handbook of multicultural counseling* (pp. 567–585). Thousand Oaks, CA: Sage.

Meyer, I. (2003). Prejudice, social stress, and mental health in lesbian and bisexual populations: Conceptual issues and research evidence. *Psychological Bulletin*, 126(5), 674–697, doi:10.1037/0033–2909.129.5.674.

Owen, J. (ed.). (2013). Early career perspectives on psychotherapy research and practice: Psychotherapist effects, multicultural orientation, and couple interventions. *Psychotherapy*, 50, 496–502, doi:10.1037/a0034617.

Owen, J., Tao, K. W., Drinane, J. M., Hook, J., Davis, D. E., & Kune, N. F. (2016). Client perceptions of therapists' multicultural orientation: Cultural (missed) opportunities and cultural humility. *Professional Psychology: Research and Practice*, 47(1), 30–37. doi:10.1037.pro0000046.

Owen, J., Tao, K., Leach, M. M., & Rodolfa, E. (2011). Clients' perceptions of their psychotherapists' multicultural orientation. *Psychotherapy Theory, Research, Practice, Training*, 48(3), 274–282, doi:10.1037/a0022065.

Schmidt, C. K., Miles, J. R., & Welsh, A. C. (2011). Perceived discrimination and social support: The influences on career development and college adjustment of LGBT college students. *Journal of Career Development*, 38(4), 293–309, doi:10.1177/0894845310372615.

Singh, A. A., Merchant, N., Bogusia, S., & Ingene, D. (2012). Association for specialists in group work: Multicultural and social justice competence principles for group workers. *The Journal for Specialists in Group Work*, 37(4), 312–325, doi:10.1080/01933922.2012.721482.

Sue, D. W., Capodilup, C. M., Torino, G. C., Bucceri, J. M., Holder, A. M. B., Nadal, K. L., & Esquilin, M. (2007). Racial microaggressions in everyday life: Implications for clinical practice. *American Psychologist*, 62(4), 271–286, doi:10.1037/0003-066X.62.4.271.

Sue, D. W., & Sue, D. (2012). *Counseling the culturally diverse: Theory and practice* (8th ed.). Hoboken, NJ: Wiley.

Welch, P. J. (1996). In search of a caring community: Group therapy for gay, lesbian, and bisexual college students. *Journal of College Student Psychotherapy*, 11 (1), 27–40.

Woodford M. R., & Kulick, A. (2015). Academic and social integration on campus among sexual minority students: The impacts of psychological and experiential campus climate. *American Journal of Community Psychology*, 55(1–2), 13–24, doi:10.1007/s10464–10014–9683-x.

Yalom, I. D., & Leszcz, M. (2005). *The theory and practice of group psychotherapy* (5th ed.). New York: Basic Books.

Yarhouse, M. A., & Beckstead, A. L. (2011). Using group therapy to navigate and resolve sexual orientation and religious conflicts. *Counseling and Values*, 56(1–2), 96–120, doi:10.1002/j.2161-007X.2011.tb01034.x.

6 Social Identities Explored in Therapy Groups

Michele D. Ribeiro

Introduction

University life whether as an undergraduate or graduate student is often filled with excitement for new experiences that lie ahead, as well as anxiety for being able to complete educational requirements. Along with studies, however, come so much more personal development that often intersects with identities related to who we are as social beings. Erikson (1968) specifically coined the term for this stage of psychosocial development as "intimacy versus isolation." Aspects of identity that are often examined in domestic students within higher education include race, culture, class, sexual orientation, gender identity, and spiritual/religious development, to name a few. In addition to the social identities that domestic students navigate, Zhuzha (2018) highlights that international students have additional factors that have the potential to further complicate their psychological wellness. These additional issues are cultural, linguistics based, social, and legal system adjustment related, and may contribute to stress and impact well-being (Chen, 1999; Johnson & Sandhu, 2007; Mori, 2000; Olivas & Li, 2006). The stress often associated with succeeding academically for both domestic and international students can interplay with psychological factors that cause attaining a degree much more difficult than predicted when first starting a program of study. Many students find themselves seeking supportive services at counseling and health centers for therapy and/or medication management.

According to the 2015 Annual Survey of the Association for University and College Counseling Center Directors, there were more than 800 member centers providing services in the survey period (2014–2015), and these counseling centers provided care for 5,738,922 students (Reetz, Krylowicz, Bershad, Lawrence, & Mistler, 2015). Between Fall 2009 and Spring 2015, counseling center utilization increased by an average of 30–40 percent, while university enrollment increased by only 5 percent. Of those 800 centers, 70.8 percent reported offering therapy groups of one kind or another. Thus, group therapy is a highly utilized and effective treatment modality in college counseling center settings. Many Students of Color and international students attending Predominantly White Institutions (PWIs) may struggle with invalidating experiences related to race, culture, and/or nationality, and group therapy can provide a supportive forum for managing difficult affective experiences related to these and other social identities (Cone-Uemura & Bentley, 2018). This chapter will focus on the impact of group psychotherapy, and in particular interpersonal process groups, on supporting college student development related to social identities that interplay with their success as a student in higher education. Several examples will be provided for reference in discussing social identity issues within group psychotherapy contexts.

Need for Attachment

Attachment or the need for security is necessary across all cultures and societies. Bowlby (1982) identified the notion of internal working models as sets of beliefs that guide behavior, emotion regulation, and future relationships with the self and others. The family or early attachment figures in a person's life becomes the basis for these internal working models; and whether someone may feel secure and trusting or have more difficulty with actually connecting to others. Marmarosh (2009) specifically talks about the opportunities for college students within higher education to work through these early ruptures within the therapy group and during social contexts that are equally salient to academic life and success.

Issues of attachment can be disrupted and cause distress socially and academically within relationships with roommates, romantic partners, parents, friends, advisor/major professor for graduate students, to name a few. It is within the realm of interpersonal process groups, however, that these disruptions can be processed, validated, and possibly worked through. Group is powerful in that there are numerous transferences that members can experience whether toward the leader(s) and/or other members. Members can feel a sense of connection to their peers likening to that of a familial sibling relationship and/or to an even more obvious one, of the leader as the "parent" of the group. A recent example involved a White 21-year-old cisgender female who joined an interpersonal process (IP) group to help her readjust to social situations that were altered after the traumatic death of her older sister. (She died less than a year before this member started the group.) Initially she was closed off from sharing her struggles with grief in this group, but as she developed more trust and felt cared for, she began to open up more to members in the group. As the group held her with compassionate feedback, she almost seemed to take on a sisterly role to some of the first-year students in the group. She highlighted how she had struggled as a first-year student also and expressed that she wanted to show them a better way to manage college. Her social identity as a sister seemed to get reactivated in what appeared to be healthy ways, both as a service to her own healing and to the healing of those younger group members.

Group members in general can experience the re-emergence of a familiar struggle or conflict within the group. This struggle can provide an opportunity to work through rather than play dramas from earlier life experiences. In order for this working through to occur, the student needs to be willing to stay engaged in the process. If attachment is too insecure or disorganized (Bowlby, 1982), the student may choose isolation over connection. A recent example involves a Middle Eastern cisgender 28-year-old undergraduate student who reportedly had difficult relationships with his family in his youth and lived with an uncle when he was an adolescent. He later left his country to study abroad in Europe and eventually the U.S. He expressed feeling alone in his experience, adding that interactions with people, even those from his culture, felt distant, almost like a thin veneer separated him from them. This author shared her appreciation for the vulnerability he demonstrated in opening up to this therapist. She wondered if he might be willing to join a therapy group to explore this deep wound of isolation with others who may be able to connect to his feelings of loneliness. He agreed. This was the first step in working on his attachments. He attended the first group and at the end disclosed appreciation for and connection to a similar struggle with feeling isolated and disconnected shared by several of the group members, and then never returned. When asked in a later individual session why he didn't come back to group, he commented that it was too difficult to share his struggle despite knowing that others could relate.

Attachment across Identity Markers

Attachment can also be strengthened as a result of familiar social identity status and may include class, identifying as a Person of Color, in a religious/spiritual context, as LGBTQ, and/or international, to name a few. Analyses of data collected through the Healthy Minds Study (Cleveland, 2013) at this author's university showed a 450 percent differential for anxiety and depression between students who reported current financial struggles with those who reportedly had none. Students who are faced with housing and/or food insecurities (class issues) may particularly benefit from group therapy as a result of feeling less alone in their experiences and feeling that, in spite of their financial situation, they belong in higher education and can feel supported in attaining their degree. One example involved a young White bisexual 20-year-old mother of a four-year-old who transferred to a four-year university after attending a rural community college several hours away from the present university. To help foster an increase in her self-concept, this writer felt that she should begin individual therapy first. Later she agreed to join a group and despite feeling that her experiences were not relatable, this client received admiration for her strength and determination, qualities that were inherent to her, from other members who were not parents. The group provided her with a secure base to further explore her own worth and identities related to class and belonging at the university.

Pre-group Preparation

Examining social identities in group therapy initially occurs in the pre-group meeting. During the pre-group meeting, it is helpful if the leader checks in with clients about social identities they may want to explore, particularly if their goals do not highlight these issues. Initially clients may not have specific goals surrounding the examination of their social identities in an interpersonal process group. However, even if clients do not foresee a need to examine such issues immediately, they are encouraged to express the need as the group moves forward.

Example of Connection through Sharing Faith

A recent example in group related to religiosity with a young first-year White, male identified college student. He reported that he wanted to feel less socially anxious and decided to make this a goal of individual therapy. He described what he referred to as an automatic tendency to shut down, turn red from the throat up to his face, and almost need to remove himself from most social situations. This author asked if he might trial group therapy. Upon identifying the goal of taking small risks to share himself with others, he reluctantly agreed. During the second group meeting, a member who strongly identified with her faith shared that she had a desire to know how other members felt about religion. The socially anxious young man, who happened to have a rosary wrapped around his hands, stated, "I think about religion a great deal and find myself comforted by my faith." These statements provided a springboard for the group members to explore their relationship to religion, both past and present. For the young man, his disclosure around his faith demonstrated a level of vulnerability and ultimately helped him take the first step with forming a relationship with others in the group.

Example of Connection across Different Abilities

A White identified, cisgender male student (X) who identified as blind sought therapy due to feeling lonely and socially isolated. He was referred to this author's IP group and was recognized by a member of the group with whom he had attended camp as a youth. Visibly surprised and delighted, he confirmed that he indeed had attended the camp. The warmth displayed in this initial group created a sense of safety and cohesion for the group members. Increased by their desire to help X understand more of what he might have otherwise missed nonverbally, the progressing group members developed a more vividly verbal way of expressing themselves. X shared how lonely he feels walking on campus when no one says anything to him. This leader and members learned that saying hello across campus would be a wonderful experience for X, and would also let him know that he was seen and a valued member of the campus community. Yalom and Leszcz (2005) speak to X's example when they identify the therapeutic factors of cohesion, universality, the experience of acceptance, and instillation of hope as key experiences that are reinforced in the therapy group. Rutan, Greene, and Kaklauskas (2019) further acknowledge the alliance that occurs between group members; the group can help build a "sense of safety and promotes risk-taking, engagement, and commitment to the work of the group" (p. 120). These precise factors coupled with the group's alliance helped create a sense of safety for X, allowing him to feel like he belonged among his peers. It also taught this leader and his peers the value of expressing ourselves verbally and descriptively, particularly when interacting with people who have visual impairment.

International Students' Need for Connection

More than 450 million people of all ages around the world suffer from a mental illness. Depression is the leading cause of disability across the world today (World Health Organization, 2012). According to the Institute of International Education (2017) more than a million foreign students are currently studying in the U.S. This is an increase of almost 30 percent since 2011. Given the almost epidemic numbers of depression worldwide and the increasing numbers of international students studying abroad and in the U.S., an examination of the mental health status of international students is important. Mori (2000) identified unique stressors faced by international students that include but are not limited to: high expectations of self, language barriers, cultural differences, and sensory overload, and may contribute to various states of mental health. In addition, Mori identified a number of barriers that international students face regarding the perception/acknowledgment of the need for mental health services, and how to access those services. As an example, international students may hold stronger stigmatized beliefs regarding mental illness and the utilization of mental health services (i.e. Hyun, Quinn, Madon, & Lustig, 2007; Golberstein, Eisenberg, & Gollust, 2008). Stark differences in cultural beliefs and practices may also affect how international students perceive mental health problems. According to Mori (2000), international students are more likely to report mental health problems as physical symptoms rather than emotional ones, and are more likely to see mental health problems as personal inadequacies.

According to researchers, international students often experience relational difficulties that include shyness, isolation, difficulty making friends, and loneliness. There is also evidence that their concerns with adjusting socially may be more significant than those of domestic students (Hechanova-Alampay, Beehr, Christiansen, & Horn, 2002; Nilsson, Berkel, Flores, & Lucas, 2004; Owie, 1982; Parr, Bradley, & Bingi, 1991; Zhuzha,

2018). Data further suggests that international students have better mental health outcomes and lower stress when social support and connection occur between themselves and with domestic students (Atri, Sharma, & Cottrell, 2007; Lee, Koeske, & Sales, 2004; Mallinckrodt & Leong, 1992; Wang, Wei, & Chen, 2015; Wei, Liang, Du, Botello, & Li, 2015; Yeh & Inose, 2003). This finding is particularly useful when considering group psychotherapy as a modality of treatment for international students.

Many counseling centers attempt to offer international student support groups or psychoeducational groups specifically for this population. However, given the research that supports the notion that interactions with domestic students may produce better outcomes for international students, practitioners may want to regularly include international students in all types of therapy groups rather than offering only homogeneous groups exclusively. Interpersonal process groups whether structured (Johnson, 2009) or unstructured are particularly great vehicles for international students to learn how to interact within the host culture and for learning interpersonal effectiveness with domestic students. The following is an example of one student this author worked with in group who benefitted from an interpersonal process experience. A 28-year-old Japanese international undergraduate student (Y) was referred to this author's interpersonal process graduate and non-traditional undergraduate group. He had been seen in individual therapy with a Japanese therapist who felt he was ready for more interaction with his peers. Y presented as very depressed and isolated, and identified that his main goal in therapy was to increase his social interaction with others. He reported uncertainty regarding his major and also having a poor relationship with his parents who were very high achieving doctors living in Japan. By default, the group comprised a total of seven male identified graduate and non-traditional undergraduate students. One of the seven members, a South American student (pursuing his PhD), who left his country as a successful farmer to learn more about agricultural practices in the United States, also struggled with isolation. The remainder of the group was comprised of domestic U.S. White identified students or Men of Color. What occurred in this group was remarkable. The men provided a space for one another that held empathy and compassion. The Japanese student, who had presented initially with paucity in speech due to his anxiety and depression, began to share that the pressure of his family had thwarted his growth as a person. He and the others each shared the challenges they faced academically but the more salient topic revolved around their strong desire for intimate relationships. The men remained in group for six months before there was a change in membership, with the majority of the initial group staying for the whole academic year. What they created was a holding environment, where their sense of security and attachment was fostered and strengthened.

Domestic Students of Color and Need for Connection

Although White Euro American males are only 33 percent of the U.S. population, they occupy 80 percent of tenured positions in higher education and 90 percent of public school superintendents (Sue, 2019). Thus, Students of Color are especially likely to be brought up in an educational system that is either highly informed and/or dominated by Eurocentric values. This is particularly true in Predominantly White Institutions (PWI), which tend to dominate across the United States. Although members of IP (interpersonal process) groups may not start off with a specific goal to process issues related to discrimination, they can become prime safe spaces to engage in race-related dialogues. The ways in which a leader opens group can set the stage for the members to feel that social identities are an important aspect of what can be discussed in group. Below is an example of the dialogue between the group leader and the members at the start of session two; introductions and identification of goals are discussed. (All names are pseudonyms, some demographics were changed to protect identity, and permission was granted by group members to use the material in this transcript.)

LEADER: So welcome back, I know Cate missed last week so we want to spend just a few minutes to go around and introduce ourselves again. We will want to repeat goals because part of what this group does is to listen to each other's goals and try to help each other work towards accomplishing these. What we also did last week was identify any salient social identities that are important to you and that you would like the group to know about, including your gender pronouns. Please share any of these identities after you identify your name, your year in school, and your major. So who would like to start?

MARY: My name is Mary and I'm a kinesiology major. I'm a senior this year. Gender pronouns, she/her. I'm also a student and I work. My goals are to be more outgoing and be able to start up conversations more easily and to keep the conversation going. To work on and improve my relationships with my boyfriend and my family.

SARAH: My name is Sarah and I am a science major. My gender pronouns are she/her/hers. I'm a Woman of Color and my goal is to be able to be comfortable being vulnerable in my relationships with men for whom I have feelings.

CONAN: I'm Conan. I want to work on being more engaged. I'm an engineering major. It's my senior year as well. Pronouns are he/him. And I'd also like to be more comfortable with intimacy, I guess.

RICH: Alright, I'm Rich and I'm a junior. My pronouns are he/him. Engineering major and since I'm autistic, I'm trying to learn how to understand other people better and I'd like to be better at starting conversations and not being quite as shy.

JUNIOR: I'm Junior, I'm a second-year pre-med major, and I'm multiracial and bisexual, and I go with he/him/his. My goals are to work on my anxiety, not be as defensive, not shut down as easily, to relate and gain trust with people.

CATE: My name is Cate and I am also a senior, graduating. I'm a double major in merchandise management and design. My pronouns are she, her, and hers. I identify as Asian American. And my goals this term are to gain some perspective on how everyone else deals with their mental health issues and people's defense mechanisms and see how that relates to the relationships in my life.

RAYNA: I'm Rayna. I'm a third year and she/her/hers. I'm a psychology and education double major. Um, I also identify as Asian American and my goals are to practice being more authentic, not be so malleable in social situations, and to also release some of my defense mechanisms because I don't always recognize when they come up and I very frequently step into shame. And then that kind of guides my personality. Basically, I just don't like how malleable I am. I'd rather just be authentically me and accept myself in conversations and just in general.

As the group became more comfortable with hearing similar themes around insecurity in relationships, members seemed to be more open to sharing vulnerable aspects of their personal experiences. Here is an example of where this general IP group went after approximately 40 minutes into this second group meeting. For context, one of the members shared her experience of racism and being the target of a micro-aggression. Here is an excerpt from the group:

SARAH: I had problems with my roommate who was White and grew up very sheltered. Although I felt triggered by what she said to me, I had to make sure that I said something or I'd hate myself later. It's like I'm dealing with all this emotion right now not just with her but others too.

JUNIOR: So I have a question, what kind of questions did she and others ask?

SARAH: So they'll ask me about religion. So I come from Islam but I'm not religious. And then they'll just get like "is your dad a terrorist?"

GROUP: Oh God!

SARAH: And then, "does your mom wear the head scarf," or um, just stupid shit like that. And they, I don't know. I can't blame them for thinking that Syria is a Third World country, that it's not civilized at all, but they just already assume that. I was called terrorist like all my life. Just recently when I came to college I realized that it wasn't okay.

RAYNA: That sounds really painful.

SARAH: Yeah, yeah.

RAYNA: It's like bullying.

SARAH: Yeah, at the time it wasn't because it was okay. Everyone called me that and it was fine cause it ... I don't know it was a joke. I thought it was funny. And we all thought it was funny. Then I came here and I realized, oh, they're not joking, like there was a small part of them that believed that, you know.

LEADER: Sarah, it sounds like you experienced a microaggression.

SARAH: Yeah, yeah.

LEADER: I'm wondering how the group feels as they listen to Sarah share this painful experience.

JUNIOR: What I try to do for the most part, as long as they don't shut me down is ... I don't block it out like it's not real. There was someone that said to me that race doesn't exist. I try to engage with them as long as they don't shut me down. So when a lot people call me Nazi, I go hey my family was Jewish by the way, so not every Austrian was that.

SARAH: Yeah.

JUNIOR: So they usually don't know what to say anymore.

SARAH: Right.

JUNIOR: So they just realize, but I try to keep them engaged and educate them.

SARAH: Yeah. I mostly just experience people getting defensive. There was one time where there was like ... it was the guy who I really liked, and we were having a really good time, and it was last summer. He made a really weird comment, and I tried very hard to ... it wasn't even like trying to educate him ... I was just trying to be like you know that doesn't really make sense what you're saying. Like most stereotypes that people will say it just doesn't make sense. Like very uneducated, like they think they're funny. And he was very defensive and I was very hurt.

LEADER: (Rich shakes his head and looks down.) Rich it looks like you are having a reaction to what you are hearing?

RICH: I'm just trying to process it, sorry.

LEADER: Like disbelief? Kind of feeling like how could that happen for someone to say that?

RICH: Kind of ...

SARAH: Were you more surprised that people would say that?

RICH: I mean it's like yes and no, I've never personally experienced that much of that and it's like, yeah, I'm aware that stuff like that happens but its hurtful when you hear about it.

RAYNA: So you were feeling sad?

RICH: I think I feel sad for you (looking at Sarah) about that.

SARAH: Is it weird that I don't like people feeling sad for me? To me it's just whatever. I think that someone said that to me but I don't associate with them.

LEADER: Sarah, you might have defended against the sadness in the past, so it might be helpful for you to just sit with people feeling sadness that you had to experience that. And it could be useful for you to not feel sad around it, but it might also be useful for you to know that people also feel sad that you had that experience.

JUNIOR: I understand that too, though. When people feel sad for me and you just get by and you're like, I don't really care. I understand that too.

CONAN: Do you appreciate their honest attempt for empathy?

JUNIOR: I don't know, it's like why do they care? I used to face it a lot, yeah, a lot in high school.

LEADER: Conan what you said about empathy, I'm wondering if you want to check in with how Sarah is feeling?

CONAN: How are you feeling?

SARAH: I'm feeling fine. I don't know.

CONAN: When you had that interaction with the guy over the summer, did you say those ... did you tell him why you were leaving?

SARAH: No, I never said anything.

CONAN: Ah, but you said something the other day with your friend?

SARAH: I did. And that was a big step for me. And it was very powerful for that. And he was immediately like you are so right, that was so bad for me to say and that was just like rewarding. I was like, after I said that, like the feeling I get when you do say something it's like Oh my God did I make a big deal out of it? You think, did I just overreact with what I said, did I just make everything up? Uh, when I sent that text and he didn't respond for hours it was kind of like really early in the morning. I was thinking that I just made a big deal out of nothing. Like, he's going to be defensive and it's going to hurt me really, really badly and the second he defended I will just shut down. But he wasn't, which is good.

LEADER: You had a corrective experience with your friend?

SARAH: Yeah, yeah, cool.

MARY: When you say that getting defensive kind of hurts you more than them, how do you communicate that to them?

SARAH: Um with the guy when I just tried, I didn't outwardly say what you said is wrong, I just didn't imply that at all, so maybe that was on me that I should have started with what you said was wrong, I just try to use logic. Or to show them that what they're saying isn't making much sense so that they can be like, oh that doesn't make sense and I can be like, yeah it was also racist. But I try not to bring up race first especially with, um, Caucasians because I know they get defensive.

CONAN: We do, but I would want to know that it hurts you so I can learn what my impact is on others.

CATE: I feel you made an impact by saying something so that is good.

LEADER: What's coming up for you Cate?

CATE: I felt bad for you and I also felt like even though that situation didn't feel good for you, I think you made an impact, if not just a tiny bit, like a little bit of good came out of that.

SARAH: For sure.

JUNIOR: I understand not wanting to bring race up a lot. When I did it in the last group I felt like, why am I bringing it up?

SARAH: The stuff always gets brought up.

JUNIOR: I shouldn't be talking about this.

CATE: This is like your truth.

CONAN: But if it's important to you, you should bring it up.

JUNIOR: Yeah but the same thoughts pop up, like why am I talking about this, I'm bringing it up and making a big deal about this. The exact same thought process came up for me too.

RAYNA: One way I've minimized defensive responses is just saying how I'm processing in that moment. Like instead of approaching it with the educational side because people get defensive about that, like even me personally, if I feel like someone's talking down to me about my thing, like kind of implying that I'm stupid and I don't know something I get kind of defensive. So sometimes especially with the race thing I'll just say like that kind of offends me that you said that or like it kind of hurt that you assumed that I am like every other Asian.

SARAH: Yeah, it's mostly just, am I allowed to be offended right now?

RAYNA AND OTHERS: Yeah, I think, yeah, you have a right to feel offended!

SARAH: But then, if you have that thought then obviously you were offended but it's just I kind of have to review what they said in my head two or three times to be like okay.

RAYNA: That makes me feel sad that this is like something we have to ask ourselves, like is it okay for me to announce how I'm feeling?

SARAH: I feel sad about that too.

RAYNA: Yeah.

SARAH: 'Cause I do that to other people too, yeah I appreciate it, say it. Totally that was wrong, that was not okay for them to say like say whatever is on their mind. If someone came up to me and called me a terrorist that's like 100 percent racism but with microaggressions like that it's a lot harder to measure whether I should say something or not.

SARAH: With my friend recently, I said it the day after I texted him. It was good I was able to process it. 'Cause sometimes not saying it in the exact moment is fine as long as you say something within a good timeframe I guess. But just being like what you said the other day was wrong, um, in the moment, doesn't give you time to process it and really think about how you want to say it. Or you know, like figure out your emotions.

CONAN: What would be bad about saying it immediately or calling out?

CATE: The situation is hard. How you're feeling in the moment on whether to comment or not.

RAYNA: When inside you don't feel that way.

SARAH: Yeah, I admire you so much.

RAYNA: Thanks.

CATE: There's a lot of support in here, it feels good.

LEADER: What are you appreciating?

CATE: I appreciate the way you are here for us and, like, you want everyone to be better and I don't even know you guys and I just met you guys (Rayna laughing) and that's great. I feel that way. You guys don't even know each other and you're supporting each other and it's great.

RAYNA: Yeah.

CATE: It's an awesome group.

It should be noted that, although issues of racism and microaggressions would not be resolved in this one group, members appeared to understand that these topics were open for discussion and could be useful in understanding what keeps them from their goals of intimacy with others in their lives. This excerpt displays a few issues. First, People of Color often hold doubt and go through so much questioning around their experiences of racism and microaggressions. Sue (2019) states "it is not the old-fashioned racism, sexism, and heterosexism that is most harmful to People of Color, women, and LGBT persons but the contemporary forms known as microaggressions." Microaggessions can be defined as "brief and commonplace daily, verbal, behavioral or environmental indignities, whether intentional or unintentional, that communicate hostile, derogatory, or negative slights, invalidations and insults, to an individual or group because of their marginalized status in society" (Sue, 2019). The group was able to validate and affirm that it was okay for Sarah to feel the way she did regarding the microaggression she experienced, and to take the next step and express it. Sue et al. (2019) further identify the need for micro-interventions that validate the experiences of people who hold minoritized identities. Group therapy can be a productive space to practice micro-interventions and build allies across diverse and often targeted social identities such as race. Conan, the White male in the group, validated Sarah by admitting that White people do get defensive, but that it is also okay to let people know how she (Sarah) felt.

National conversations have opened up around White dominance, and the overwhelming need White people have to maintain a sense of "goodness" with their intentions and actions, something DiAngelo (2011) identifies as a kind of White fragility. Additionally, several researchers (Kivel, 2011; Spanierman, Todd, & Anderson, 2009) have identified the personal costs of racism to White people and that loss exists for everyone when inequitable societies persist as a way to motivate White people to move into social action. Therapy groups can be hit or miss around these sensitive issues on race; depending on the racial identity salience of all members involved (Helms, 1990; McRae, 1994). Thus, having a sense of group members' ability to understand their own racial identity development can provide some basis for what the group can productively explore and the leader can effectively facilitate. Utilizing the pre-group meeting to assess for racial identity development particularly when populating groups with varied racial groups could be a good first place to assess for sensitivity to issues on dominance and marginalization. D'Andrea (2014) highlights that trust across racial groups and developing secure group attachments can be more successfully accomplished by having several minority group members share a cultural identity. He further goes on to delineate that often connections to one's ethnic group can create a sense of belonging in the group. Thus, when leaders populate groups with members, it is helpful to have members who can share specific social identities particularly if they are minoritized identities related to race, nationality, and sexual orientation. Additionally, group leaders have a responsibility to regularly engage in diversity dialogues themselves as well as participate in ongoing peer consultation and supervision, so as to know how to manage these and other types of difficult issues in group. As leaders, we need to be ready to create the foundation for our clients to trust in sharing vulnerable emotional issues related to social identity examination as well as manage their need to be heard and validated.

Conclusion

Although psychoeducational and support groups are helpful in exploring social identity, the interpersonal process group is a particularly useful vehicle for examining these issues. This chapter highlighted the value of the interpersonal process group in college counseling center settings. It also identified the value these groups provide in creating a space for attachment styles to be examined and potentially for secure attachment to be experienced. Interpersonal process groups can become an ideal context for having dialogue across differences related to social identities. This is particularly true with college students who are faced with social relationship and more salient marginalized identity issues (e.g. Person of Color, People with disabilities). Further, because we live in a conflicted sociopolitical world, it is the responsibility of the group therapist to become versed in diversity dialogues so that a space can be created to explore germane societal issues. As group practitioners we can create an environment that builds a bridge between our group members so that we become more united than divided around our differences.

References

Atri, A., Sharma, M., & Cottrell, R. (2007). Role of social support, hardiness, and acculturation as predictors of mental health among international students of Asian Indian origin. *International Quarterly of Community Health Education, 27* (1), 59–73, doi:10.2190/IQ.27.1.e.

Bowlby, J. (1982). *Attachment and loss vol.1: Attachment.* New York, NY: Basic Books.

Chen, C. P. (1999). Common stressors among international college students: Research and counseling implications. *Journal of College Counseling, 2*(1), 49, doi:10.1002/j.2161-1882.1999.tb00142.x.

Cleveland, S. (2013). *The Oregon State University 2013 Healthy Minds Study Results Report.* Unpublished manuscript. Corvallis, OR: Counseling and Psychological Services.

Cone-Uemura, K., & Bentley, E. S. (2018). Multicultural/diversity issues in groups. In M. D. Ribeiro, J. M. Gross, & M. M. Turner (eds), *The college counselor's guide to group psychotherapy* (pp. 21–35). New York: Routledge.

D'Andrea, M. (2014) Understanding racial/cultural identity development theories to promote effective multicultural group counseling. In D. A. Gerrity, C. R. Kalodner, & M.T. Riva (eds) *Handbook of group counseling and psychotherapy* (2nd ed.) (pp. 196–208). Thousand Oaks, CA: Sage.

DiAngelo, R. (2011). White fragility. *The International Journal of White Pedagogy, 3* (3), 54–70.

Erikson, E. H. (1968). *Identity, youth and crisis.* New York: W.W. Norton Co.

Golberstein, E., Eisenberg, D., & Gollust, S. E. (2008). Perceived stigma and mental health care seeking. *Psychiatric Services, 59*(4), 392–399.

Hechanova-Alampay, R., Beehr, T. A., Christiansen, N. D., & Horn, R. K. V. (2002). Adjustment and strain among domestic and international student sojourners: A longitudinal study. *School Psychology International, 23*(4), 458–474, doi:10.1177/0143034302234007.

Helms, J. (1990). *Black and White racial identity: Theory, research & practice.* New York: Greenwood.

Hyun, J., Quinn, B., Madon, T., & Lustig, S. (2007). Mental health need, awareness, and use of counseling services among international graduate students. *Journal of American College Health, 56*(2), 109–118.

Institute of International Education (2017). *Open Doors 2015 "fast facts".* Retrieved from: https://www.iie.org/Research-and-Insights/Open-Doors/Fact-Sheets-and-In fographics/Fast-Facts.

Johnson, C. V. (2009). A process-oriented group model for university students: A semi-structured approach [Special Issue]. *International Journal of Group Psychotherapy, 59*(4), 511–528.

Johnson, L. R., & Sandhu, D. S. (2007). Isolation, adjustment, and acculturation issues of international students: Intervention strategies for counselors. In H. D. Singaravelu, & M. Pope (eds), *A Handbook for counseling international students in the United States* (pp. 13–35). Alexandria, VA: American Counseling Association.

Kivel, P. (2011). *Uprooting racism: How White people can work for racial justice.* Gabriola Island, BC: New Society Publishers.

Lee, J. S., Koeske, G. F., & Sales, E. (2004). Social support buffering of acculturative stress: a study of mental health symptoms among Korean international students. *International Journal of Intercultural Relations, 28*(5), 399–414, doi:10.1016/j.ijintrel.2004. 08. 005.

Mallinckrodt, B., & Leong, F. T. (1992). International graduate students, stress, and social support. *Journal of College Student Development, 33*(1), 71–78.

Marmarosh, C. (2009). Multiple attachments and group psychotherapy: Implications for college counseling centers [Special Issue]. *International Journal of Group Psychotherapy*, 59(4), 461–490.

McRae, M. (1994). Interracial group dynamics: A new perspective. *The Journal for Specialists in Group Work*, 19(3), 168–174, doi:10.1080/0193392940814361.

Mori, S. (2000). Addressing the Mental Health Concerns of International Students. *Journal of Counseling & Development*, 78, 137–144.

Nilsson, J. E., Berkel, L. A., Flores, L. Y., & Lucas, M. S. (2004). Utilization rate and presenting concerns of international students at a university counseling center. *Journal of College Student Psychotherapy*, 19(2), 49–59, doi:10.1300/J035v19n02_05.

Olivas, M., & Li, C. (2006). Understanding stressors of international students in higher education: What college counselors and personnel need to know. *Journal of Instructional Psychology*, 33(3), 217.

Owie, I. (1982). Social alienation among foreign students. *College Student Journal*, 16(2), 163–165.

Parr, G., Bradley, L., & Bingi, R. (1991). Directors' perceptions of the concerns and feelings of international students. *College Student Journal*, 25(3), 370–376.

Reetz, D. R., Krylowicz, B., Bershad, C., Lawrence, J. M., & Mistler, B. (2015). *The Association for University and College Counseling Center Directors annual survey*. Retrieved from: http://www.aucccd.org/director-surveys-public.

Rutan, J. S., Greene, L. R., & Kaklauskas, F. J. (2019). Basic leadership tasks. In F. J. Kaklauskas, & L. R. Greene (eds), *Core principles of group psychotherapy: An integrated theory, research, and practice training manual* (pp. 111–121). New York: Routledge Press.

Spanierman, L. B., Todd, N. R., & Anderson, C. J. (2009). Psychosocial costs of racism to Whites: Understanding patterns among university students. *Journal of Counseling Psychology*, 56(2), 239–252.

Sue, D. W. (2019). The detrimental impact of microaggressions. Keynote Address at the Society for Humanistic Psychology Conference, Corvallis, OR.

Sue, D. W., Alsaidi, S., Awad, M. N., Glaeser, E., & Calle, C. Z. (2019). Disarming racial microaggressions: Microintervention strategies for targets, White allies, and bystanders. *American Psychologist*, 74(1), 128–142.

Wang, K. T., Wei, M., Chen, H. H. (2015). Social factors in cross-national adjustment: Subjective well-being trajectories among Chinese international students. *The Counseling Psychologist*, 43(2), 272–298, doi:10.1177/0011000014566470.

Wei, M., Liang, Y. S., Du, Y., Botello, R., & Li, C. I. (2015). Moderating effects of perceived language discrimination on mental health outcomes among Chinese international students. *Asian American Journal of Psychology*, 6(3), 213–222, doi:10.1037/aap0000021.

World Health Organization (2012). World Health Statistics 2012. Retrieved from: https://www.who.int/gho/publications/world_health_statistics/2012/en/.

Yalom, I. D., & Leszcz, M. (2005). *The theory and practice of group Psychotherapy* (5th ed.). New York: Basic Books.

Yeh, C. J., & Inose, M. (2003). International students' reported English fluency, social support satisfaction, and social connectedness as predictors of acculturative stress. *Counselling Psychology Quarterly*, 16(1), 15–28, doi:10.1080/0951507031000114058.

Zhuzha, K. (2018). International students' intentions to seek group therapy and self-stigma: Effects of informational and therapist rapport interventions (unpublished dissertation). Auburn, AL: Auburn University.

Section III
Working with Specific Populations in Groups

7 Athletic Identity: A House of Mirrors

Cindy Miller Aron

Introduction

"Athletic identity is the degree to which an individual identifies with the athlete role and looks to others for acknowledgement of that role. ... as a self-concept, athletic identity can define the way in which an individual evaluates their competence or worth" (Brewer, Van Raalte, & Linder, 1993). Elite athletes and the supporting culture can inflate winning in sport as a means of achieving immortality. The resulting idolatry justifies the meaning of their existence through their sport participation (Watson, 2010). This can operate for the athlete on a less than conscious level, yet is experienced consciously as a "pressure to succeed."

An athlete can have a strong athletic identity, which can have little to do with their internal experience of self. Identification as an athlete poses challenges in therapeutic settings for a multiplicity of reasons. The visibility of being identified as an athlete incites images and stereotypes, which often have little to do with the athletic individual's experience of their life. This can be intertwined with racial, ethic, socioeconomic, and gender identities. The projections upon an individual with an athletic identity is based upon performance; in other words, "what the person does." This can spark accompanying attributes that are not necessarily based upon "who they are." Assumptions can be a source of confusion for the athlete, as late adolescence/young adulthood is a period of time in which identity formation is part and parcel of the developmental tasks. Athletic identity can pose a significant distraction for providers as well as group therapy members, based upon the cultural idealization of the athlete as a heroic symbol of struggle. Often the visible struggle, determination to triumph, that the athlete has in their sport, is a significantly different experience than their internal and interpersonal struggles. For example, it is not uncommon for athletes of unusual height and/or stature to be approached about their physical size. It can be difficult to appreciate the burden of this level of visibility when struggling with depression or anxiety. In a group setting the athletes' sheer physical presence takes up more space than the typical individual, which can pose distractions for the leader as well as other members. Immediately this can place the athlete in a position of "other," especially when intersecting racialized dynamics also occur, which can challenge the task of integration, in the service of developing group cohesion, unless appropriately addressed.

Developmental Tasks and Athletic Culture

Erikson (1968) conceptualized the developmental task of adolescence as that of "identity versus role confusion;" the existential question of "who am I and what can I be." Individuals need to re-establish their boundaries as they venture into this unknown territory of life away from home. Erikson asserts the importance of having the "time and space" to openly explore and experiment, out of which may emerge a solid sense of identity and awareness of self. The kind of commitment elite athletes are asked to make, prior to having had the opportunity to explore and develop a sense of self away from home, creates systemic obstacles to the more typical societal leeway that is given to a late teen, young adult's need to "find themselves." In addition to the remarkable time commitment athletes are expected to make, they must adhere to rigid schedules, strict rules, travel demands, sport-related regulations and ongoing performance expectations. This can present deflections to growth resulting in an unconscious temporizing of this important developmental process. Chickering (Chickering & Reisser, 1993) expanded the tasks of late adolescence to include the development of advancing integrity. The development of identity, autonomy, and integrity are normative maturational processes that can create unconscious stressors, given the systemic constraints, which then work against the resolution of tasks. This can be particularly challenging for African Americans who attend predominantly White institutions in White towns or small cities. It is not uncommon for non-athlete African Americans to have other students assume they are athletes. By the same token, the assumption that you are an athlete (versus there for an education) creates its own battleground of oppression for African American Student-Athletes. The level of objectification for these individuals can be potent. Football players in particular, for no other reason than the fact it is the sport they play, garner attention whether they like it or not. "I'm African American, from the city. This is a White university and a White town. I am looked at wherever I go, with suspicion. This is in contrast to the rush of fans after a football game who want my autograph, even though I didn't play, and they do not know my name. I don't know who I am anymore. It is depressing. I feel lost, I'm really nobody I recognize." On the surface this can be flattering, but underneath it holds little valence and serves a minimal purpose in the search for self and meaning.

Athletes function in what are essentially closed, top-down, autocratic systems. Conforming to the standards set is often linked to the athletes' scholarship/participation, hence a literal dependence that positions athletes to submit to what is expected. Over-conformity to an identity can be considered normative (Hughes & Coakley, 1991). "These systems place tremendous pressure on college athletes, which manifests as a variety of psychological risks" (Moore, 2016). Kissenger et al. (2015) noted in their research on athletic identity that "the predominant 'sports first' theme was grounded in the student athlete's perception of their role and responsibilities as principally athletic in nature" (p. 14). This role and their responsibilities toward their sport create a tension, for the individual who wishes to learn; who wishes to embrace their identity as a college student unrelated to their identity as an athlete. The student who wishes to pursue an area of interest/major that their practice schedule does not allow is often faced with an untenable dilemma. "I want to be in a major that cannot work out with my sport because of conflicting practice schedules. Both involve performing. This is just one more thing that contributes to me feeling depressed." Frequently athletic academic advisors will discourage athletes from either majoring in their interest or pursuing a minor in a difficult subject area. The oppression of the system flies in the face of what can be viewed as the "privilege" athletes have. An athlete who formerly might have been a confident student is inadvertently undermined, reducing their role as primarily being "an athlete."

Jay Coakley has written extensively about the constraints of the social system athletes function within, contributing to what is a "developmental dead-end" (Coakley, 1992). The disempowerment that can ensue from no longer having control of their lives in developmentally appropriate ways can create "personal troubles" for the individual. The tightly controlled schedules of elite athletes are non-negotiable. This can create disempowerment (Coakley, 1992) during a time when an increased sense of power and competency is necessary; and when the athletes' peers are experiencing the joys and challenges of navigating the environments of academia and the workplace.

It is important for providers of mental health services to understand and appreciate the unusual demands the system sports' culture asks of teens and young adults. In addition to appreciating these demands providers need to understand the fidelity that is asked of the athlete to the system and the power differential that exists between player and coach. These are complex roles to navigate at this vulnerable, developmental time. The demand for fidelity to the athletic system and acculturation necessary for performance can work to the detriment of the completion of the developmental tasks. It is not uncommon for athletes to be seen in college counseling centers and be assigned to providers unfamiliar with the culture of athletics. Often the suggestions are to "talk to the coach about cutting back on training," if the athlete is feeling overwhelmed. That kind of response from a mental health provider can result in the athlete feeling profoundly misunderstood or viewed somehow as not appropriately asserting themselves. In a top-down authoritarian system this kind of request from an athlete is not an option unless it is medically driven, in which case the sports medicine doctor would make the recommendation.

Athletes and Identity

A substantial body of literature has been produced over the last 35 years addressing the complex issue of athletes and identity. Brewer et al. developed the athletic identity measurement scale in 1993. It is the most widely used and cited scale. Sturm et al. (2011) suggest that

> when student-athletes find it difficult to balance the contexts of academics and athletics, usually athletic identity takes precedence over the student identity noting that previous research with Division I student-athletes has suggested that their athletic identity for these students may be stronger than their student identity.

The demand for commitment to their role within their sport places college athletes at a greater risk for identity foreclosure reducing them to only the role of athlete (Murphy et al., 1996). The kinds of self-exploratory options that are afforded other university students are simply not available to those with this demanding dual role, as well as limitations that the structure of the role requires. Identity foreclosure happens when individuals prematurely make a firm commitment to an occupation or ideology (Marcia, 1980). This results from not being allowed to explore their internal needs and values, rather conceding to the demands of their environment and acquired social role identity. Poucher and Tamminen (2017) found that athletes with a stronger "Athletic Identity" were more likely to neglect other parts of their lives to fulfill their athletic role, which can impede the development of a more multidimensional self-concept. As a person's athletic identity grows they often begin the process of identity foreclosure, in which they dissociate with other important aspects of their social identity (Good et al., 1993). Athletic identity is a dominant identity and the level of identity foreclosure increases with the level of sports participation, which is high with elite athletes. Individuals participating at highly competitive levels have a higher athletic identity versus student identity and higher identity foreclosure levels than those who participate at less competitive levels (Brewer et al., 1993).

Lurking underneath what is considered to be a solidified athletic identity can be considerable role confusion. This is further compromised by the lack of flexibility and ability to explore different aspects of self. Most students arrive at college surrounded by other students who do not know their history, their accomplishments or lack thereof, which sets a nice stage for the exploration and development of self. The college athlete has quite the opposite circumstance with a history of accomplishments as well as expectations created in a public arena. In addition to the fan base developed at a college or university, athletes often have "fans and family" at home who are emotionally invested in their athletic success. This "responsibility" weighs heavily on the heart of the athlete who does not wish to "let people down" by not fulfilling what is expected athletically. Additionally, it is not uncommon for absent parents in some students' lives to contact them at this time, which can be remarkably unsettling.

The greatest challenge athletic advisors face when working with college athletes is with students in the foreclosure stage (Ross, 2016). The foreclosure stage is one of four identity stages as described by Marcia (1980). The foreclosure stage is characterized by a commitment made without proper exploration. Often these students have made a commitment to a major, likely at the suggestion of someone else without questioning it; in a sense, a default due to circumstance. Additionally, when a foreclosed athlete is unable to perform in the chosen major, advisors find that they often are not open to suggestions about another course of study (Berk, 2006). Athletic eligibility becomes an issue, forcing the athlete to choose another major. This can find students shifting, again, without much exploration, choosing the path of least resistance to sustain the goal of maintaining academic eligibility at any cost.

African American male athletes can struggle to negotiate two salient self concepts, one being African American and one being an athlete. This presents unique complications for this population as a result of the role sport plays in the African American community (Bimper & Harrison, 2011). The attraction to sports begins at an early age and is often viewed as a perceived route to success, to the exclusion of other routes; a means for upward mobility. From a critical race perspective, the legacy of discriminatory policies and practices combined with the social-cultural factors contribute to Black student athletes' emphasis on sports pursuits rather than academic success (Hodge et al., 2008). Critical race scholars assert that racial advances transpire only when it supports White self-interest. This is in reference to the integration of Black athletes into the revenue generating sports in the '70s. Often African American athletes are accepted under "special admission" programs which do not necessarily emphasize the importance of academics, only what is needed to "get by" (Hodge et al., 2008). Additionally, it is less likely for African Americans to graduate from college compared to their White counterparts. This reinforces the strong athletic identity which may cause the athlete to be less invested in their education (Bimper & Harrison, 2011). It also can dominate their alternative social and personal identities (Bimper & Harrison, 2011).

Athletic Injury, Identity, and Fallout

There is considerable research on the perils of orthopedic injury and psychiatric risk. This is intrinsically related to the developmental task of identity, for elite athletes. Once an athlete is no longer able to participate in training, play their sport, be a part of their team, the psychological adjustment issues are far greater than rehabilitating the injury. The separation from the peer group (team) that they have been part of brings into question their value and self-worth. Concern about re-injury, questions about competency, diminished sense of self-efficacy, in addition to the loss of athletic identity can be a consequence of injury. Injured athletes report more symptoms of depression and anxiety compared with non-injured athletes (Reardon et al., 2019).

Athletes frequently use their sport as a way to manage emotions through intensive exercising. When this ability vanishes, the resulting anxiety and depressive symptoms are intensified, as this primary, overdeveloped coping skill is gone. A profound social isolation can ensue as a result of family and friends not being able to appreciate how all-encompassing the loss of physical function is for the individual. It is also possible that mental health providers will lack an appreciation for the significant meaning injury has for the individual. Elite athletes typically have a "warrior" mentality of relentless toughness in the face of hardship. Consequently, they may not reveal the degree to which they are suffering physically or psychologically. Dr Antonia Baum, sports psychiatrist, reports that athletes with higher levels of success subsequently have higher levels of depression and suicidal ideation after injury (Baum, 2013).

Stereotypes

There is social dissonance when athletes behave in ways contrary to the heroic image and cultural wish (Reid, 2008). Athletic performances can be heroic, but must be separated from the individual who has mortal thoughts, feelings, uncertainties, inadequacies, and fears like anyone else (Reid, 2008). Without a humanized way of relating to the individual, who is also an athlete, a profound interpersonal isolation can ensue.

Hegemonic masculinity as defined by "masculine traits, such as strength and toughness, are celebrated in the media coverage of sport and operate to reaffirm the myths of male prowess" (Boyle & Haynes, 2009, p.136), can be supported within athletic college culture by the focal value upon the revenue generating sports, which are football and basketball. This consciously and less than consciously creates a bind for a young man who is trying to find his way in the world of interpersonal relationships. "Guys assume I have it easy with girls since I am a football player. But that does not help with my confidence and the fact that I have no sexual experience. It feels like people don't want to hear about that."

Black male athletes in particular suffer from the cultural way athletics and the institution of sport has defined acceptable forms of heterosexual masculinity, which plays into the stereotype of Blacks being physically more capable than Whites (Anderson & McCormack, 2010). This poses complications for any gay athlete but particularly complicated for the Black male gay athlete. The intersection of race, sexuality, gender, and sport contributes to the idea that Black American male athletes are necessarily heterosexual, and that gay athletes are exclusively White (Anderson & McCormack, 2010). This is driven by the stereotype that gay athletes are involved in what are considered feminized sports such as ice skating, gymnastics, diving, and so on. In combination with the higher degree of homophobia in the Black culture, which is supported by White cultural images and definitions of gay men, keeps Black gay athletes from coming out (Anderson & McCormack, 2010).

Male athletes experience considerable stereotyping related to the "dumb jock" image. This is commonly encountered by athletes with their professors, at times experiencing reduced academic expectations and patronizing offers by fellow students to help with coursework. The "dumb jock" research has demonstrated that the negative stereotype of academic incompetence was higher for African Americans than White counterparts (Sailes, 1993). This is painful for athletes across the board and there is evidence this can become a "stereotype threat" that can incite a self-fulfilling prophecy around performance (Dee, 2014). Scholarly athletes, regardless of ethnicity, who are in honors programs and/or have high GPAs routinely encounter surprise that this is the case. "It is not uncommon when someone asks me about my major and I mention the honors college, for them to be surprised and comment 'Oh, I didn't imagine that.'" "People are very surprised that I am pre-med and have a 4.0 GPA." A bi-racial athlete who appears African American is an honor student with a 3.86 GPA, and is routinely asked by White peers or professors if he needs "help" with his homework. Additionally, there was a question about whether he could "manage" minoring in a challenging field along with the challenging choice of major.

Female athletes are subjected to stereotypes about femininity and possibly assumptions that they are lesbian as a result of a lack of conformity to hegemonic femininity (Kauer et al., 2006). Female athletes can struggle with their self-image as their muscle mass increases. It is common for the media emphasis on female athletes to be heterosexual and feminine. This can lead to an overemphasis on feminine characteristics, such as wearing ribbons during competitions, in order to avoid the prejudice and discrimination they can receive. The bind shifts further when appearing too feminine; sexualization can occur, resulting in a trivializing of their athletic activity. The media is adept at photographing female athletes in positions that stereotypically can be viewed as "sexual" by men. The media routinely photograph the athletes in what would outside of sport be considered sexually suggestive positions. "As a gymnast I have gotten used to having my picture or a picture of a teammate taken when we are in a performing a maneuver with our legs spread apart. You do not see these kinds of pictures of men on the sports pages." At a time of heightened self-consciousness these visible and public experiences can complicate the very private task of experiencing oneself as a female, sexual being.

Fantasies, Unconscious Illusions, and Projections

Carl Jung's (1980) conceptualization of *archetypal events*, such as separating from one's parents, and *archetypal figures*, such as the hero, provide a platform for understanding the unconscious binds described in this chapter. The developmental period of late adolescence/young adulthood is about the separation from one's family of origin. The athlete as a representative figure of heroic struggle, hence archetypal figure, can contribute to an unconscious resistance to truly joining the person on an exploration of internal struggle. The human need for idealized figures belies the reality of a struggling and perhaps all too human hero. In the same way we do not wish to acknowledge our own weaknesses, there may be unconscious resistance to acknowledging the weakness of the heroic figure. One then has to reconcile the shattering of the illusion that the athletic hero can transcend human frailties. This is largely based upon ignorance; the less we know about an athlete, the easier it is to idealize them; projecting individuals' needs to manufacture images to meet their own needs, which have little to do with the athletes' experience.

This ignorance can take the form of voyeurism; a wish to be on the "inside" of athletics. The interest that a provider and/or group member has might relate more to the athlete's sport than it does to the individual. It is not uncommon for athletes to wish to talk about anything but their sport, since sport occupies most of their waking hours. An athlete expressed the family and community preoccupation with his sport. "One of the reasons I do not like to go home for holidays is that all my relatives wish to talk about is football. They do not know football like I do, nor do they understand that this is personal for me, not 'interesting,' and that I do not wish to talk about it." Another athlete spoke about the family's tendency to over identify with the athlete and actually see their progress in the sport intertwined with the family's success. "As I began to have more and more success and broke into the national spotlight, friends and family would describe what I did as 'we.' I wondered 'who is we?' I'm the only one doing this and yet somehow they were taking credit and using it as a badge of honor in their lives."

Group therapists in particular need to be aware of groups' unconscious dynamics that can lead to more primitive levels of functioning. Bion's theory of assumptive cultures describes the working group culture as the times when the group is focused upon its tasks. Group members are communicating honestly and openly, reacting rationally rather than emotionally. Bion observed groups shifting rapidly in the face of conflict and/or other anxieties. Bion's (1948) three "basic assumptions" can derail a group from its tasks. He named the three assumptions "dependency," "fight/flight," and "pairing." As an idealizing of a member or members begins to occur the group could find itself in a "fight/flight" mode, the most basic of defenses for the purpose of survival; this could involve an unconscious resistance to weakness in self, in other, and perhaps the leader. Additionally, an idealized member, namely an athlete, could easily become sucked into a role that contributes to the assumption of "pairing." The group's preponderant needs focus upon the fantasy of an idealized couple who will "save" them from the peril of their fears and anxieties; projecting group success upon how the "pair" can, for example, save them from the inadequacies of the leader. Group leaders can work with these enactments by addressing group members' unexamined anxieties, which often revolve around tolerance for difference. Typically the most effective approaches at this time in the life of a group is to use "group as a whole" interventions.

Conclusion

Elite athletes struggle with the same developmental challenges as their peers. The difficulties of this stage are complicated by their immersion and fidelity to the culture of athletics. An athletic identity is viewed as an identity of privilege and an idealized assumption of power. This can create cultural blinders to the human struggles that athletes have, which further complicate the completion of these important developmental tasks.

Likely issues for athletes in a therapeutic environment will have to do with difference – difference residing in the multiple identities an athlete can have, as well as the difference between the internal experience of the athlete and the external perception. Similar to other identities addressed in this text, it is important for mental health providers of individual and group therapy to be aware of the unique opportunity looking at social identities provides for us. Assumptions and transferential feelings are powerful parts of the individual and group therapy experience. Social identities being particularly potent as a result of cultural and historical narratives. As individual and group leaders, it is crucial to appreciate the skill needed to navigate the, at times, treacherous territory of difference. It is also an opportunity for good faith, which therapists and group members alike share in the hopes for what is possible. Gitterman (2019) recommends addressing differences during the early stages of group – to aid clients' abilities to talk about difference from the beginning. This is in contrast to the regressive and expected "pull" for similarity as a foundation for cohesion. Gitterman asserts that ultimately cohesion depends upon the ability to work with difference. He states that there can be a loss of connection when social identities create hierarchies that perpetuate oppressive systems. It is important that the system of our therapy groups avoids this trap of avoidance and silence. Commonality regarding our differences and perhaps even similar experiences of oppression can be powerful forces for repair and transformative possibilities. Theoretical models and therapeutic approaches aside, acknowledgment of how we are identified by others as well as how we identity are crucial links to the developmental task of late adolescents/young adult elite athletes.

References

Anderson, E., & McCormack, M. (2010). Intersectionality, critical race theory and American sporting oppression: Examining Black and gay male athletes. *Journal of Homosexuality*, 57(8), 949–967.

Baum, A. L. (2013). Suicide in athletes. In D. A. Baron, C. L. Reardon, & S. H. Baron (eds), *Clinical sports psychiatry: An international perspective* (pp. 79–88). Oxford: Wiley-Blackwell.

Berk, L. E. (2006). *Child development* (7th ed.). Boston, MA: Allyn & Bacon.

Bimper, A. Y., & Harrison, L. (2011). Meet me at the crossroads: African American athletic and racial identity, *Quest*, 63(3), 275–288.

Bion, W. R. (1948). Experiences in groups: I. *Human Relations*, 1(3), 314–320.

Boyle, R., & Haynes, R. (2009). *Power play: sport, the media and popular culture* (2nd edn). Edinburgh: Edinburgh University Press.

Brewer, W. B., Van Raalte, J. L., & Linder, D. E. (1993). Athletic identity: Hercules' muscle or Achilles' heel? *International Journal of Sport Psychology*, 24, 237–254.

Chickering, A. W., & Reisser, L. (1993). *Education and identity* (2nd edn). San Francisco, CA: Jossey-Bass.

Coakley, J. (1992). Burnout among adolescent athletes: A personal failure or social problem? *Sociology of Sport Journal*, 9, 271–285.

Dee, T. S. (2014). Stereotype threat and the student-athlete. *Economic Inquiry, Western Economic Association International*, 52(1), 173–182.

Erikson, E. H. (1968). *Identity, Youth and Crisis*. New York: W.W. Norton Co.

Gitterman, P. (2019). Social identities, power, and privilege: The importance of difference in establishing early group cohesion. *International Journal of Group Psychotherapy*, 69(1), 99–125, doi:10.1080/00207284.2018.1484665.

Good, A. J., Brewer, B. W., Petitpas, A. J., Van Raalte, J. L., & Mahar, M. T. (1993). Identity foreclosure, athletic identity, and college sport participation. *Academic Athletic Journal*, 8, 1–12.

Hodge, S., Burden, J., Robinson, L., *et al.* (2008). Theorizing on the stereotyping of Black male student-athletes: Issues and implications. *Journal for the Study of Sports and Athletes in Education*, 2(2), 203–226.

Hughes, R., & Coakley, J. (1991). Positive defiance among athletes: The implications of overconformity to the sport ethic. *Sociology of Sport Journal*, 8, 307–325.

Jung, C. G. (1980). *The archetypes and the collective unconscious*. Princeton, NJ: Princeton University Press.

Kauer, K., Krane, K., & Williams, L. (2006). "Scary dykes" and "feminine queens": Stereotypes and female collegiate athletes. *Women in Sport and Physical Activity Journal*, 15(1), 42–55.

Kissenger, D. B., Newman, R. E., & Miller, M. T. (2015). Hope, Trust, and Dreaming Big: Student Athlete Identity and Athletic Divisional Reclassification. Paper presentation at the 38th Annual Meeting of the Eastern Educational Research Association, Sarasota, Florida.

Marcia, J. E., (1980). Identity in adolescence. In J. Adelson (ed.), *Handbook of adolescent psychology*. New York: John Wiley & Sons.

Moore, M. A. (2016). Taking a timeout to ensure well-being: Social work involvement in college sports. *Social Work*, 61(3), 267–269.

Murphy, G. M., Petitpas, A. J., & Brewer, B. W. (1996). Identity foreclosure, athletic identity, and career maturity in intercollegiate athletes. *The Sport Psychologist*, 10(3), 239–246.

Poucher, Z., & Tamminen, K. (2017). Maintaining and managing athletic identity among elite athletes. *Journal of Sport Psychology*, 26(4), 63–67.

Reardon, C. L., Hainline, B., Aron, C. M., et al. (2019). Mental health in elite athletes: International Olympic Committee consensus statement. *British Journal of Sports Medicine*, 53, 667–699.

Reid, H. (2008). Olympic epistemology: The athletic roots of philosophical reasoning. *Proceedings of the XXII World Congress of Philosophy: Philosophy of Sport*, 47, 19–28, doi:10.5840/wcp22200847216.

Ross, K. (2016). Applying career and identity development theories in advising. In S. Brown & R. Lent (eds), *Career development and counseling: Putting theory and research to work* (pp. 71–100). Hoboken, NJ: John Wiley & Sons.

Sailes, G. A. (1993). An investigation of campus stereotypes: The myth of Black athletic superiority and the dumb jock stereotype. *Sociology of Sport Journal*, 10 (1), 88–97.

Sturm, J. E., Feltz, D. L., & Gilson, T. A. (2011). A comparison of athlete and student identity for Division I and Division III athletes. *Journal of Sport Behavior*, 34, 295–306.

Watson, N. J. (2010). Identity in sport: A psychological and theological analysis. In J. Parry, M. Nesti, & N. J. Watson (eds) *Theology, ethics and transcendence in sports* (pp. 107–148). New York: Routledge.

8 Prisoners in Group

Healing Processes at the Intersections of Race, Gender, and Age

Miriam M. Ribeiro

Introduction

Prisons in the form of dungeons have existed for centuries. Although penal incarceration dates back to the 1500s, imprisonment on a massive scale and as a form of criminal punishment is a relatively new development in our society. The number of people incarcerated in the United States of America increased to an all-time high between 1980 and 2015 (The Sentencing Project, 2019a). Statistics show that over that 35-year period, there was a 500 percent increase in the number of incarcerated people, from approximately 500,000 to over 2.2 million (National Association of the Advancement of Colored People, 2019; The Sentencing Project, 2019a), in large part due to changes in law enforcement policies and the war on drugs (Alexander, 2012; The Sentencing Project, 2019b; Toldsen, 2002). Today the U.S. comprises roughly 5 percent of the world's population, yet it incarcerates 21 percent of the world's prisoners (National Association of the Advancement of Colored People, 2019). Some form of correctional supervision including but not limited to probation and parole occurs for 1 in 37 adults in the United States (National Association of the Advancement of Colored People, 2019; The Sentencing Project, 2019a). Racial disparity occurs specifically with African American males (Alexander, 2012), who are reportedly six times more likely to be incarcerated than White males and 2.5 times more likely than Hispanic males (The Sentencing project, 2019b). In 2015 African American and Hispanic males made up 32 percent of the population of the U.S.A., yet comprised 56 percent of all incarcerated people for that year (National Association of the Advancement of Colored People, 2019). The disproportionate focus on Brown-skinned people (Alexander, 2012; Novek, 2014) contributes to California's state prison population demographic. In 1998 Blacks comprised 3 percent of California's population, yet made up 40 percent of the state prison system's inmate population (Toldsen, 2002). Projected outcomes in relation to these trends anticipate that one in every three Black American males may go to prison in his lifetime, compared to one in six Hispanic males, and one in seventeen White males (Sentencing project, 2019b). It is obvious based on these startling statistics that a colossal problem exists, leaving those who wish to be a part of its amelioration feeling overwhelmed. As therapists we can play a significant role in how treatment is disseminated within prison groups and can help inmates on their journey toward healing wounds related to recent as well as ancestral trauma.

Overview

This chapter aims to identify the demographics of individual systems that make up a series of subgroups that in turn comprise the larger group of incarcerated inmates within a California medium security male prison. It further examines treatment methodologies and their results by specifically illuminating attachment styles of racially diverse inmates who fit a traditional masculine stereotype. In addition, it looks at how humanizing the offender impacts the individual inmate and how it can influence the group as a whole, both within the therapeutic milieu and beyond. A brief exploration of transference and countertransference and what can be triggering for inmates and group facilitators is examined followed by a look at the importance of supportive supervision and consultation.

Subgroups within the Larger Group

Groups of many sorts have existed within our society and throughout the world since the beginning of humankind. It should be of no surprise that prisons and prisoners alike have both constructed and imposed a variety of groups based on an array of factors including but not limited to social-, racial-, and age-related strata. Prisoners foster group system dynamics as identified by Agazarian and Peters (1981) through several interdependent interactions of individual systems (Badia, 1989). Each inmate on a prison yard has a part in the development of the group as a whole (Agazarian & Peters, 1981; Badia, 1989).

Incarcerated scholar Francisco Wills, as reported by Novek (2014), describes the dual stratification of the prison environment. The first part of this stratum looks at the hierarchy of crime from a vertical position: inmates create a value system that informally disseminates punishment based on the types of offenses committed by fellow prisoners (Novek, 2014). In examining the first stratification, inmates create a hierarchy of crime or pecking order that labels the acts of the rapist and pedophile as the most heinous and egregious of all violent acts, including murder. The pedophile, in particular, is considered the "lowest of the low" and not worthy of living. This value system propagates a culture whereby inmates who are known as "shot callers" request "the papers" (the paperwork identifying the crime for which the inmate is serving time) of inmates who have recently arrived in a particular yard. The prison culture not only justifies but encourages and applauds the murdering of an inmate whose offense history involves molestation of a child under the age of 14. The bottom rung of this pecking order designated for sex offenders, specifically child molesters, is the only crime that has an overt and ubiquitous unifying retaliatory effect on the inmate population. Prison politics alleviate other crimes including theft and murder, seeing them through a less judgmental eye.

The second part of the stratification delineates and constrains group membership among inmates through a horizontal stratum that constructs rigid boundaries of division based on race, religion, and culture (Novek, 2014). The prison structure endorses and propagates division over unification from the larger group of inmates to smaller groups, with racial segregation being the most noticeably salient among the subgroups. Although the self-imposed segregation of inmates based on race is the glaring cultural mores within most prison systems, subgrouping based on gang affiliation also exists. It is common to see inmates who share the same skin color and ethnic background exclusively associating with one another in a yard. Within this racially homogenous group a bifurcation occurs causing these subgroups to lash out in violent and destructive ways. Dilution of racial connectivity due to gang affiliation is seen in examples of notorious gang rivalries including The Crips versus The Bloods, The Nortenos (Neustra Familia) versus The Surenos (Mexican Mafia), and the Aryan Brotherhood.

Race is not the only subgroup within California's prisons; the elderly are a growing population and the fastest growing age group within the prison system today (Blankenship, del Rio Gonzalez, Keene, & Groves, 2018). According to the Public Policy Institute of California (2019), the population of prisoners 50 years of age and older grew from 4 percent to 23 percent between 2000 and 2017, while the proportion of prisoners aged 25 and younger has decreased from 20 percent to 10 percent, leaving the average age of all prisoners within California's Department of Corrections and Rehabilitation (CDCR) close to 40 years of age (Public Policy Institute of California, 2019). Studies show that chronic health conditions are disproportionately common among the incarcerated due in large part to life experiences involving significant stress and trauma, a lifespan of limited access to quality health care and education, and a history of substance abuse and homelessness (Bedard, Metzger, & Williams, 2017; Greene, Ahalt, Stijacic-Cenzer, Metzger, & Williams, 2018; Maschi, Gibson, Zgoba, & Morgen, 2011; Williams, Goodwin, Baillargeon, Ahalt, & Walter, 2012). Some researchers and professionals purport that the cumulative burden of multiple chronic conditions and adverse health risks expose prisoners to premature and/or accelerated aging (Aday, 2003; Greene et al., 2018; Williams et al., 2012).

These aging prisoners can be further grouped into smaller categories or subgroups based on the accommodations their increasing limitations necessitate, including functional, sensory, and mobility impairments. Functional impairments typically involve activities of daily living and may require prompting in the specific areas of hygiene. Sensory impairments may involve the use of corrective lenses and hearing aids and require the asking of specific questions to ensure effective communication is achieved. Additional provision of accommodations specific to the inmate's mobility, including canes and wheel chairs, is necessary for aging inmates. Of equal importance is the assessment of the inmates' ability to assimilate and process information. Ascertaining what provision of special accommodation, i.e. slow, simple, and/ or repetitive speech, is necessary for the inmate's full participation. In addition to the aforementioned limitations, many aging inmates have debilitating chronic medical conditions including but not limited to hypertension, diabetes, cancer, lung disease, heart disease, stroke, and arthritis, as well as HIV and Hepatitis C. These medical conditions and the medical care and attention they require pose copious challenges for the inmates and their ability to ameliorate and/or manage their symptoms, while simultaneously placing a burden on the system as a whole.

Separation by gender is yet another way in which subgrouping occurs within the California prison system. Separating male and female cisgendered inmates is standard. Inmates who are transgendered are not separated based on their gender identity but are categorized and then housed based on the sex they were given at birth. Until recently, these transgendered inmates were a subgroup that had the option of being placed in designated prisons within Sensitive Needs Yards (SNY) for further protection. Formerly the inmate chose this designation, and then was classified as an SNY inmate. Pedophiles and gang drop-outs are additional inmate subgroups that were historically victimized and thought to be at greater risk of harm. Some inmates requested subsequent placement under the SNY umbrella, so as to provide them with greater protection. Over the years, inmates in the general population have viewed SNY inmates in an unfavorable way, referring to them as "snitches" or from the perspective of a hierarchy, lower-tier inmates. In Spring 2019 the Department of Corrections decided to dismantle the SNY subgroup due to the formation of gangs on these Special Needs Yards and because no noticeable decrease in violence was observed.

How does this system of subgrouping impact clinical treatment offered and utilized? Research shows that men utilize helping services less frequently compared to women (Addis & Cohane, 2006; Fitzpatrick, 2016; Rule & Gandy, 1994) and reluctance to seek help is reportedly linked to a greater endorsement of traditional masculine gender roles (Blazina & Watkins Jr, 2000; Fitzpatrick, 2016).

Masculinity, Race, and Attachment

Our development hinges on the attachments we create in our human relationships. Not only can our attachment styles influence the level of vulnerability we are willing to show in groups, but ethnicity and culture also play an influential role with the group facilitator and as part of the group therapy process (Marmarosh, Markin, & Spiegel, 2013). Prisoners naturally mistrust people based on their history, the larger societal para-digm of racism, and their current environment. Developing a sense of trust in an environment that is generally inhospitable and with people who have histories of perpetration is a pervasive challenge faced by inmates and therapists alike. The experiences of racism, animosity, and discrimination felt by group members of color may also breed a sense of majority cultural mistrust (Marmarosh et al., 2013) and result in the display of avoidant attachment styles among group members within groups. Group providers should be aware of a tendency toward over-pathologizing different racial groups and their attachment-seeking behaviors; discernment is encouraged to help mitigate such tendencies (Marmarosh et al., 2013).

Group therapy research links more avoidance in groups to African Americans and Asian Americans when compared to Whites (Marmarosh et al., 2013) and to men who endorse a higher traditional masculine image (Fitzpatrick, 2016). Since prison populations in California disproportionately represent African Americans who largely fit the traditional masculine male stereotype, it is not a surprise that emotion-based risk taking and vulner-ability are not standard within most group therapy settings within prisons. The ubiquitous White Eurocentric therapeutic paradigm and the standard for what constitutes "healthy attachments" are currently what mental health programs in the California prison system are endorsing and disseminating. It should be noted for the purposes of this chapter, when referring to "healthy attachment", this writer is referring to the White Dominant Culture's definition.

Marmarosh et al. (2013) link behaviors that prioritize autonomy and individualism to the Euro American dominant culture and label this presentation as one that is healthy and belonging to someone who is securely attached. Endorsement of such priorities, including indepen-dence as well as self-reliant and self-soothing problem-solving techniques, can be in direct conflict with the more anxious attachment styles demonstrated by Asian American and Hispanic American inmates (Mar-marosh et al., 2013). Marmarosh et al. (2013) further highlight Sue and Sue's (2003) research of Hispanics and their value of interdependence, collectivism, and family orientation and how more likely they are to seek social approval and to depend on others to meet their needs thus experiencing the Euro American paradigm as threatening to their attach-ment bonds (Marmarosh et al., 2013). This writer's experience has shown that African Americans who present as more dismissive and with higher self-esteem often struggle to allow themselves to develop connections with other group members and are known to say things like "I don't need anyone" and "I love me," when presented with the concepts of trust and low self-esteem respectively. These same inmates, over time and with sustained engagement in long-term groups, often begin to express their vulnerabilities and recognize that their past tendency toward self-reliance was more of a defense mechanism that no longer serves them.

So how does the clinician foster healthy attachments among racially and culturally diverse prisoners in an environment that endorses traditional masculine stereotypes, and necessitates dominance and violence to survive?

One initial and vital step often involves a thorough screening process where the assessment of an inmate's stage of change (Miller & Rollnick, 2002) is explored and identified. Those inmates who are at the denial stage (Miller & Rollnick, 2002) are typically uninterested in looking at changing themselves and therefore are generally not engaged in the treatment process. Group providers will want to recognize this and to remember that one of the most salient therapeutic approaches for this inmate is one that nurtures and cultivates the therapeutic alliance (Miller & Rollnick, 2002). It will also be important for the provider to contemplate whether the other members can create enough ambivalence in their peer to motivate him to begin to change. If this is not something the group provider can predict with some certainty, she/he should possibly consider whether this member is a good fit for this particular group at this particular time. Communicating the expectation of the group's projected time length is also essential during the screening process.

Research has shown and experience has proven that another important way to foster healthy attachments is through the longevity of a group's membership. The length of the group and the longer retention of voluntary membership can help lower anxious and avoidant attachment styles among group members (Fitzpatrick, 2016) while creating changes in behavior (Miller & Rollnick, 2002), thereby dismantling self-imposed walls. Exploring the manner in which these walls have served a purpose and may have played an essential role in the inmate's survival is important, as is the reality that those same walls that may have protected them may have also created a world of loneliness and isolation for them.

Lowering anxious and avoidant interactive styles among group members can be accomplished by having them examine the sociocultural factors that contribute to their attachment type. Rapport building between group members, both minorities and White members (Marmarosh et al., 2013), and the facilitator is essential and can be accomplished in many ways including by addressing racism and discrimination in the group. Retraumatization among marginalized group members may be prevented (Marmarosh et al., 2013) by a skillful facilitator who addresses racism and subsequently navigates and leads the group as a whole to a safe harbor.

Through the delivery of services that are respectful of and responsive to the beliefs and cultural and linguistic needs of all inmates, we can begin to establish a sense of safety and security within the group. Once this sentiment is created, vulnerability is more likely to occur. Once inmate group members show up, put down their weapons, take off their armor, and let themselves be seen (Brown, 2012, p. 112), vulnerability can exist among group members and as part of the group process. Healthy attachment and connection has a greater chance to embed itself, as well.

In groups the overarching goal for the facilitator is to assist in the cultivation of healthy and secure attachments. Similar to Bowlby (1982) and Object Relations, secure attachment within groups is fostered through the development of a secure base. This writer has found that practicing shame resilience as identified by Brown (2012), in a group that feels safe, creates an atmosphere where members are more willing to go to the edge of their comfort zone. This edge might include the exploration of concepts and connections, made within the group, to outside the therapeutic milieu and onto the yards and housing tiers. This exploration is then followed by a return to the secure base of group a week later for reassurance. With each passing week, the inmate ideally begins to feel more secure and comforted, and thereby is encouraged to explore beyond a newer edge. The more reliable and consistent the secure base/safe haven of the group, the more likely the member, in times of distress, will learn to self-regulate.

Like a guardian the facilitator must respond to and repair mistakes related to the attunement of the group members. In a group co-led by this writer, a member expressed not feeling seen by this group leader after he joined other group members in revealing sexual trauma he suffered as a child. By acknowledging her oversight with that specific group member, the group leader was able to facilitate a repair to the rupture between her and the group member while creating a greater sense of safety for the group as a whole. This writer has found that such positive experiences in group can play an influential role with traditional male prisoners and has helped alter the relationships with many inmates and their peers, as well as with their romantic partners, other group members, and within their families of origin (Fitzpatrick, 2016).

Humanizing the Offender

Our mental and physical health in many ways is connected to how we are treated as both individuals and as a collective. Since California's prison system disproportionately houses People of Color, it is important that clinicians consider the growing body of clinical and empirical research illuminating the psychological and physiological effects on People of Color and Indigenous individuals (POCI) who experience racism, discrimination, and microaggressions (Alvarez, Liang, & Neville, 2016; Comas-Diaz, Nagayama Hall, & Neville, 2019). Intersectional oppression is a contributor to the cumulative effects of racial trauma and includes microaggressions involving race, gender, sexual orientation, and xenophobia (Comas-Diaz et al., 2019). Research shows that dehumanizing people through cumulative racial trauma can leave lasting scars and can not only impact the mental and physical well-being of POCI (Comas-Diaz et al., 2019) but can be life-threatening to them as well. Since all inmates of color have been members of the free society at some point in their lives, it is fair to assume they have experienced some form of racial trauma both in the community and the prison system, and subsequently have felt dehumanized at some point. Many inmates of all races have shared how dehumanizing the experience of incarceration is and that the belittlement they experience on a daily basis by many staff is demoralizing and impacts their sense of self-worth and esteem.

Society, as a whole, has acted and continues to act as a poor attachment object to POCI (D'Andrea, 2014) and inmates on the whole, with greater affliction placed on inmates of color. Society's overarching attitude reflects that these men are not people of value and that their needs and feelings are not important enough and worthy of an adequate nurturing and supportive response. How can the group facilitator cultivate a more human-centric approach to treatment within the criminal justice system?

Research illuminates the importance of a culturally sensitive clinician who offers culturally responsive and racially informed interventions (Comas-Diaz et al., 2019; Helms, Nicholas, & Green, 2012) that encourage individual resilience (Comas-Diaz et al., 2019) within the group.

This writer has also found that humanizing the offender with whom she works, recognizing him as more than the crime(s) he has committed, and seeing him as someone who has aspirations, dreams, feelings, and emotions, allows the door to intra-individual and interpersonal healing and wellness to open. The co-operative group facilitator, who encourages, listens, validates, and offers support while modeling kindness and demonstrating the inmates' worthiness, not only helps foster the construction of a therapeutic alliance but encourages exploration beyond the boundaries of group and to other relationships within the inmates' lives. The group leader must be patient, committed, and should consult frequently to process feelings that may elicit countertransference.

A process group that can meet once a week, ideally for two hours, with intermittent individual follow-up sessions, can gradually create a culture of trust, and can foster the opportunity for depth work to commence. An inmate from a group conducted at a medium security prison stated that once he knew someone cared, he was able to remove his mask and begin to peel away the layers. Helping the inmate tap into his empathy and compassion allowed him to see the beautiful human being that exists behind the mask.

Cross-Cultural Identity, Transference, and Countertransference

There is an overwhelming majority of White counselors in the United States (D'Andrea, 2014; D'Andrea & Daniels, 2001). These White group leaders have a responsibility in understanding how their racial identity development influences their therapeutic orientation and group interventions (D'Andrea, 2014). Since Whites have greater privilege and power than persons in devalued racial groups (D'Andrea, 2014), it is essential for White group leaders to understand racial privilege so as to become culturally competent providers. Most inmate group members of color have past experiences involving marginalization and humiliation at the hands of White people in positions of power. Their past can influence and project expectations of being treated in a shaming, uncaring, and rejecting manner by their White group facilitator, further causing the inmate to reject the leader first by putting him or her down so as to protect himself from receiving rejection and establishing closeness (D'Andrea, 2014). Inmates of color who do not openly trust the White Dominant Culture may experience transference, and project their lack of trust onto their White facilitator.

Overcoming lack of trust in the process, and in the group as a whole, can be accomplished through the development of a secure group attachment to a new group with minority members who share a cultural identity (D'Andrea, 2014). Connection to one's ethnic group creates a sense of belonging (D'Andrea, 2014) for many inmates within group. In a long-term group, members can begin to feel safe, thereby pushing up against these negative feelings of transference, and taking risks to express their honest feelings about their White facilitator(s). Inmates in such a group expressed a learned paradigm taught to them by their communities of color regarding White people and the perception that they are not trustworthy. These same group members, after trust and safety were established a year later, expressed how surprised they were that this White writer and her White co-facilitator were able to guide them on their journey toward self-discovery and healing. This subsequently helped to create meaningful and heartfelt connections with their families for the first time.

Other transference issues that project mother and/or guardian onto the facilitator can arise with all races of inmates. Many of the inmates have had a history of conflicted relationships often with their mothers and/or absent fathers, so it should not be surprising to the leader when transference occurs in general, but especially in long-term groups where deeper relationships are formed. Many inmates have suffered sexual trauma at the hands of male and female family members, friends, and/or strangers. On one occasion, this White female group facilitator experienced an African American offender overtly sexualizing her. The situation involved a projection of the inmate's childhood White female perpetrator on this White facilitator, during a one-on-one session as follow up to the group. Unresolved and deeply seeded trauma that this inmate suffered as a child initially played out in a sexualized presentation in the session. Later the inmate's response turned submissive, and was eventually followed by grief and finally anger toward the facilitator. The potential consequences of the inmate's verbalized desires to act out in a sexually inappropriate way were explored with the inmate and later processed by this writer in a peer consultation group she facilitated.

Transference also occurs between inmates. On more than one occasion, middle-aged and elderly inmates have expressed disbelief to this writer with regard to the lack of respect shown to them by their younger inmate cohort. The majority of these older inmates have spent a large portion of their lives incarcerated. Many have spent between 20 and 40 years imprisoned and away from their families. In many cases these inmates were never physically present for their children who often comprise the younger inmate population between 18 and 35 years of age.

These older inmates have been known to say things like, "These youngsters, today, are so disrespectful. When I was young I had the utmost respect for the OGs" ("Ole Gangstas" – an affectionate and respectful term used to describe significantly older inmates). Therapists can promote healing on multiple levels by encouraging these elderly inmates to be curious about their younger cohort and ask themselves, why are these younger inmates not respectful? Older inmates may begin to see that their complaints and disdain are merely a mask veiling pain and hurt felt, due to their younger peers' rejection of them. Therapists can play a meaningful role in changing their narrative and helping them create a new purpose. Exploration and empathic curiosity often illuminates an understanding that these elders were not physically present in the lives of these young men. Pointing out that their absence may have cultivated feelings of anger and a lack of trust in people and in the world as a whole can be helpful for an inmate who either has a level of self-awareness and/or has begun to embark upon an introspective journey. The therapist can help the elderly population see that the feelings of anger by the younger inmates are often projected or transferred onto these older men and can play out in disrespectful attitudes and behaviors. The acknowledgment of this possibility has often fostered compassion in the older inmates toward their younger peers and subsequently has inspired many of them to change their perspectives. It is common for these aforementioned older inmates to seek out the young and begin mentoring them. This mentorship allows for the mending and eventual crossing of a bridge that may have historically divided these age groups in prison and beyond.

Countertransference exists on the part of the facilitator with the inmate population as much as it does in any therapeutic milieu that provides care. It is essential that the facilitator seek consultation to allow for the processing of both positive and negative inmate regard. Many years ago, at the beginning of this writer's career, she experienced a strong countertransference with one older pedophile who had expressed ongoing and overt criticism toward her in group. In response to the criticism, this writer projected her unresolved father issues on this inmate and, prior to seeking consultation, attempted to receive positive favor and approval from the offender by directing a lot of her attention to him in group.

Through curiosity and self-exploration coupled with consultation, she examined the dynamic and was able to recognize her role in their inter-action and ultimately change it. Working in a traditionally masculine and male-dominated environment can trigger countertransference with both male and female facilitators. Facilitators should suspend judgment and instead exercise curiosity when they notice themselves having a reaction to an inmate with whom they have been working.

The Importance of Supervision and Consultation

Consultation is essential when working with an inmate population. Like any and all people, inmates can be manipulative. It is important for the group facilitator to process thoughts, feelings, and issues that may arise within him or herself in relation to the group members and the group process. This writer facilitated a monthly peer consultation group in which colleagues who were struggling with challenging cases congregated for support, guidance, and a place to process. Therapists working in a prison setting should prioritize and structure time for consultation.

Supportive supervisors that have an open-door policy are also essential to a healthy therapeutic milieu. Supervisors are taxed; however, it is imperative that they carve time out of their schedules to provide a sounding board for their supervisees. By being available to offer a listen-ing and supportive ear, supervisors can benefit not only the clinicians providing direct care, and the inmates receiving that care, but have the potential to transform the entire prison environment.

Conclusion

Scholars, activists, human rights advocates, and all people of conscience consider the criminal justice system of the U.S.A to be fragmented and in drastic need of transformation. The threat of mass incarceration of Americans in general and People of Color in particular requires immedi-ate action and reformation. It is easy to feel overwhelmed and paralyzed by the fact that its roots stem from bigger systemic problems like racism and classism. We might think, "there is not much I can do." By acknowledging the privilege, both overt and covert, that we hold as clin-icians; by educating ourselves so as to be culturally competent; and by seeking support and consultation so that our best and most empathic selves show up every day, we therapists can begin to plant seeds of reconciliation and restoration one male prisoner at a time and one group at a time. As each inmate within group takes a risk to connect to his group members, hearts are opened and healing can begin to take place.

A Black Lifer in a Lifer's group this writer facilitated took a similar risk recently and told a White group member that he admired him and the transformation that he had observed the inmate implementing in his life. The Black inmate asked if he could get up and shake the hand of the White inmate. The White inmate responded by acquiescing and the two men, Black and White, walked to the center of the room. The Black inmate went from shaking the White inmate's hand to embracing him. Shortly following this monumental exchange another inmate requested that the men engage in a group hug. This writer sat with tears in her eyes as she observed ten men serving life sentences holding one another. In this moment she was reminded of the power of group and its awesome potential to heal the heart of an inmate, and to transform the prison culture, one group at a time.

References

Aday, R. H. (2003). *Aging prisoners: Crisis in American corrections.* Westport, CT: Praeger Publishers.

Addis, M. E., & Cohane, G. E. (2006). Social scientific paradigms of masculinity and their implications for research and practice in men's mental health. *Journal of Clinical Psychology,* 61, 633–647.

Agazarian, Y., & Peters, R. (1981). *The visible and invisible group: Two perspectives on group psychotherapy and group process.* London: Routledge & Kegan Paul.

Alexander, M. (2012). *The new Jim Crow: Mass incarceration in the age of colorblindness.* New York, NY: The New Press.

Alvarez, A. N., Liang, C. T. H., & Neville, H. A. (2016). *Cultural, racial, and ethnic psychology book series. The cost of racism for People of Color: Contextualizing experiences of discrimination.* Washington, DC: American Psychological Association.

Badia, E. D. (1989) Group-as-a-whole concepts and the therapeutic milieu on the inpatient psychiatric unit. *Group-as-a-whole,* 13(3–4), 165–172.

Bedard, R., Metzger, L., & Williams, B. (2017). Aging prisoners: An introduction to geriatric health-care challenges in correctional facilities. *International Review of the Red Cross,* 1–23, doi:10.1017/S1816383117000364.

Blankenship, K. M., del Rio Gonzalez, A. M., Keene, D. E., & Groves, A. K. (2018). Mass incarceration, race inequality, and health: expanding concepts and assessing impacts on well-being. *Social Science & Medicine,* 215, 45–52.

Blazina, C., & WatkinsJr, C. E. (2000). Separation/individuation, parental attachment, and male gender role conflict: Attitudes toward the feminine and the fragile masculine self. *Psychology of Men and Masculinity,* 1, 126–132.

Bowlby, J. (1982). *Attachment and loss vol.1: Attachment.* New York, NY: Basic Books.

Brown, B. (2012). *Daring greatly.* New York, NY: Penguin Random House.

Comas-Diaz, L., Nagayama Hall, G., & Neville, H. A. (2019). Racial Trauma: Theory, Research, and healing: Introduction to the special issue. *American Psychologist,* 74, 1–5, doi:10.1037.

D'Andrea, M. (2014). Understanding racial/cultural identity development theories to promote effective multicultural group counseling. In J. L. DeLucia-Waack, C. R. Kalodner, & M.T. Riva (eds), *Handbook of group counseling and psychotherapy,* (2nd ed.) (pp. 196–208). Thousand Oaks, CA: Sage.

D'Andrea, M., & Daniels, J. (2001). Facing the changing demographic structure of our society. In D. C. Locke, J. E. Myers, & E. L. Herr (eds), *The handbook of counseling* (pp. 529–539). Thousand Oaks, CA: Sage.

Fitzpatrick, B. (2016). Men in groups: attachment and masculinity (doctoral dissertation). Available from ProQuest Dissertation Publishing (UMI No. 10259251).

Greene, M., Ahalt, C., Stijacic-Cenzer, I., Metzger, L., & Williams, B. (2018). Older adults in jail: High rates and early onset of geriatric conditions. *Health Justice*, 6, doi:10.1186/s40352- 018-0062-9.

Helms, J., Nicolas, G., & Green, C. E. (2012). Racism and ethnoviolence as trauama: Enhancing professional and research training. *Traumatology*, 18, 65–74, doi:10.1177/1534765610396728.

Marmarosh, C. L., Markin, R. D., & Spiegel, E. B. (2013). *Attachment in group psychotherapy*. Washington, DC: American Psychological Association.

Maschi T., Gibson S., Zgoba, K. M., & Morgen, K. (2011). Trauma and life event stressors among young and older adult prisoners. *Journal of Correctional Health Care*, 17(2), 160–172, doi:10.1177/1078345810396682.

Miller, W. R., & Rollnick, S. (2002). *Motivational interviewing: Preparing people for change*. New York, NY: The Guilford Press.

National Association of the Advancement of ColoredPeople (2019). Incarceration trends in America. Racial disparities in incarceration. Retrieved from: www.naacp.org/criminal- justice-fact-sheet/2019.

Novek, E. (2014). The color of hell, reframing justice in the age of mass incarceration. *Atlantic Journal of Communication*, 22, 1–4.

Public Policy Institute of California (2019). Just the facts California's prison population. Retrieved from: https://www.ppic.org/publication/californias-changing-prison-population/.

Rule, W. R., & Gandy, G. L. (1994). A thirteen-year comparison in patterns of attitudes toward counseling. *Adolescence*, 29(115), 575.

Sue, D. W., & Sue, D. (2003). *Counseling the culturally diverse: Theory and practice* (4th ed.). New York, NY: John Wiley & Sons.

The Sentencing Project (2019a). Criminal justice facts. Retrieved from: https://www.sentencingproject.org/criminal-justice-facts/2019.

The Sentencing Project (2019b). Racial disparity. Retrieved from: https://www.sentencingproject.org/issues/racial-disparity/2019.

Toldsen, I. A. (2002). The relationship between race and psychopathy: an evaluation of selected psychometric properties of the psychopathy checklist – revised (PCL-R) for incarcerated African American men (doctoral dissertation). Retrieved from ProQuest Dissertations Publishing (UMI No. 3040365).

Williams, B. A., Goodwin, J. S., Baillargeon, J., Ahalt, C., & Walter, L. C. (2012). Addressing the aging crisis in U.S. criminal justice health care. *Journal of the American Geriatrics Society*, 60(6),1150–1156, doi:10.1111/j.1532–5415.2012.03962.x.

9 Managing Microaggressions within Veterans' Psychotherapy Groups

Miguel Lewis

Introduction

The Veterans Health Administration (VHA) is the largest integrated health care system in the United States, providing care at 168 VA medical centers and 1,053 community-based outpatient clinics. In 2017, more than 1.7 million Veterans received mental health treatment in a VA mental health program (U.S. Department of Veteran Affairs, 2018). Further demographics of the VA indicate that in 2018, of the 5,453,256 total male service users, 25.4 percent were confirmed with a mental illness. In the same year, there were 501,281 total female service users, 41.7 percent were confirmed with a mental illness (Greenberg & Hoff, 2019). As of 2017, Vet Pop 2016 estimates 1.9 million of the 19.6 percent living Veterans are women, or 9.5 percent of all living Veterans (U.S. Department of Veterans Affairs, 2019). According to the Veterans Health Administration report (U.S. Department of Veteran Affairs, 2017), in respect to age variations for those serving in the last three wars [Operation Enduring Freedom (OEF), Operation Iraqi Freedom (OIF), and Operation New Dawn (OND)], 48.4 percent are between the ages of 30 and 40 years; 24.6 percent are between 40 and 50 years; 18 percent are between 50 and 60 years; and 5.4 percent are over 60 years old. The racial make-up of Veterans, not necessarily those receiving mental health treatment, are: 75 percent identifying as White, 13 percent as African American, 7.7 percent as Latino, 1.6 percent as Asian American, 7 percent as Native American, 3 percent as Mixed Race, and 2 percent as Pacific Islander. Moreover, the Minority Veterans Report (U.S. Department of Veteran Affairs, 2017) stated that in 2014 racial and ethnic minorities made up 21.6 percent of the total Veteran population in the United States. In the year 2040, this number is projected to make up 35.7 percent of all living Veterans. Given this diversity, there is ample opportunity for intersecting identities around race, gender, and class to be examined as they interplay with presenting mental health concerns.

Many of the over 1.7 million Veterans receiving mental health services also receive group therapy in outpatient departments including primary care behavioral health, substance abuse, PTSD, and mental health. Group therapy also occurs within the inpatient psychiatric units and residential programs for PTSD and substance abuse. There are numerous types of group therapy offered including: Dialectical Behavioral Therapy, Cognitive Behavioral Therapy, Cognitive Processing Therapy, Problem Solving Therapy, Acceptance and Commitment Therapy, and Seeking Safety. Other types of therapy groups address anger management, substance abuse, PTSD, as well as coping skills, moral injury, and bereavement, to name a few.

While the VA offers 16 types of evidence-based therapy for individual therapy, there is no national training for group therapy. In addition, many providers offering group therapy may not have had the adequate training even within their graduate school programs. In fact, group therapy is inconsistent among doctoral psychology programs and internships (Butler & Fuhriman, 1986; Markus & King, 2003). However, there is evidence that with particular types of programs such as PsyD and counseling psychology doctoral programs, there is a greater presence of group therapy training (Fuhriman & Burlingame, 2001; Weinstein & Rossini, 1998). Thus, the training in group psychotherapy varies.

Given the limited group therapy training in graduate programs and the lack thereof within Veterans Administration settings, this author wonders how many providers are able to adequately handle complicated situations that occur in group therapy, such as managing bias and prejudices given the differences in gender, race, and age across clients in the VA. Further, due to the minority of clients representing the female gender and who identify as People of Color, one can further speculate that microaggressions may regularly occur and therapists may not have the skills to manage them when they are manifested.

This chapter aims to raise the issue of microaggressions and examine the impact they can have on members who participate in groups offered through the Veterans Administration. Of particular focus will be an examination of microaggressions in two groups led by this author –a long-term men's process group and a short-term mixed group utilizing Acceptance and Commitment Therapy. These examples include the inevitability of microaggressions between members. Finally, the chapter will highlight the importance of consultation with the intent to repair ruptures with clients, when they will unfortunately occur.

Microaggressions

Sue and colleagues defined racial microaggressions as "brief and commonplace daily verbal, behavioral, or environmental indignities, whether intentional or unintentional, that communicate hostile, derogatory, or negative racial slights and insults to persons of color" (p. 271). Within the broad term of microaggressions, there are specifically three types: microassaults, microinsults, and microinvalidations (Sue, Capodilupo, Torino,

Bucceri, Holder, Nadal, & Esquilin, 2007). However, for the purpose of this chapter, only the last two will be defined. According to Sue et al. (2007), a microinsult is "characterized by communications that convey rudeness and insensitivity and demean a person's racial heritage or identity" (p. 274). Examples include: 1) when a man calls a woman "sweetie" or "baby" in a professional context, and 2) when a White employee follows a Black customer around a store for no apparent reason. A microinvalidation is "characterized by communications that exclude, negate, or nullify the psychological thoughts, feelings, or experiential reality of a person of color" (p. 274). For instance, when someone tells a Black person, "We are all human beings," the result may be experienced as minimizing or negating the Black individual's experience as a racial/cultural being (Helms, 1992). Other examples include someone saying, "I can't be racist, I have a friend who is Black." Since being a Veteran is often a salient and unifying identity for clients and the therapist working with the group, there often may be less focus on other intersecting social identities (e.g. being a vet and a woman; having a disability and being a Man of Color). Because these social identities may be overlooked by the therapist, the potential for microinsults and/or invalidations to occur may be more likely.

Leader Identity Awareness

My own mother began speaking to me in Spanish when I was very young. She stated when I was around the age of four, however, that I expressed not wanting to learn the language anymore. So she stopped teaching me. As an adult, I regretted the loss of learning my mother's native language. As a result, I traveled to Guatemala twice to learn Spanish, and I now consider myself fluent. Even though I learned Spanish, however, I still somehow did not own my Latin identity.

When consulting about this chapter over the phone, a colleague asked me the question, "How do you identify yourself?" Having only thought of this question briefly from time to time, I explained to her that my mother was from Puerto Rico and my father was White American. I explained that while in college I met a male from Puerto Rico who asked if I had ever been to Puerto Rico. I explained to my colleague that I had replied to this man by saying that I had not been there, and that I did not speak Spanish well. I then revealed to her that what this young male said to me still creates shame and pain to this day. I shared that this man said, "You are the sorriest Puerto Rican I know." Sharing this with my colleague brought me into a state of quiet. I then felt a lump in my throat and tears began to develop in my eyes. I had not realized how those words still hurt me to this day. Later in our conversation, I revealed that I nearly began to cry as I stated this. After she provided an empathic comment, she noted this was a microaggression against me. That struck me, as I had never realized that before. I elaborated by stating that I had often struggled with not "feeling" Latin, partly because I was not around Latin groups growing up. In addition, my Latin grandparents, cousins, and an aunt lived in New York and we only saw them once a year. Yet another reason may have been that this microaggression led me to place my culture underground. At that moment and with pride in my voice, I then revealed to her a statement that I wished I had told that male long ago, "Just because I learned Spanish as an adult and have never been to Puerto Rico, it does not erase that I am still Latin." She wholeheartedly agreed and asked, "Who gets to determine if you are a Man of Color?" I finally realized something – I did.

Case Example: Microaggressions within a Men's Process Group

I currently lead a men's interpersonal process group for Veterans. Because of this type of group, which is more process-oriented than psychoeducational or skills-based, the possibility to explore intersections of identity that are raised are increased. The following paragraphs provide an example of a microaggression that occurred in this group of seven men, two of whom were African American, and five of whom were White identified.

Two African American men spoke of racism during the same group session. The first African American group member brought up an incident of racism that he experienced while in the military. He spoke of a racist joke he overheard that scared him: "How do you get a _igger out of a tree? You cut the rope." The second African American group member then shared another example of marginalization. He indicated that he can't even stand in his front yard without being interrogated. He then gave a recent example where someone asked him in a threatening manner what he was doing while he was standing in his own front yard. He went on to explain that he felt as though he couldn't say or do anything for fear that he would be arrested.

Completely out of context after each of these two men spoke, another group member, who identified as a White male, shared that when he lived in Vermont, he rarely saw any "Black people." Another older White group member then spoke for about five minutes about how he knew someone in Vermont who was Black and a business owner.

Facilitating this group, I found this exchange bizarre and was thinking about the following:

1   *Did the two White males just hear the African American's emotional pain?*
2   *What would lead these two White group members to respond in this way?*
3   *Was the first individual nervous and unsure of how to respond to the African American's anger; thus, he brought up a neutral issue of race?*
4   *What was happening with the second White group member? Was he following along with the first group member's theme of avoidance regarding the African American's fear/anger?*
5   *What impact did this avoidance have on the African American group member?*

6   As the leader, if I don't respond, would the group be experienced for the Men of Color as unsafe; and, for the White men, as collusion?

7   How does the group view this leader in terms of racial identification?

One of the African American men then responded to the second White group member with the following:

"That's an asterisk and patronizing. It shouldn't be I know a Black man and he did good. I don't say I know a White man ..."

The White group member then stated, "You should let things go," which understandably resulted in the African American man becoming angry.

As a facilitator, I felt the need to slow down the process to understand what could be happening. What came to awareness was how this example, in which a Person of Color brings up an incident involving racism, is then met with denial and/or resistance from White people (Sue & Zane, 1987). Additionally, this interaction demonstrates how this group member's viewpoint, which represented the Dominant White Culture, displayed implicit power and privilege (Sue, 2015).

When the White group member stated, "You should let things go," this type of microaggression could be experienced as a microinvalidation, which negates the thoughts, feelings, and racial realities of People of Color, and in this incident, the African American man in the group (Sue, Capodilupo, & Holder, 2008). Fortunately, another White member, as well as this author, came to his support. Although the African American man did come back to the group the following week, he noted he had thoughts of not doing so. He voiced that he came back so as not to leave the other African American in the group alone. Surprisingly, he noted that he did not want the group, or the group member who committed the microinvaliation, to think he was upset. I voiced appreciation that he returned to the group, as I was worried about him. Since it appeared initially that the group wanted to avoid the incident that occurred the previous week, this leader had to encourage the group to discuss and unpack what may have happened.

Returning to microaggressions/racial discrimination and essentially looking to repair ruptures is extremely important for the group as a whole and is strongly supported in the research. Leaving microaggressions undiscussed or unexamined can lead to a myriad mental and physical health consequences, including depression and anxiety, PTSD, and overall poor health outcomes for People of Color in particular (Williams, Neighbors, & Jackson, 2003).

Other questions raised internally by this group facilitator included:

1   What kept me from asking why he didn't want the other Black group member to be alone in the group as a reason for why he returned?

2   What was the impact of this microinvalidation on the veteran during and after the group?

3   How did he cope with this microaggression after the group and prior to the next group?

4   How was the safety of the group compromised as a result of this microinvalidation?

Consulting about Microaggressions

Consultation for group therapists is critical for many reasons, but particularly when navigating difficult affective states that can occur as a result of microaggressions. The following are a few reasons why consultation is necessary when leading diverse groups in the VA, but essentially in any setting. First, consultation reduces the isolation that one can often feel as a clinician. Second, consultation addresses the need for additional training that is necessary for ethical and effective practice in psychology. Third, consultation addresses the need for self-care from the emotional intensity of clinical work and provides solutions to clinical problems (Counselman & Weber, 2004). Fourth, group consultation can reduce the shame that clinicians may feel related to mistakes that occur when leading therapy groups (Counselman & Gumbert, 1993). That is, they can hear how others also make errors or miss opportunities from time to time. Finally, consultation for group therapy plays an extremely valuable role as group facilitators learn to become more effective generally and particularly when dealing with microaggressions.

As a result of the value attained through consultation, I have been a member of a clinical peer supervision group for the past 2.5 years. This consult group includes five experienced group therapists (including myself), and a consultant who is a Certified Group Psychotherapist and is Board Certified in Group Psychology. Specific to this group, I described concerns for not only the microaggression that affected the African American group member, but concerns for the White group member as well. That is, I would describe incidents within the group to gain a broader perspective of members' behaviors. One example that I brought up included examining why some group members would laugh in regard to a particular topic, but one particular older White group member failed to join the laughter. Two questions were raised within the consultation group: 1) was the lack of empathy by this older White man toward the African American group member due to a cognitive decline issue? Or, 2) was the response by this older White male considered normal based on his race, age, and background?

Discussions and questions ensued in the consultation group that included the following: Was the White group member taking away from the quality of the group in addition to injuring the one African American group member in which he had a disagreement? Further discussions led to recommendations for this author to have an individual session with the White member to discuss what he was missing in terms of opportunities to connect, bond, and grow closer to other group members. Discussions also highlighted that cognitive issues could also be making it more difficult to relate to others and neuropsychological testing was recommended as a possibility to assess for further cognitive issues. There was agreement within the consult group that conducting cognitive testing with this member would allow for a more informed decision on what was most beneficial for this member and the group as a whole.

Two sessions thereafter, this White male decided to leave the group. He expressed finding his ability to walk declined significantly, and that he needed more time for himself. Again, without the cognitive testing, it was difficult to know whether this was neurologically based or whether his intense interaction with the African American group member also influenced his decision. Unfortunately, due to this member prematurely leaving the group, there was a lost opportunity for the White group member to work through his beliefs about the Black group member, for the group to see the rupture repaired, and for the group to fully process the microaggression, and ultimately a loss for both the White and African American men to possibly find connection (Zaharopoulos & Chen, 2018).

Potential After-effects of Microaggressions on a Group's Development

The premature departure of one of the White group members left the group with only five members for a few months. This pause in new membership in part was due to my hesitancy to add more members to what felt like a racially wounded group. As a result of consultation, however, I came to realize that I was trying to protect the group from any possible further damage by not adding new members. Yet, this fear was also holding back the group from experiencing new connections through the addition of new group members and new perspectives (Cohen & Rice, 1985).

After a few months, I decided it was time to add another member to the group. The potential new member identified as White and prior to joining the group shared with me that he supported the current U.S. president's policies. This was in direct contrast to a current group member who identified as African American, and had recently spoken out negatively about this same president. I raised the initial logical question of: How does this difference and potential conflict that often arises in political party support get managed in a therapy group? Other questions noted by this group facilitator included:

1   *Would there be a heated exchange with this new White member and this current Black group member about their contrasting viewpoints of the president?*
2   *Would we have another incident where an African American group member speaks up about racism and they would be hurt again by this potentially new White group member?*

Group consultation became a good source of support again, by providing a variety of perspectives and ideas for possible interventions. A key suggestion was utilizing the pre-group meeting to gain a better understanding of this potential new member's views and whether his joining would "fit" the current group culture (Ribeiro, Gross, & Turner, 2018). Other questions were posed to help determine how flexible the potential group member could be in regard to certain topics involving race and differences. Some examples included asking this potential member:

1   *What would happen if some of the group members brought up how they were anti-Trump? How would you react?*
2   *How do you feel about being in a group with people different from you?*
3   *We're all impacted by what is happening in our society, and sometimes people want to talk about cultural issues like their experience of racism and discrimination. How would that be for you?*

Group consultation solidified common themes for my therapy group including: 1) addressing microaggressions shows the affected group member and the group as a whole that attending to these ruptures is important and could benefit from further discussion/examination; 2) fears of adding group members because of differences should not stop the facilitator from adding new members, but it needs to be intentional and thoughtful; 3) the importance of effectively screening group members to determine good fit for the group; 4) prioritizing safety and the need for it to be re-established prior to differences re-emerging in the group; and 5) group cohesion needs to be a primary focus to increase readiness for exploring difficult issues at a later point in group.

As a result of learning through consultation based on experiences within this author's group, the following are a few recommendations for group clinicians to consider:

1   When a microaggression occurs in a group, it is important to discuss White power and privilege and how statements such as "let it go" not only show insensitivity but also deny a Person of Color's experience.
2   It is important to ask the affected party, which may include others in the group as well as the person receiving the microaggression, how the microaggression affected them at the moment it occurred and during the week prior to the next group. It is also important to ask what strategies they used to cope with emotions that were triggered as a result of the microaggression.
3   The idea of addressing items 1 and 2 in session can potentially lead to discussions, examination, and ultimately reparation for the person who committed the microaggression, and more importantly, healing for the recipient of the microaggression.

An Example of a Microaggression in an ACT group

I have led a 12-week Acceptance and Commitment Therapy (ACT) group. The goals of ACT are to "help the patient accept internal events (thoughts, emotions, sensations, and memories) while also helping them make and keep behavioral commitments that reflect personal values" (Walser, Sears, Chartier, & Karlin, 2012, p. 9). This group will be used to examine another microaggression that occurred and reflections that occurred as a result of the interchange.

A microaggression occurred within the first few sessions of a 12-week ACT group that consisted of six members – four men and two women. The racial/ethnic make-up of the group included an African American older male, a young Latin woman/Latina, an Italian American older male, a middle-aged White woman, an older White male, and a young White male whose mother was of Indigenous descent. During the group I described an ACT metaphor, the person in the hole exercise, which emphasizes an alternative to experiential avoidance (Hayes, Strossal, & Wilson, 2016). I then asked each member what they would do if they were in this metaphorical hole. The group members shared numerous examples. The young White male group member whose mother was of Indigenous descent stated, "Well, you could ask a few Mexicans to dig me out of the hole." In that moment, I became nervous and in my mind questioned, "Did he just say that?" My immediate concern was for the Latina in my group and wondered how she experienced the comment. At the time, I had little awareness of the impact on me as a Latino and rather was more focused on the impact on the Latina. As the leader, I thought, "What do I do in this situation?" Being unsure, I remained quiet, decided to bring it up in consultation, and let the group continue with whatever reactions came up after the microaggression occurred. None of the group members responded to what was just stated.

I shared this interaction in my consultation group. Upon processing my reactions and hearing the narrative of the group, my consultation group validated my uncomfortable reaction, named the comment as a microaggression, and raised the importance of addressing this microaggression in the next group. I was reminded through this consultation that despite the lack of responsiveness of the members in the therapy group where the microaggression had occurred, as group leaders we can return to the rupture with the attempt to repair and allow healing of any group members that were offended and microaggressed against.

Taking what I processed from this author's consultation group, in the following group session, I noted that I had a reaction to a comment in the previous group. First, I provided a definition of a microaggression. I then asked the group if they knew what I was referring to from the last group or had any reactions either then or now. As a result of creating an open forum to discuss the microaggression, the group was invited to revisit and examine this difficult topic (Bemak & Chung, 2019). Initially, everyone sat in silence, so I retraced the incident that occurred the previous week.

Revisiting this microaggression gave me a new opportunity in the group to work through reactions. Fortunately, the Veteran who committed the microaggression not only apologized but spoke about how he previously engaged in a microaggression with his Jewish friend as well. He began to share his previous experience and noted: "My needs were not met at the drive-through today and I said to the employee, 'what is this, a circus?'" The group member went on to explain how the person who attended to him seemed to have an intellectual disability as they then asked their boss the same question. The member shared how the boss then confronted the group member about his question, which the member noted resulted in feelings of shame. I praised the Veteran for owning his mistake. I then asked the Latina in the group about her thoughts of his comment the previous week. She responded (to the multiracial male that she presumed was White, who committed the microaggression) in an angry manner, "What are we your slaves?" She then asked if he had ever been picked on in his life. He affirmed that he had. He also revealed in their discussion that he was multiracial (part White and part Indigenous), since his mother was of Indigenous descent.

New reflections came to me at this moment including:

- What impact did hearing this disclosure have on the Latina and on the group as a whole? The Latina had thoughts of leaving the group, which she revealed to me in an individual session, yet she stayed until the end. Did my addressing this issue as the leader cause her to stay in the group?

By bringing up this issue, the Latina likely had the experience of being seen and validated (Schmidt, 2019). Additionally, the positive response led to group understanding and individual growth by the Latina, in that she had an opportunity to verbalize her feelings of the microaggression to the perpetrator of the microaggression. Also vital was the learning that occurred for other group members regarding microaggressions and effectively communicating when difficult topics occur.

A Revisiting of an Initial Microaggression in the ACT Group

In the same ACT group described above, Stan (pseudonym), the man who identified himself as multiracial (Indigenous and White), shared having had a difficult time with his feelings of self-worth. In week three or four of the group, I had Stan engage in an exercise to weaken the word "worthless" in his mind by having him, and the group, repeat it over and over for one minute. The purpose of this metaphor was to create more flexibility and have the veteran hopefully realize that they don't have to be as attached to this word/belief, with the intention to create more flexibility when the word arises again (Hayes, Strossal, & Wilson, 2016). In week 11 of this 12-week group, one White group member, Jerry, apologized to Stan. Jerry went on to detail that he previously mocked in a joking tone, "Stan is worthless" when Stan shared feeling worthless with the group. Due to Stan being out of town for a few weeks, Jerry noted that he had been waiting to apologize to him but lacked the opportunity until this moment. Stan stated, "You don't have to apologize. I feel bad now that you have feelings like that."

After hearing Stan's response, Jerry then noted to the group that because the two of them formerly knew each other from another group, "we can joke like that." Although this leader reflected on this interchange, nothing was stated overtly to unpack the exchange. Stan continued to share more in the group a little later. He noted that he has a tendency to become "too worked up." He described an incident with someone over money and that his girlfriend said he was becoming too upset.

Later in the session, Jerry stated he was diagnosed with Borderline Personality Disorder.

After Stan described his incident over money, he stated, "I think you have Borderline Personality Disorder."

A White male group member interjected and asked, "You mean like being two people?"

Jerry stated with a smile on his face: "Yeah, Mexican and Indian."

As the leader, I felt a surge of anxiety and wondered whether another microaggression was happening again.

A White female member, who described her trauma in previous sessions, shook her head as she looked downward and stated, "That's a bad joke."

The Latina member also shook her head showing disapproval.

Leader (speaking toward the White woman): "What are your thoughts about what he said?"

White woman: "It was a bad joke."

Fortunately, Stan agreed and stated, "Yeah, it was a bad joke."

Leader (speaking toward the Latina): "I wonder what your thoughts are regarding what has been said?"

Latina: "It's okay as the other member said two people," she remarked. (I was surprised to hear her not address this issue.)

Just then another group member asked, "He's Indian?"

The White group member then stated again, "He's Indian and Mexican."

I then became involved and wondered if this was true. Thus, I asked, "Are you Indian and Mexican?"

"Only Indian," Stan replied. He then quickly changed the topic and discussed his girlfriend.

I was surprised Stan did not address this offensive remark. The group went on to discuss other material. As the leader, I felt again that I could have said more, but was thrown off by the comments. That is, I could have asked Stan about his feelings regarding this comment and/or addressed a similar microaggression that occurred in the second week of the group when Jerry called Stan Mexican as a result of his brown skin. Micro-aggressions frequently have so much emotional power to them that leaders and group members often go silent in the moment or move to another topic to manage the emotional overload that is felt from the microaggression.

A Follow-up Individual Session with the Microaggressor

Unfortunately, I never did address that particular microaggression in the group. In retrospect, perhaps this had to do with my feelings of avoiding the issue as the last group would focus on termination. Perhaps I feared that Jerry would become angry, as he had demonstrated some irritation with others in earlier groups. And perhaps, rationalizing to myself, I wanted our last session to be free of conflict. In hindsight, I now see this was a mistake. I was quick to point out when this Veteran committed a microaggression, but I did not become more involved when a micro-aggression was committed against him. Again, in retrospect, I could have pushed this further by asking why he was bringing up a different topic after he stated "Only Indian." Even if the Veteran avoided it again, I could have posed a question to the group whether anyone felt that another micro-aggression could have occurred. This query would have allowed the group to examine whether the comment was perceived as hurtful and would have modelled an openness to staying engaged rather than staying silent and potentially shutting off a strong affective experience.

Although the group didn't process this microaggresssion, fortunately I did have a follow-up appointment with Stan. Here is an overview of our conversation:

THERAPIST: So what were your feelings when so-and-so mentioned you were Mexican and Indian?

STAN: It didn't bother me. I didn't think about it. He doesn't know or understand and has no clue what is going on.

THERAPIST: What do you mean?

STAN: To a Hispanic it would have been offensive to say this. We have to watch what we say. Someone else could've taken offense to that. When I was younger people used to say to me, "what's up chief?" Many knew I was Indian and they would still say it, which bothered me. He then stated that this other group member who committed the microaggression against him came up with the Mexican part on his own. I then raised his awareness by stating that he first brought up the term Mexican in group during the second week of this 12-week group.

STAN: Did he do that to stir the pot? To get me to say something about Mexicans? We already went down that road. That's why I quickly changed the topic when he stated that. He may have problems with that. Stirring things up. He then spoke of his growth in the group in that he is now cautious and mindful of what he says.

STAN: You have to be careful of what you say. (After some reflective silence) I felt bad when I said that comment to Jerry. I praised him for how he reacted in the group previously. That is, he owned the comment which led to healing for the Latina.

He also noted he could have made a joke about that comment in regard to Mexicans or become angry at the individual. Instead, he chose to shift the focus and remain quiet. Although the group was not advantaged in having closure regarding the hurtful microaggressions that occurred, the interchange between Stan and this author seemed to bring some closure and understanding to why he stayed quiet and redirected the conversation. Although there were several missed opportunities for the group as a whole to examine, I feel hopeful that I am more equipped in future groups as a result of the learning that occurred in these two process and ACT groups.

Conclusion

Studies show that White clinicians receive minimal or no practicum or supervision experiences that address race and are uncomfortable broaching the topic (Knox, Burkard, Johnson, Suzuki, & Ponterotto, 2003). Without multicultural supervision or consultation in addressing these potential microaggressions, racial-cultural biases can be missed (Zaharopoulos & Chen, 2018). Worse than missing them is having diverse members leave a group as a function of feeling invisible of their marginalized identities (Yalom & Leszcz, 2005). Furthermore, if group leaders fail to discuss issues of racism, discrimination, or oppression, they also deprive group members of the opportunity to examine the psychological impact of these issues on their lives (Bemak & Chung, 2019) and in the life of the group.

The microaggressions described in this chapter occurred in a men's interpersonal process group and a psychoeducational group with some process (Acceptance and Commitment Therapy). Group leaders can easily overlook or ignore microaggressions such as these, given the unfamiliar terrain of managing and processing microaggressions in a group. This chapter highlighted the importance of learning how to address microaggressions in group therapy through peer consultation. Without my consultation group, I may have ignored the microaggression within my group. While I would have realized something hurtful had occurred in the group, I would have been at a loss as to how to address it. My consultation group provided me the education and courage to address the microaggression in the group. Although I was tense when addressing them, inviting examination of the microaggressions within the group was worth the initial tension that most felt in the group. Another key as the leader is demonstrating the value of not ignoring microaggressions, and rather highlighting the importance of having them addressed and explored.

In addition to consultation, research suggests ongoing education in cultural competence through workshops, trainings, readings, and conferences, and how growing in cultural sensitivity and humility is our ethical responsibility as group therapists (Comas-Diaz, 2012). A goal of mine that aligns with training is to encourage all group therapists in the Veterans Health Administration to become a certified group psychotherapist. A key requirement for this certification is to obtain 75 hours of group supervision. Embedded in this goal of supervision is to also examine topics such as how to detect and confront microaggressions, as well as understand the impact of microaggressions on the individual, group, and group therapists. These opportunities to learn as group therapists ultimately help us be better in our work and lead to greater understanding and healing for our clients.

Author's Note

The opinions expressed are those of the author and in no way represent the opinions of the United States Department of Veterans Affairs or the Veterans Health Administration.

References

Bemak, F., & Chung, C. (2019). Race dialogues in group psychotherapy: Key issues in training and practice, *International Journal of Group Psychotherapy*, 69(2), 172–191, doi:10.1080/002077284.2018.1498743.

Butler, T., & Fuhriman, A. (1986). Professional psychologists as group treatment providers: Utilization, training, and trends. *Professional Psychology: Research and Practice*, 17(3), 273–275, doi:10.1037/0735-7028.17.3.273.

Cohen, S. L., & Rice, C. (1985). Maximizing the therapeutic effectiveness of small psychotherapy groups. GROUP: *Eastern Group Psychotherapy Society*, 9(4), 3–9.

Comas-Diaz, L. (2012). *Multicultural care*. Washington, DC: American Psychological Association.

Counselman, E., & Gumbert. P. (1993). Psychotherapy supervision in small leader-led groups. *Group: Eastern Group Psychotherapy Society*, 17, 25–32.

Counselman, E. C., & Weber, R.W. (2004). Organizing and maintaining peer supervision groups. *International Journal of Group Psychotherapy*, 54(2), 125–143.

Fuhriman A., & Burlingame. G. (2001). Group psychotherapy training and effectiveness. *International Journal of Group Psychotherapy*, 51(3), 399–416. doi:10.1521/ijgp.51.3.399.49889.

Greenberg, G., & Hoff, R. (2019). FY 2018 Female and Male Veterans Data Sheet: National, VISN, and VAMC Tables, West Haven, CT. Northeast Program Evaluation Center. Annual (FY 2010 – Present).

Hayes, S. C., Strossal K. D., & Wilson, K. G. (2016). *Acceptance and commitment therapy: The process and practice of mindful change* (2nd ed.). New York, NY: The Gilford Press.

Helms, J. E. (1992). *A race is a nice thing to have: A guide to being a White person or understanding the White persons in your life.* Topeka, KS: Content Communications.

Knox, S., Burkard, A. W., Johnson, A. J., Suzuki, L. A., & Ponterotto, J. G. (2003). African American and European American therapists' experiences of addressing race in cross-racial psychotherapy dyads. *Journal of Counseling Psychology*, 50, 466–481.

Markus, H. E., & King, D. A. (2003). A survey of group psychotherapy training during predoctoral psychology internship. *Professional Psychology: Research and Practice*, 34(2), 203–209, doi:10.1037/0735-7028.34.2.203.

Ribeiro, M., Gross, J., & Turner, M. (2018). *The college counselor's guide to group psychotherapy.* New York, NY: Routledge.

Schmidt, C. (2019). Anatomy of racial micro-aggressions. *International Journal of Group Psychotherapy*, 68(4), 585–607, doi:10.1080/00207284.2017.1421469.

Sue, D. W. (2015). *Race talk and the conspiracy of silence: Understanding and facilitating difficult race dialogues.* Hoboken, NJ: Wiley.

Sue, D. W., Capodilupo, C., Torino, G., Bucceri, J., Holder, A., Nadal, K., & Esquilin, M. (2007). Racial microaggressions in everyday life, Implications for clinical practice. *American Psychologist*, 62(4), 271–286, doi:10.1037/003–066X.62.4.271.

Sue, D. W, Capodilupo, C., & Holder, A. (2008). Racial microaggressions in the life experiences of Black Americans. *Professional Psychology, Research and Practice*, 39(3), 329–336.

Sue, D. W., & Zane, N. (1987). The role of culture and cultural techniques in psychotherapy. A critique and reformulation. *American Psychologist*, 42, 37–45. doi:10.1037/0003-066X42.1.37.

U.S. Department of Veterans Affairs (March2017). *Minority Veterans report: Military service history and VA benefit utilization statistics.* Data Governance and Analytics. Washington, DC: Department of Veterans Affairs.

U.S. Department of Veteran Affairs (March2019). *Profile of Veterans: 2017.* National Center for Veterans Analysis and Statistics.

U.S. Department of Veterans Affairs (June2018). *VA office of mental health and suicide prevention guidebook.* https://www.mentalhealth.va.gov.

Walser, R. D., Sears, K., Chartier, M., & Karlin, B. E. (2012). *Acceptance and commitment therapy for depression in Veterans: Therapist manual.* Washington, DC: U.S. Department of Veterans Affairs.

Weinstein, M., & Rossini, E. (1998). Academic Training in Group Psychotherapy in Clinical Psychology Doctoral Programs. *Psychological Reports*, 82(3), 955–959.

Williams, D. R., Neighbors, H. W., & Jackson, J. S. (2003). Racial/ethnic discrimination and health: Findings from community studies. *American Journal of Public Health*, 93(2), 200–208.

Yalom, I. D., & Leszcz, M. (2005). *The theory and practice of group psychotherapy* (5th ed.). New York, NY: Basic Books.

Zaharopoulos, M., & Chen, E. (2018). Racial-cultural events in group therapy as perceived by group therapists. *International Journal of Group Psychotherapy*, 68 (4), 629–653, doi:10.1080/00207284.2018.1470899.

10 Group Art-Making Therapy for Mothers of Young Children

Massiel M. Abramson

Introduction

Mothers are the primary breadwinner in approximately 40 percent of families in the U.S. and a quarter of mothers are raising children on their own (Geiger, Livingston, & Bialik, 2019). These rates are higher for Black, Latinx, and low-income families (Geiger, Livingston, & Bialik, 2019). Therefore, mothers play a critical role in raising future generations. However, the numerous responsibilities and limited resources can cause mothers to suffer from stress, anxiety, and other mental health issues. Given their significant role as caregivers, good and stable maternal health is crucial in order for the community to continuously thrive. Given the impact and risks of motherhood, maternal mental health has been given more attention in mental health over the past few years. Maternal mental health focuses on the impact of pregnancy, labor and delivery, post-partum issues and life adjustment needs when a mother has a pregnancy or child aged five or younger. Non-bipartisan funding has been allocated to programs that serve the maternal and early childhood population (Health Resources and Services Administration, 2017; World Health Organization, 2019); Mendoza, 2018). Yet, while access to mental health has increased over the past decade, barriers to treatment still exist.

This author has worked to support maternal health through in-home therapy focused on early motherhood – mothers with children from birth to five years. In addition to in-home therapy, this author also conducted a five-week art-making group with mothers, which is the focus of this chapter. More specifically, the purpose of this chapter is to present the related literature on maternal health, group therapy, and the therapeutic benefits of art-making. Specifics of the five-week workshop, which include details on the collage and the framework that guided the facilitation, will be explored. By the end of this chapter, clinicians should further understand the importance of therapy for new mothers, the therapeutic benefits of art-making – specifically collage-making – and how to facilitate the workshop in ways that center on the mothers and encourages them to invest in therapy, and their well-being more generally.

Literature Review

Mothers

Mothers face unique challenges in our society. A high number of people in poverty in the U.S. include young children and their mothers. According to the Kids Count Data Center, 20% of children between birth and six years of age live in poverty. These mothers face immense financial burdens, at times raising their children without the support of another working adult – contributing to parental distress and instability (The Annie E. Casey Foundation, 2019; Geiger, Livingston, & Bialik, 2019). The assessment, Adverse Childhood Experiences (ACEs), indicates that poverty and other stressful life experiences are linked to mental and physical health problems in adulthood (Steele et al., 2016). These stresses can cause a mother to ignore her child's needs and her own self-care. Specifically, mothers of young children are at a risk for post-partum depression (PPD). In the United States, the prevalence of depression among new mothers can range from 5 percent to almost 40 percent (Easterbrooks et al., 2013; Howells & Zelnick, 2014) with an increased prevalence among Latina and low-income mothers (Lewis-Fernandez et al., 2005; Rich-Edwards et al. 2006). As cited by Abrams, Dornig, and Curran (2009), the rates of PPD are likely higher because mothers frequently go undiagnosed and undetected (Murray et al., 2003).

Depression in new mothers can have negative consequences on them, their partners, and their children. For mothers, untreated depression can worsen over time, lead to social isolation, and cause relationship strains with their partners (Letourneau, Salamani, & Duffett-Leger, 2010; Letourneau et al., 2012; Meadows, McLanahan, & Brooks-Gunn, 2007). For children, a mother's depression can lead to low receptive vocabulary, inattention, physical aggression, and anxiety (Letourneau, Tramonte, & Willms, 2013). Perry et al. (2011) studied 217 Latina mothers and found that lower depression symptoms predicted stronger attachment between mothers and their infants. Mothers are in a critical role in supporting the healthy emotional development of their children (Hartup & Rubin, 2013; Novick & Novick, 2010). Meins (2013) highlights how attachments to a mother early in life improve the child's social flexibility and self-efficacy. As shown in this body of literature, depression among mothers can be quite common and have dire consequences on families.

While we understand that Black, Latina, and low-income mothers face numerous mental health issues, their participation in mental health services is still a struggle. Black and Latina women cite lack of compassion from their practitioner and lack of a trusting relationship as a barrier to reporting mental health symptoms (Edge, 2011; Gardner et al., 2014; Lara-Cinisomo et al., 2014). Post-partum help-seeking behaviors are low, due in part to the view of difficulties in motherhood as normal and fears of being judged negatively for pursuing support (Rouhi et al., 2019; Abrams, Dornig, & Curran, 2009). Mothers are more willing to get support when it is recommended by a family member or the referral is coming from a trusted source, yet there is a lack of social networks who can offer this support (Callister, Beckstrand, & Corbett, 2011). When no formal mental health care is taken, mothers often resort to self-care practices such as emotional strategies (e.g. self-expression), cognitive practices (e.g. planning, prayer), and behavioral practices (e.g. reflective journaling) (Abrams, Dornig, & Curran, 2009). While these informal practices may help alleviate some stress, group therapy and an alternative way of expression (e.g. art-making) can help mothers explore underdeveloped aspects of their themselves.

Group Therapy

Social networks are often perceived as lacking for mothers (Callister, Beckstrand, & Corbett, 2011; Sheng, Le, & Perry, 2010), especially for those living in urban environments (Vigod et al., 2013). Therefore, group therapy can help mothers connect with other people who are in similar circumstances and build social bonds. A systemic review on group therapy by Goodman and Santangelo (2011) found that group treatments significantly improved symptoms of depression in post-partum mothers. A limitation in the research is that many studies on interventions focus on children and less on how mothers individually address their mental health and their thoughts regarding motherhood – particularly in group therapy. Social networks provide support to mothers and it can come in the form of a group where individuals can understand stressors better and gain coping skills (Taylor, 2011). People learn from each other in these settings, especially those going through specific developmental milestones like early parenthood. Groups can be a resource for mothers to decrease their social isolation and depression (Vigod et al., 2013; Ugarriza, 2004; Goodman & Santangelo, 2011). Along with developing community, mothers in group therapy can reflect on their experiences and learn to identify symptoms, coping skills, and other basic aspects of psychology (Ugarriza, 2004).

Art-making: Collages

Art-making is a therapeutic strategy that allows for nonverbal engagement and meaning-making. Art-making in therapy has been shown to be an effective tool in processing self-awareness, allowing clients to make connections they had not made before (Howells & Zelnick, 2014; Simmons & Daley, 2013). Art-making can also support a healthy and interactive relationship between the client and their therapist (Simmons & Daley, 2013). In one program review by Perry, Thurston, and Osborn (2008), mothers described the art treatment as providing a safe, relaxing and supportive space. Art in therapy is often used to treat depression and its associated symptoms (Van Lith, 2016).

Yet there are gaps in the literature on art in therapy. There is not much research on the prompts and instructions so that replication of the practice is possible (Van Lith, 2016). Many differences among the reviewed art-making literature is found; symptoms being addressed, duration of the group, and the art activity itself (Slayton, D'Archer, & Kaplan, 2010; Van Lith, 2016). Nonetheless, art treatments are shown to be helpful.

Collaging or assemblage is a form of art treatment. Art treatments, when they are the key focus of treatment, can benefit self-discovery, self-expression, and relationships (Slayton, D'Archer, & Kaplan 2010). Collage making can free one's thinking and create space for making connections one has not made before (Simmons & Daley, 2013). Collage allows one's thinking to be more explicit (Simmons & Daley, 2013). The materials used in collaging serve as facilitators to enhance conceptualizations of the self and relationships (Kay, 2013). Collage is also helpful for populations that do not have a strong command of the language (Van Schalkwyk, 2010).

My Collage-making Mother Group

As a clinician working in child–parent psychotherapy (CPP), this author saw a gap in services for mothers. In CPP, parents were able to attend to relational needs and enhance attachment, but more reflection on how attachment has evolved in their life and new understanding of identity was difficult to make time for. Parents go through tremendous changes and traumas when they transition to parenthood. Although services exist for the child and their parenting, there was little structured time for mothers to reflect on their own mental health, identity development, and coping skills. Given mothers' social isolation, often with no grandmother or experienced mother to offer guidance, the adjustments to motherhood are often fleeting and uninformed.

My Positionality

I am an Afro-Dominican immigrant mother who has worked as a clinician for over ten years in underserved communities of color. I have also lived and raised my family in similar communities. I recognize that my physical presence and experiences allow me to connect with my clients. These similarities allow me to understand some of my clients' values and cultural practices. I also understand participants in the group may see me as culturally familiar, which can support *familismo* (dedication, commitment, and loyalty to the family) within the group. While the similarities between the participants and me can be therapeutically beneficial, I also acknowledge I have some blind spots to understanding and helping my clients. Therefore, I utilize self-reflection through journaling after sessions, supervision, and colleagues to manage the biases, assumptions, and practices that can negatively impact my clients. This reflective process helps sustain trust and empathy with clients.

The Participating Mothers

Given the lack of individualized support for new mothers and the reliance of talk therapy, I saw an opportunity to create a group for mothers of young children with an alternative form of expression – collage-making. Collaging on clinical issues provided an opportunity to be creative and reflective in a non-traditional way. Participants are recruited from families that had been a part of an in-home child–parent psychotherapy program. Of these participants, some were under my own care and the rest were in the care of a colleague. This style facilitated recruitment of members. Participants were familiar with me, the facilitator, or they were recommended by their trusted in-home visitor. They were initially told by their in-home visitor, then given the flyer with more information, and finally contacted a few days before the first group.

In addition to being mothers, participants also came from marginalized and underserved communities. Most of the participating mothers were Latinx and all the mothers were low-income at the time of the workshops. Additionally, many of them had traumatic pasts. Given their demographics and experiences, I relied on the literature on intersectionality to design and facilitate the workshops. For one, I refrained from using language that may have judgmental overtones and assumptions. For example, I did not ask questions such as, "What is your fondest memory as a child?" because they may have struggled to identify a happy moment in their traumatic past. Instead, I would ask, "As a child, what did you do with adults who were important to you?" because it can support engagement from participants without traditionally defined parents, and the question is open enough for participants to identify memories with a wide range of feelings and emotions. In addition to considering participants' pasts, I decided on a group setting because it generally aligns with the Latinx community's collective cultural practices (Comas-Diaz, 2006; Tamura & Lau, 1992). Lastly, I prompted participants to use imagery to tell their stories in the collage. The focus on imagery allows people with varying language capabilities to engage in the workshop.

Facilitating the Group

The group was held at the local library. This allowed clients access to a local service closer to a bus route, and provided a less confrontational environment than a clinic. The group was scheduled to be once a week for an hour and a half (11:00–12:30pm) for five weeks. This time allowed for mothers to be able to take their kids to school and pick them up after the group. Weekly meetings allowed for intentional and focused attention on each topic. Each week participants focused on a new quadrant and the last week involved finalizing and presenting the finished collage to the therapist.

Materials available to participants included a canvas sized 16 × 20 inches, liquid glue called Mod Podge, paint brushes, scissors, pencils, and flashcards. Light snacks and beverages were also provided. The room was set up with the purpose of all participants having adequate table space, direct view of the facilitator, and access to extra magazines. The tables were set up in a U shape with the therapist in front of the room rotating among the group. The purpose of this set-up was also so that participants could bounce ideas and share questions with the therapist. The collage process is an internal and reflective process that can be distracted by others' processes. Aware of this, a facilitator can redirect participants who show signs of disengagement from the collage.

Each session started with an experiential exercise. The purpose was to practice observational skills, enhance feelings and perceptions, and utilize grounding techniques. This would in turn support the participant in transitioning to the collage. One activity involved observing pieces of art and scaffolding up in their description and feelings towards the art. First, they answered the question of shapes and colors they see in the piece. Next, they processed what could be happening in the piece of art. Finally, they reflected on how the piece of art made them feel and what personal meaning it had for them. Another week the initial activity involved listening to three different songs. Participants were prompted to reflect on the energy of the song, what feelings were elicited in them, and whether they liked it or not. Participants wrote their reflections on paper without the expectation of presenting or passing it on to the rest of the group. This form of free association provoked connection to feelings and engagement with material outside of themselves.

The collage was intended to be full of images that included colors, texture, people, nature, and places. The use of text was limited with the thought it would allow for more interpretation. It is important to note that participants were still drawn to using text and this was allowed. Participants were encouraged to tear or cut images. Some participants asked for help as to how to put the art together. They were encouraged to either put down the images all at once, and then paste or start with one image and work around it. They were reminded that it was difficult to make a major mistake since they could paste over images and use water to remove adhesive.

The Collage's Four Quadrants

There were four areas of focus for the collage group. The four areas included reflections on the self, their relationships, the past, and the future. The collage is broken down into these areas because it covers the constellation of changes that occur for a person when they are in a challenging part of their life. During a chaotic time of development, verbal forms of describing or understanding the problem are not always at the precipice. The four-quadrant structure of collage was created to give order to the reflective process.

A narrative form of inquiry was utilized, coupled with prompts and questions throughout the collage process. Narrative therapy involves making meaning of your life, processing life challenges, and processing development (McAdams, 2006; Van Schalkwyk, 2010). Collaging with question prompts from the therapist guides the clients to reflect on their lives. The nature of the questions was intentionally asking about positive and negative life aspects. This was crucial to elicit realistic observations of relationship dynamics.

The Self

A shift in identity occurs when a woman becomes a parent (Prinds et al., 2014). This change that occurs in the self can be life-altering and traumatic. A person re-evaluates their responsibilities and competence in themselves and their role as a parent (Geiger, Livingston, & Bialik, 2019). The struggle is particularly challenging throughout the first years of a child's life when the most difficult adjustments in the adult's life occur (Novick & Novick, 2010).

The shift of becoming a parent is important for mothers to reflect on in terms of their identity. Reflection during times of transition better equips mothers to manage the stress and changes they undergo. Coping skills and personal strengths can be emphasized through a visual format. To build on the group's confidence, "The Self" as the first quadrant was chosen because it pulls on personal strengths and knowledge which may be more easily transferred from thought to image. Prompts and questions to guide the selection of images for "the Self" quadrant are included in Table 10.1.

Table 10.1 Prompts and Questions for the Self Quadrant

Pick images that represent who you are. What items would we find in your room?
What are images that bring you relaxation or peace?
What images are inspiring to you?
What are your coping skills?
What is something you have accomplished?
What is a challenge for you? Make some space for something you want to improve in yourself.

In the group, participants are active in this topic. Mothers are given magazines and brochures that are representative of them (e.g. Spanish language, Women of Color, parents). The results of this quadrant showed coping skills, interests, and individual personality factors. Given that it is the first session, some people may be hesitant to start to paste. The therapist can encourage participants to make commitments to pasting early in the session so as to build confidence and fully start the process.

Relationships

The second quadrant in the collage is relationships. Motherhood is a relationship. All mothers have a type of relationship with their child. A common saying in early childhood mental health is, "there is no such thing as a baby ... there is a baby and someone." This quote exemplifies that children only thrive because of their relationship with another person, who is primarily their mother. The demands of a child's survival and development depend on their mother.

It is crucial for the mother to reflect on her relationship with her child. Healthy early connections inoculate children against life-long risks (Lieberman & Van Horn, 2011). Reflecting on the relationship, the attachment, and empathizing with your child supports a parent with having less parental distress in the face of challenges. Table 10.2 includes the questions and prompts for "the Relationships" quadrant.

This quadrant was more difficult for participants. How do you capture relationships with a color? How do you pick an image that represents connectedness? How do people understand the word empathy? Reframing questions is helpful and allows participants to slow down and consider their relationship with their child.

The Past

Trauma experiences are high amongst low-income mothers (Steele et al., 2016). Exposure to trauma increases parental distress (Steele et al., 2016). There is an intergenerational transmission of unhealthy parent–child relations among children of parents exposed to traumatic life experiences

Table 10.2 Prompts and Questions for the Relationships Quadrant

What are my family traditions? What did I do for fun as a kid?

What activities do I enjoy with my children?

What is difficult about parenting or motherhood? What comes easily or is enjoyable?

What does it look like to be connected to another?

What images make you think of understanding another person (i.e. empathy)?

(Fraiberg, Adelson, & Shapiro, 1975; Steele et al., 2016). Decreasing maternal depression can inoculate children from the negative effects of trauma the child experiences (Aisenberg et al., 2007).

This quadrant is just as much about the trauma of the child as it is about the trauma of the mother. In order for mothers to decrease the incidence of trauma for their child, it is important for them to reflect on the feelings of trauma they experienced themselves (Fraiberg, Adelson, & Shapiro, 1975). What feelings would they never want their child to go through? Table 10.3 highlights questions for "the Past" quadrant.

This quadrant was impactful for the participants. The questions and images of the past and strong emotions made it tearful and intense for many mothers. The collages included images of parental figures, childhood memories, and mixed emotions.

The Future

Collages in current times are often utilized for planning out future goals and brainstorming on projects. There is a belief that if you visualize your future, your outcome will be closer to your desires. Many of the mothers expected the collage to be future oriented. One person made most of her boards about ideal scenarios for their relationships and themselves.

This was the last quadrant presented in the collage group. Participants were well versed in the process. One participant selected images of roads and a car, stating that she really wants to get her driver's license. Another participant put herself surrounded by animals because her dream is to work with animals. There were also images about dreams of traveling and home ownership. Given that the prompts and questions, included in Table 10.4, were individualistic, the section of the collage was centered on a mother's personal goals.

Collage Presentation

At the end of the group, the participants presented their collages. They each took about seven minutes to show their collage and talk about images that meant the most to them, and what they felt they gained from the process. Fellow group members reflected on what they liked or felt strongly about in the collages.

Table 10.3 Prompts and Questions for the Past Quadrant

Choose images that represent a high and a low point in your life.
What childhood memories were important to me?
What negative emotions did I face as a child?
Who was an important role model for me as a child?

Table 10.4 Prompts and Questions for the Future Quadrant

What motivates you?

Where do you see yourself in one year?

What creative activity or hobby do you like to engage in?

If something changed for the better in your relationship with your child, what would it be?

How would your relationship look differently?

A limit to the group was the lack of time to process difficult topics that came up in the collage. Topics related to historical trauma, relationship fallouts, and even aspirations for the future fueled conversations and insights that were only touched on the surface in the group. To help with this issue, therapists could encourage participants to process the collage further with their personal support people.

Considerations

Clinicians should take into account a few considerations when designing and executing similar collage workshops. For one, my initial intentions were to guide participants to use only images as a way to move away from traditional therapeutic language. However, I learned some participants were drawn to text and I did not want to discourage any forms of expression. Instead, I shifted my approach and encouraged participants to primarily rely on images to create their collages, but to also consider texts and words if they felt a deep connection with the text. I also learned I needed to ask clarifying questions about texts in order to fully understand participants' collages. For instance, one participant used the words "turn myself on." I found out she did not mean to become sexually aroused; rather she saw the text as a wake-up call to strive for her own goals. In another instance, a participant used a large bold word that read "ESTABLISHMENT." To her, this signified a dream of being a professional and a responsible family woman. As seen in these examples, I treated the text in the same manner as the images and did not take the text for granted, as it can have different meanings to different people – especially in my groups where English is often people's second language.

Another consideration is in regard to location. This author facilitated the workshops at a public library that was accessible via public transportation. A library or comfortable public space is less intimidating and less medicalized than the clinical setting. Also, the library may have additional programming and resources, which can be an added benefit for participants and their children. However, there can be personal challenges when using other settings (e.g. time it takes for a clinician to get there from work setting), so these choices need to be carefully thought through prior to leading groups outside of a clinical setting.

Conclusion

Mothers go through tremendous life stress when they are raising young children. They require a social network and a community of supportive therapists that spike their interests, address their barriers to treatment, and impact their therapeutic goals. Collage art-making groups with other mothers conducted in an easy to understand and accessible manner is an avenue that can be supportive to them, and provide an effective alternative therapy to traditional talk therapy methods.

References

Abrams, L. S., Dornig, K., & Curran, L. (2009). Barriers to service use for postpartum depression symptoms among low-income ethnic minority mothers in the United States. *Qualitative Health Research*, 19(4), 535–551.

Aisenberg, E., Trickett, P. K., Mennen, F. E., Saltzman, W., & Zayas, L. H. (2007). Maternal depression and adolescent behavior problems: An examination of mediation among immigrant Latino mothers and their adolescent children exposed to community violence. *Journal of Interpersonal Violence*, 22(10), 1227–1249.

Callister, L. C., Beckstrand, R. L., & Corbett, C. (2011). Postpartum depression and help-seeking behaviors in immigrant Hispanic women. *Journal of Obstetric, Gynecologic & Neonatal Nursing*, 40(4), 440–449.

Comas-Diaz, L. (2006). Latino healing: The integration of ethnic psychology into psychotherapy. *Psychotherapy: Theory, Research, Practice, Training*, 43(4), 436.

Easterbrooks, M. A., Bartlett, J. D., Raskin, M., Goldberg, J., Contreras, M. M., Kotake, C., Chaudhuri, J. H., & Jacobs, F. H. (2013). Limiting home visiting effects: Maternal depression as a moderator of child maltreatment. *American Academy of Pediatrics*, 132(Suppl 2), 126–133.

Edge, D. (2011). 'It's leaflet, leaflet, leaflet then, "see you later"': Black Caribbean women's perceptions of perinatal mental health care. *British Journal of General Practice*, 61(585), 256–262.

Fraiberg, S., Adelson, E., & Shapiro, V. (1975). Ghosts in the nursery: A psychoanalytic approach to the problems of impaired infant-mother relationships. *Journal of the American Academy of Child & Adolescent Psychiatry*, 14(3), 387–421.

Gardner, P. L., Bunton, P., Edge, D., & Wittkowski, A. (2014). The experience of postnatal depression in West African mothers living in the United Kingdom: A qualitative study. *Midwifery*, 30(6), 756–763.

Geiger, A. W., Livingston, G., & Bialik, K. (2019, May 8) 6 facts about U.S moms. Retrieved from: https://www.pewresearch.org/fact-tank/2019/05/08/facts-about-u-s-mothers/.

Goodman, J. H., & Santangelo, G. (2011). Group treatment for postpartum depression: a systematic review. *Archives of Women's Mental Health*, 14(4), 277–293.

Hartup, W. W., & Rubin, Z. (2013). *Relationships and development*. London: Psychology Press.

Health Resources and Services Administration (2017, September 19). HRSA awards $342 million to support families through the maternal, infant and early childhood home visiting program. Retrieved from: https://www.hrsa.gov/about/news/press-releases/hrsa-awards-342-million-miechv-program.html.

Howells, V., & Zelnick, T. (2014). Making art: A qualitative study of personal and group transformation in a community arts studio. *Psychiatric Rehabilitation Journal*, 32(3), 215–222.

Kay, L. (2013). Bead collage: An arts-based research method. *International Journal of Education & the Arts*, 14(3).

Lara-Cinisomo, S., Wisner, K. L., Burns, R. M., & Chaves-Gnecco, D. (2014). Perinatal depression treatment preferences among Latina mothers. *Qualitative Health Research*, 24(2), 232–241.

Letourneau, N. L., Dennis, C-L., Benzies, K., Duffett-Leger, L., Stewart, M., Tryphonopoulos, P. D., Este, D., & Watson, W. (2012). Postpartum depression is a family affair: Addressing the impact on mothers, fathers, and children. *Journal of Issues in Mental Health Nursing*, 33(7), 445–457.

Letourneau, N. L., Salamani, M., & Duffett-Leger, L. (2010). Maternal depressive symptoms and parenting of children from birth to 12 years. *Western Journal of Nursing Research*, 32(5), 662–685.

Letourneau, N. L., Tramonte, L., & Willms, J. D. (2013). Maternal depression, family functioning and children's longitudinal development. *Journal of Pediatric Nursing*, 38(3), 223–234.

Lewis-Fernandez, R., Das, A. K., Alfonso, C., Weissman, M. M., & Olfson, M. (2005). Depression in US Hispanics: Diagnostic and management considerations in family practice. *The Journal of the American Board of Family Practice*, 18(4), 282–296.

Lieberman, A. F., & Van Horn, P. (2011). *Psychotherapy with infants and young children: Repairing the effects of stress and trauma on early attachment*. New York: Guilford Press.

McAdams, D. P. (2006). The role of narrative in personality psychology today. *Narrative Inquiry*, 16(1), 11–18.

Meadows, S. O., McLanahan, S. S., & Brooks-Gunn, J. (2007). Parental depression and anxiety and early childhood behavior problems across family types. *Journal of Marriage and Family*, 69(5), 1162–1177.

Meins, E. (2013). *Security of attachment and the social development of cognition*. Hove, East Sussex: Psychology Press.

Mendoza, L. (2018, February 18). One year after MIECHV reauthorization, advocates look to a bright future for successful home visiting services. Retrieved from: https://www.ffyf.org/one-year-after-miechv-reauthorization-advocates-look-to-a-bright-future-for-successful-home-visiting-services/.

Murray, L., Woolgar, M., Murray, J., & Cooper, P. (2003). Self-exclusion from health care in women at high risk for postpartum depression. *Journal of Public Health*, 25(2), 131–137.

Novick, K. K., & Novick, J. (2010). *Emotional muscle: Strong parents, strong children*. Bloomington, IN: Xlibris Corporation.

Perry, C., Thurston, M., & Osborn, T. (2008). Time for me: The arts as therapy in postnatal depression. *Complementary Therapies in Clinical Practice*, 14(1), 38–45.

Perry, D. F., Ettinger, A. K., Mendelson, T., & Le, H-N. (2011). Prenatal depression predicts postpartum maternal attachment in low-income Latina mothers with infants. *Journal of Infant Behavior and Development*, 34(2), 339–350.

Prinds, C., Hvidt, N. C., Mogensen, O., & Buus, N. M. (2014). Making existential meaning in transition to motherhood – a scoping review. *Midwifery*, 30(6), 733–741.

Rich-Edwards, J. W., Kleinman, K., Abrams, A., Harlow, B. L., McLaughlin, T. J., Joffe, H., & Gillman, M. W. (2006). Sociodemographic predictors of antenatal and postpartum depressive symptoms among women in a medical group practice. *Journal of Epidemiology & Community Health*, 60(3), 221–227.

Rouhi, M., Stirling, C., Ayton, J., & Crisp, E. P. (2019). Women's help-seeking behaviours within the first twelve months after childbirth: A systematic qualitative meta-aggregation review. *Midwifery*, 72, 39–49.

Sheng, X., Le, H. N., & Perry, D. (2010). Perceived satisfaction with social support and depressive symptoms in perinatal Latinas. *Journal of Transcultural Nursing*, 21(1), 35–44.

Simmons, N., & Daley, S. (2013). The art of thinking: Using collage to stimulate scholarly work. *Canadian Journal for the Scholarship of Teaching and Learning*, 4(1), 2.

Slayton, S. C., D'Archer, J. D., & Kaplan, F. (2010). Outcome studies on the efficacy of art therapy: A review of findings. *Art Therapy: Journal of the American Art Therapy Association*, 27(3), 108–118.

Steele, H., Bate, J., Steele, M., Dube, S. R., Danskin, K., Knafo, H., Nikitiades, A., Bonuck, K., Meissner, P., & Murphy, A. (2016). Adverse childhood experiences, poverty, and parenting stress. *Canadian Journal of Behavioural Science*, 48(1), 32–38.

Tamura, T., & Lau, A. (1992). Connectedness versus separateness: Applicability of family therapy to Japanese families. *Family Process*, 31(4), 319–340.

Taylor, S. E. (2011). Social support: A review. *The handbook of health psychology*, 189, 214.

The Annie E. Casey Foundation (2019). Kids Count Data Center. Retrieved from: https://datacenter.kidscount.org.

Ugarriza, D. N. (2004). Group therapy and its barriers for women suffering from postpartum depression. *Archives of Psychiatric Nursing*, 18(2), 39–48.

Van Lith, T. (2016). Art therapy in mental health: A systematic review of approaches and practices. *The Arts in Psychotherapy*, 47, 9–22.

Van Schalkwyk, G. J. (2010). Collage life story elicitation technique: A representational technique for scaffolding autobiographical memories. *The Qualitative Report*, 15(3), 675–695.

Vigod, S. N., Tarasoff, L. A., Bryja, B., Dennis, C. L., Yudin, M. H., & Ross, L. E. (2013). Relation between place of residence and postpartum depression. *Canadian Medical Association Journal*, 185(13), 1129–1135.

World Health Organization (2019). Maternal and child mental health. Retrieved from: https://www.who.int/mental_health/maternal-child/en/.

Section IV

Structural and Institutional Components of Groups

11 Spirituality as a Resource in Group Psychotherapy

Alexis D. Abernethy

Introduction

Given that best practices in the delivery of psychological treatment includes attentiveness to varied aspects of patients' social identities (American Psychological Association, 2017), including their spiritual identity, the question is not whether, but how to engage in spiritually informed care, and spiritually informed group therapy, in particular (Abernethy, 2012). "Religion" generally refers to specific doctrinal and institutional features, whereas "spirituality" is often defined as one's subjective experiences in an effort to understand life's ultimate questions and find meaning/purpose (Pargament, Mahoney, Exline, Jones, & Shafranske, 2013). Religiousness and spirituality have been associated with health and well-being, but certain aspects have been associated with negative outcomes. For example, religious comfort refers to a feeling of being loved by God, a sense of belonging to a religious community, and a sense of being forgiven (Exline, Yali, & Sanderson, 2000). Religious comfort may buffer the negative effects of stressors such as depression (Abernethy, Allen, & Carroll, 2018; Cook, Aten, Moore, Hook, & Davis, 2013) and contribute to perceived posttraumatic growth (Ogden et al., 2011). In contrast, opposite findings have emerged in research focusing on religious strain, defined as experiencing alienation from God and one's religious community, pervasive feelings of fear and guilt, and perceived or actual conflicts with other religious individuals and beliefs (Exline, Yali, & Sanderson, 2000). Inverse associations have been found between religious strain and psychological well-being in several cross-sectional studies (Exline, Yali, & Sanderson, 2000; Harris et al., 2008, 2012).

Establishing the Group Frame

As noted above, although studies of spirituality and religiousness have been associated with positive outcomes, negative associations have been found. In social conversations, religion and politics are frequently avoided as discussion topics in settings where particular views are not shared.

For many, strong convictions may foster argumentative and intensely conflictual interactions; this poses a potential challenge in groups, but attentiveness to the group frame and conflict management in particular ways offers the potential for a more constructive outcome. Addressing the stages of group is an essential task of the group leader: Creating safety and establishing norms, framing constructive conflict as an essential path to intimacy, fostering the group's developing maturity and deepened collaboration, and working through issues of termination are all important phases of group (Yalom & Leszcz, 2005). For the purposes of this chapter, the first two phases of establishing norms and addressing conflict will be a particular emphasis. Indeed, if leaders have not attended to specific ways of framing the group as a "safe enough" place to incorporate members' spiritual identities, chaos may ensue or important aspects of members' identities may be avoided. I, as well as others, have sought to articulate varied approaches that help to create a frame for the group in engaging these issues as they emerge in the group process and content (Abernethy, 2012; Jacques, 1998; Rizzuto, 1979).

In work that sought to create a safe place for pastoral supervision, Jay Foster, Sharon Engebretson, and Jane Litzinger first coined the term, "courageous conversations." Four key elements include the following: stay engaged; speak your truth *in love*; be willing to experience discomfort; and expect and accept non-closure (DeLong, 2010; Singleton & Linton, 2013; emphasis added). This framing in addition to common agreements of confidentiality, respectful engagement, and suspending judgment help to create a context to engage issues that are typically avoided. In addition, it is important that the leader orient the group members in assessment and preparation for participation in a group that will include the opportunity to engage with all aspects of one's identity including ethnic, racial, and spiritual dimensions, as it is salient for the individual (Abernethy, 2012).

In addition, Miroslav Volf, a theologian, has made an important contribution in his work, *Exclusion and Embrace: A Theological Exploration of Identity, Otherness, and Reconciliation* (1996). He offers a clear metaphorical example of the role of bias and subjectivity in understanding others that may encourage a stance of cultural humility: A "lifelong process of self-reflection, self-critique, continual assessment of power imbalances, and the development of mutually respectful relationships and partnerships" (Gallardo, 2014, p. 3). Volf recommends that we use "double vision" to see the world not only from our perspective, but from the perspective of others. He challenges the notion that we can see our own or others' perspectives from a purely objective standpoint.

> Instead of seeing the self and the other or the two cultures and their common history from no perspective we should try to see them *from*

both perspectives, both "from here" and "from there" ... But what does it take to see "from there," from the perspective of others? First, we *step outside ourselves* ... Second, we *cross a social boundary and move into the world of the other* to inhabit it temporarily (MacIntyre, 1993). We open our ears to hear how others perceive themselves as well as how they perceive us. Third, we *take the other into our own world*. We compare and contrast the view "from there" and the view "from here." Fourth, we *repeat the process*.

(Volf, 1996, pp. 250–252)

This insight reframes the discussion from polarizing differences and competing opinions to an opportunity for deepened understanding. In training graduate students in diversity where they participate in small groups and in training group therapists to engage diversity in their groups, this has been an invaluable lens and invites members to engage in interpersonal learning with one another not only in expected areas in group therapy, such as interpersonal skills, but in the development of their multicultural competence (Cross, Bazron, Dennis, & Isaacs, 1989), and in this case related to their spiritual selves. This encourages a posture of humility, curiosity, and compassion for the leader and members to attend to the story and context of others.

Addressing Similarities and Differences

In addition to encouraging a non-judgmental, narrative, and contextual approach to hearing others' stories and life journeys, the leader's recognition of the extent to which all persons are, to some degree, like all other persons, like some other persons, and like no other person is a helpful perspective (Murray & Kluckhohn, 1953). This view highlights the presence of universality, group commonalities, and individuality. Many groups focus on individuality and universality, but may ignore group commonalities. Sometimes universality becomes a central focus in the formation of groups as it is assumed that homogeneity and similarity foster a sense of belonging whereas individual or group differences might impede early group development. Drawing on Pinderhughes' work (1989) that emphasizes the importance of addressing the psychology of difference, members' avoidance of difference is not only related to some of the potential challenges associated with cultural and spiritual differences, in particular, but also connected to their developmental histories. She argues that most early experiences of difference are met with negative responses, sometimes to the point of denigration and ostracism. Members avoid highlighting differences in fear of recreating early as well as more recently painful experiences. Modeling by the leader is critical as the leader can normalize difference as an opportunity for learning and highlight a constructive posture toward engaging difference as Volf has noted. Particularly as it pertains to spiritual differences, it can also be helpful to acknowledge and offer an empathic response toward the fear associated with this. When engagement with difference goes poorly, processes of "othering" lead to denigration, dehumanization, and scapegoating (Miller & Schamess, 2000). The leader's attentiveness to this potential from the first group is even more critical in a group where explicit permission is given to engage difference. Statements that acknowledge that "coming out in our spiritual selves may not work well outside the group, but this group offers an opportunity to be more fully present with all aspects of our lives."

In an interpersonally oriented group that had met for a number of years, there was a gay man in the group who had not come out. A new member was added who was openly gay. During the first session for this openly gay man, an original male member of the group espoused his deep commitment to his faith and his judgment about gay men for the first time. This faith commitment had not been evident in past years, but emerged in response to this gay new member. I, as the leader, was not prepared to engage this and was shocked by the strength of this member's attack on the new member. This seemed to be related to the new member's sexual orientation as well as the original member's dominating style. Unfortunately, this new member dropped out after a few weeks, but the leader was able to get consultation and work more actively to create a constructive environment for engaging the intersection of religion and sexual orientation. Other members came out in their religious identities and the longer standing gay men shared their sexual orientation. The group was able to move forward and deepen cohesion.

It is critical for leaders to take an active and vigilant stance toward the interpersonal dynamics that may emerge as members engage spiritual and religious content so that the group may constructively engage these issues as relevant to the work of the group. The role of intersectionality related to these issues further complicates the work. Researchers have found that identity varies across as well as within different cultural groups (Comas-Diaz, 2012; Hays, 2016; Tummala-Narra, 2016). The leaders' openness to exploring these issues and modeling constructive engagement play critical roles in how effectively the group is able to do its work.

Critical characteristics of therapists that influence their ability to engage in spiritual content and process include the following: Their own orientation that may range from a rejectionist stance to a pluralistic stance toward religious content (Zinnbauer & Pargament, 2000); their commitment to assessing the spiritual as well as other cultural identities of their patients during screening; their countertransferential response to the interreligious and intrareligious transferential content and reactions of group members toward one another and the therapist; their skill in using spiritual language, recognizing spiritual themes, and addressing process issues related to spiritual concerns; their openness to spiritually informed consultation when necessary; and their ability to manage scapegoating (Abernethy, 2012).

So the first task of the therapist is to engage in their own work related to their orientation toward spiritual content and process and then work to prepare themselves and their group for a culturally and specifically spiritually diverse group. In the preparation phase, leaders should assess for strong religious prejudices and consider the composition of the group in its ability to work in the midst of these voices. Leaders should also explicitly underscore the importance of diverse voices and tolerance. Norms should be established related to respectful engagement and that build on the work related to courageous conversation and Volf's "double vision."

Mimetic Theory

Mimesis

Another critical leader characteristic in maximizing spirituality as a resource in group is managing the conflicts that arise and scapegoating, in particular. When microaggressions and misunderstandings occur, the leader has an opportunity to model an empathic approach that does not promote scapegoating. René Girard is a world-renowned French historian, literary critic, and cultural theorist. He developed mimetic theory to explain a wide range of interpersonal and cultural phenomena, including understanding how human violence arises and the nature and origins of religious rituals. His mimetic theory consists of three components: 1) mimetic desire, 2) the scapegoating mechanism, and 3) the reversal of the scapegoating mechanism. In Girard's mimetic theory, he argues that desire is mimetic. People's desire for things or other people is based on imitation and is constitutionally mimetic (Girard, 1961). While this is one way that interpersonal learning and imitation works in groups in a positive way, mimesis may also have negative effects, as it may move from a constructive to a competitive interaction (Finlay, Abernethy, & Garrels, 2016). Mimetic rivalry emerges from the reciprocal desire of both the model and imitator to acquire the same object and this mimesis regularly leads to conflict. When two members desire the same object, such as the group leader, conflict emerges. Girard would argue that one member desires the group leader and another member is imitating this desire. Mimetic violence arises from unchecked desires and rivalries that perpetually escalate into intense and ongoing forms of social conflict. Girard argues not only desire but competition and violence is imitated (Girard, 1977; Girard, Oughourlian, & Lefort, 1987). Given this seemingly inevitable cycle of violence, he wondered how the world was not destroyed. Social and cultural structures, including religion, are forces that may check and stop this escalation.

Scapegoating

Girard (1977, 1986) posits further that the displacement of tension between mimetic rivals onto a scapegoat or surrogate victim was the spontaneous event that created social stability, and ultimately made a cohesive human culture possible. So when mimetic rivals who desire a similar object experience increased tension, one way this tension is resolved is that they project onto a scapegoat or third party. He argued that this occurs on an interpersonal level as well as a societal level. Girard noted that rituals, myths, and all the unique forms of human cultural and religious phenomena emerge as attempts to manage human mimetic violence. He proposed that ritual sacrifice reflected this scapegoating process. As he read religious texts, Girard noted the presence of ritual sacrifice in archaic religions. He argued that these ritualized sacrifices reflect an attempt on the part of society and religions to avert and avoid even more devastating destruction and violence. A victim, animal or human, is identified to sacrifice before the gods to appease the wrath of the gods and to resolve the chaos of the community. He posited that first religions sought to prohibit violence; when these efforts failed, ritual sacrifice became the next alternative.

Reversal of the Scapegoating Mechanism

After developing his initial perspectives on mimetic theory, Girard looked at the Hebrew Bible and Gospel narratives for mimetic phenomena. He discovered not only all the same elements of archaic myth, including stereotypes of persecution that represented scapegoating traditions, but he also found unexpectedly that these cultural narratives were actively attempting to reveal scapegoating tendencies and reverse the outcome by siding with the social victim. For Girard (1986), the cultural narratives of the Hebrew Bible represent a revelatory movement away from scapegoating, and a decisive shift toward non-sacrificial forms of cultural maintenance (Girard, Oughourlian, & Lefort, 1987). So instead of the traditional and historical focus on scapegoating and sacrifice, Girard notes a trend away from this. For Girard, these texts progressively reveal the innocence of the social victim and the attribution of violence to human, rather than divine, prerogative. This reality emerges as authors reveal a God who is ultimately on the side of the victim – a God who in fact suffers with people, rather than demanding their sacrifice. Similarly, Girard's (1986) analysis of the narratives describing the crucifixion of Christ reveal that many of the same elements of myth and texts of persecution are present, including a community in chaos and a mob's attempt to resolve the crisis through the sacrifice of a single victim (Girard, Oughourlian, & Lefort, 1987). The innocent death of Jesus makes it impossible to fully ascribe guilt to the innocent victim and reveals the hidden nature of societies to engage in violence directed toward surrogate victims. Although he argues that this scapegoating phenomenon is pervasive, societies routinely try to obscure this.

Implications for Group

In response to offense, rivalry, and violence, group members have an opportunity to follow models that encourage scapegoating and sacrifice (pursuing justified blame, including retaliation) or to imitate the desire of a God who demands mercy and not sacrifice (transcending blame) (Abernethy, 2009; Abernethy, Allen, & Carroll, 2018). Dr David F. Allen (see Chapter 14), in his transformational group work in the Bahamas with former gang leaders and those who have survived violence committed against their loved ones, has embodied this transcending blame presence which has led to reduced violence, transformation, and gratitude (Abernethy, Allen, & Carroll, 2018). Survivors shift their focus from justified anger and retaliatory violence toward transformation and healthier relationships. Anger and demands for justice are important to be expressed, but the punitive progression toward scapegoating and violence can be averted. This poses a challenging opportunity for groups and humanity to find new ways of maintaining social bonds through beliefs and practices that are not founded on the exclusion of particular individuals. Instead, members are offered vastly different models whose desires can be imitated in the service of non-exclusionary social justice and reciprocal acts of self-giving – a non-sacrificial perspective. These processes of transformation are evident in training groups as leaders learn to embody such a transcending blame presence as well as in community-based groups such as Dr Allen's (Abernethy, Allen, & Carroll, 2018).

A reasonable question might be, is an elaborate perspective such as Girard's necessary or is the main idea for group leaders to be empathic and not promote retaliation and revenge-seeking? The challenge arises when the leader seeks to retaliate or the strength of the interaction between or among members is quite powerful. Consultation can assist most leaders in this context; however, in the current political climate with the intersection of global challenges and political polarization, many group therapists experience increased tension and the relevance of political and religious issues as a source of stress in their groups (Abernethy, 2018). Strategies in working with this content in constructive ways are invaluable tools for therapists. Leaders need to not only contain these communications and explore the meaning of the communications (Jacques 1998; Rizzuto, 1979), but also consider engaging this content from a transcendent perspective. Members can sense when a leader reaches for something beyond him or herself for strength, understanding, and insight. This may be observable as an act of gratitude or compassion. The members not only feel understood, but will often use terms such as grace and joy, and have a sense of being transformed in a way that is atypical from everyday experience. This may occur even for members who are not particularly religious. In our research on spiritual transcendence and in the development of the Spiritual Transcendence Index (Abernethy &

Kim, 2018; Seidlitz et al., 2002), we describe the process of transcending an experience as:

> an experience of, or identification with, a subjective state that transcended and was unencumbered by one's limitations, psychological distress, or physical suffering, even though such limitations or distress might persist in another part of one's conscious experience.
>
> (Seidlitz et al., 2002, p. 441)

Critical Exchanges

A spiritual perspective has provided an additional lens for the posture of the leader toward forming the group and anticipating early tensions related to spiritual differences or similarities. How does this spiritually informed perspective as well as the most recent discussion of Girardian perspectives on scapegoating inform a leader's response to microaggressions directed toward the leader and members?

In a workshop that focused on cultural issues and increasing group therapists' ability to work in a culturally competent manner, toward the end of the group a statement was made by a White male participant that was experienced as a microaggression by the female African American leader (Pierce, 1970). This statement occurred at a point where processing was occurring in the large group, so the leader was not only instructor but group leader. A stereotyped comment was made about a person from the leader's racial group. The leader felt the sting of this comment and noted others' visible shudders as the statement was made. Some participants might not have perceived the toxic nature of the communication. The leader was surprised by this comment and recognized that as the session had progressed and things were proceeding well, she had become less vigilant. She felt whiplashed. She realized that until that point, she had felt quite positive about the workshop and she wondered whether part of the communication of this participant included a power play to undermine her confidence. It partly felt like a stereotyped comment based on his experiences, but it had an interpersonal dimension in the moment that felt more particularly directed as a challenge to the leader. In her fatigue and surprise, she felt less equipped and ready to respond. She felt a desire to retaliate toward him by shaming him or calling him out. She took a deep breath. With muscle memory and drawing on a spiritual presence beyond herself, she was able to experience compassion and contain his comment with equanimity. Instead of seeking to blame him, she transcended blame and sought to understand, even if briefly, how this description might have emerged from him. What was his story? In his response to her question, she gained a better sense of his context and was able to reframe his comment in a way that highlighted the potential overgeneralization in his statement without shaming him, but also with an acknowledgment from a social justice perspective that the communication as it was needed to be modified or reframed. The leader exerted her own power and skill in an effort to not be overpowered by this man, to enlarge his perspective, and to address a microaggression.

In another situation with an interpersonally oriented group, a female wife and mother who was a member of a religion that held fairly defined roles for her as a wife and mother joined the group. She led with her concern about marital and parental issues, but as time unfolded her deeper concern involved her own struggles with the demands of her religious faith. She presented initially as devout and proud of her religion. She seemed particularly vigilant for negative comments about her faith. Some microaggressive comments were made about her religion, particularly in light of what sounded like a rigid adherence on her part. Initially the co-leaders were less vigilant in response to her potential for being scapegoated as they held a more judgmental stance toward her religion. With consultation, the co-leaders examined their bias and became more open. The group was able to work with her more constructively and listen from her perspective. This allowed her to move from a defensive stance and share her own religious struggles and concerns related to her roles.

Implications

In group therapy scapegoating refers to the tendency for group members to allow one member to be marginalized and viewed as different or representing an extreme position. Without intervention, this person may be viewed negatively, ridiculed, and ultimately rejected by the group to the point of being removed from the group. In my group therapy seminars when I discuss the process of scapegoating and the therapist's role in redirecting this, a common question is whether scapegoating is universal? A similar question emerges in teaching students how to work with patients in a culturally competent way. Is there something natural, automatic, or instinctual about denigrating the other, discriminating against an entire group of people, or viewing others negatively? From a group therapy perspective, I see scapegoating as a normal process that may be destructive if not redirected. In cultural competency training, I take a developmental perspective and argue that children learn to discriminate and are socialized in this process. So, something learned may be unlearned. I do not see this discriminatory process as natural or instinctual. Now after reading some of Girard's work I would see scapegoating and the related projective processes as a more pervasive human tendency, but a tendency that may be redirected and transcended. In order to effectively draw on spirituality as a resource in group, leaders must first be vigilant and understand how the emergence of spiritual content and process may contribute to polarization and scapegoating. In addition, with specific preparation of the leader and the group, the leader may model and embody a more gracious and compassionate presence that creates more space for the group to engage in their spiritual identities and make substantive progress toward individual and collective growth.

References

Abernethy, A. D. (2012). A spiritually informed approach to group psychotherapy. In J. L. Kleinberg (ed.), *The Wiley-Blackwell handbook of group psychotherapy* (pp. 681–705). Chichester, West Sussex: John Wiley & Sons.

Abernethy, A. D. (2018). Cultural competence, spirituality, and transcendence in times of crisis. Mid Atlantic Group Psychotherapy Society Spring Conference, St. Elisabeth's Hospital, Washington, DC.

Abernethy, A. D. (2009). *Relational conflict, worship, and transformation.* Professorial Lecture. Fuller Theological Seminary. Pasadena, CA.

Abernethy, A. D., Allen, D. F., & Carroll, M. A. (2018). Adapting group therapy to address real world problems: Insights from groups offered in the Bahamas. *International Journal of Group Psychotherapy*, 68(1), 17–34, doi:10.1080/00207284.2017.1335582.

Abernethy, A. D., Currier, J. M., Witvliet, C. V. O., Schnitker, S. A., Putman, K. M., Root Luna, L. M., Foster, J. D., Spencer, A., Jones, H., VanHarn, K. J., & Carter, J. (2018). Understanding the role of religious comfort and strain on depressive symptoms in an inpatient psychiatric setting. *Psychology of Religion and Spirituality.* Advance online publication, http://dx.doi.org/10.1037/rel0000233.

Abernethy, A. D., & Kim, S-H. (2018). The Spiritual Transcendence Index: An item response theory analysis. *The International Journal for the Psychology of Religion*, 28(4), 240–256, doi:10.1080/10508619.2018.1507800.

American Psychological Association (2017). *Multicultural guidelines: An ecological approach to context, identity, and intersectionality.* Washington, DC: American Psychological Association.

Comas-Diaz, L. (2012). *Multicultural care: A clinician's guide to cultural competence.* Washington, DC: American Psychological Association.

Cook, S. W., Aten, J. D., Moore, M., Hook, J. N., & Davis, D. E. (2013). Resource loss, religiousness, health, and posttraumatic growth following Hurricane Katrina. *Mental Health, Religion & Culture*, 16(4), 352–366, doi:10.1080/13674676.2012.667395.

Cross, T. L., Bazron, B. J., Dennis, K. W., & Isaacs, M. R. (1989). *Towards a culturally competent system of care (Vol. 1).* Washington, DC: Child and Adolescent Service System Program Technical Assistance Center.

DeLong, W. R. (ed.). (2010). *Courageous conversations: The teaching and learning of pastoral supervision.* Lanham, MD: University Press of America.

Exline, J. J., Yali, A. M., & Sanderson, W. C. (2000). Guilt, discord, and alienation: The role of religious strain in depression and suicidality. *Journal of Clinical Psychology*, 56(12), 1481–1496. http://dx.doi.org/10.1002/1097-4679(200012)56:12_1481:AID-1_3.0.CO;2-A.

Finlay, L. D., Abernethy, A. D., & Garrels, S. R. (2016). Scapegoating in group therapy: Insights from Girard's Mimetic Theory. *International Journal of Group Psychotherapy*, 66(2), 188–204.

Gallardo, M. E. (2014). *Developing cultural humility: Embracing race, privilege and power*. Thousand Oaks, CA: Sage.

Girard, R. (1965). *Deceit, desire, and the novel: Self and other in literary structure.* (Y. Freccero, Trans.). Baltimore, MD: Johns Hopkins Press (original work published 1961).

Girard, R. (1986). *The scapegoat.* (Y. Freccero, Trans.). Baltimore, MD: Johns Hopkins University Press (original work published 1982).

Girard, R. (1977). *Violence and the sacred.* (P. Gregory, Trans.). Baltimore, MD: Johns Hopkins University Press (original work published 1972).

Girard, R., Oughourlian, J.-M., & Lefort, G. (1987). *Things hidden since the foundation of the world.* (S. Bann, & M. Metteer, Trans.). Stanford, CA: Stanford University Press (original work published 1978).

Harris, J. I., Erbes, C. R., Engdahl, B. E., Ogden, H., Olson, R. H., Winskowski, A. M. M., Campion, K., & Mataas, S. (2012). Religious distress and coping with stressful life events: A longitudinal study. *Journal of Clinical Psychology*, 68 (12), 1276–1286, doi:10.1002/jclp.21900.

Harris, J. I., Erbes, C. R., Engdahl, B. E., Olson, R. H., Winskowski, A. M., & McMahill, J. (2008). Christian religious functioning and trauma outcomes. *Journal of Clinical Psychology*, 64(1), 17–29, doi:10.1002/jclp.20427.

Hays, P. A. (2016). Understanding clients' identities and contexts. *Addressing cultural complexities in practice: Assessment, diagnosis, and therapy* (3rd ed.). Washington, DC: American Psychological Association.

Jacques, J. R. (1998). Working with spiritual and religious themes in group therapy. *International Journal of Group Psychotherapy*, 48(1), 69–83.

MacIntyre, A. (1993). Are philosophical problems insoluble? The relevance of systems and history. In P. Cook (ed.), *Philosophical imagination and cultural memory: Appropriating historical traditions* (pp. 65–82). Durham, NC: Duke University Press.

Miller, J., & Schamess, G. (2000). The discourse of denigration and the creation of "Other." *Journal of Sociology & Social Welfare*, 27(3), 39–63.

Murray H. A., & Kluckhohn, C. (1953). *Personality in nature, society, and culture.* New York, NY: Knopf.

Ogden, H., Harris, J. I., Erbes, C. R., Engdahl, B. E., Olson, R. A., Winskowski, A. M., & McMahill, J. (2011). Religious functioning and trauma outcomes among combat veterans. *Counselling and Spirituality*, 31(1), 71–89.

Pargament, K. I., Mahoney, A., Exline, J. J., Jones, J. W., & Shafranske, E. P. (2013). Envisioning an integrative paradigm for the psychology of religion and spirituality. In K. I. Pargament, J. J. Exline, J. W. Jones, K. I. Pargament, J. J. Exline, & J. W. Jones (eds), *APA handbook of psychology, religion, and spirituality (Vol 1): Context, theory, and research* (pp. 3–19). Washington, DC: American Psychological Association, doi:10.1037/14045-001.

Pierce, C. (1970). Offensive mechanisms. In F. Barbour, (ed.), *The Black seventies* (pp. 265–282). Boston, MA: Porter Sargent.

Pinderhughes, E. (1989). *Understanding race, ethnicity, and power: The key to efficacy in clinical practice.* New York, NY: Simon and Schuster.

Rizzuto, A. M. (1979). *The birth of the living God: A psychoanalytic study.* Chicago: University of Chicago Press.

Seidlitz, L., Abernethy, A. D., Duberstein, P. R., Evinger, J. S., Lewis, B. L., & Chang, H. C. (2002). Development of the spiritual transcendence index. *Journal for the Scientific Study of Religion*, 41(3), 439–453, doi:10.1111/1468-5906.00129.

Singleton, G., & Linton, C. (2013). *Courageous conversations about race: A field guide for achieving equity in schools.* Thousand Oaks, CA: Corwin.

Tummala-Narra, P. (2016). *Psychoanalytic theory and cultural competence in psychotherapy.* Washington, DC: American Psychological Association.

Volf, M. (1996). *Exclusion and embrace: A theological exploration of identity, otherness, and reconciliation.* Nashville, TN: Abingdon Press.

Yalom, I. D., & Leszcz, M. (2005). *The theory and practice of group psychotherapy* (5th ed.). New York, NY: Basic Books.

Zinnbauer, B. J., & Pargament, K. I. (2000). Working with the sacred: Four approaches to religious and spiritual issues in counseling. *Journal of Counseling and Development*, 78(2), 162–171.

12 Teaching Group within a Social Constructionist Framework

Carlos A. Taloyo and David W. Neal

> Where else could you put the Northern Hemisphere but on the top?
>
> C. J. Cregg

Teaching multiculturalism in group therapy can lead to questions like the one asked by C. J. Cregg, fictional character in the television show *The West Wing* (Yu, Sorkin, & Redford, 2001). In the episode where she asks this question, the Cartographers for Social Equality teach her about the inherent social inequality of the traditional, and most common Mercator Map in contrast to the Peters Projection map. Land masses are distorted, with areas closer to the poles appearing larger, South America, for instance, is almost twice as large as Europe but appears smaller on the Mercator Map. The cartographers then present an upside-down map that challenges C. J. Cregg's unconsciously and automatically held understanding of the world. A television show clip, among many teaching tools, can convey more cogently the truth about institutionalized inequality. The clip engagingly demonstrates the social construction of knowledge – a map of the world, leading to unconscious acceptance of inaccuracies that are tied to inequalities.

Introduction

The purpose of this chapter is to provide teachers with a multicultural framework from which to consider the dynamic processes in teaching group psychotherapy. The chapter's approach in addressing issues of multiculturalism is embedded in an understanding of the social construction of cultural identities and the concepts of discourse and positioning. The authors are nested in systems and discourse around professional psychology. Thus, the multicultural approach of this chapter is also informed by the American Psychological Association's (APA) Multicultural Guidelines (American Psychological Association, 2017). Additionally, training in professional psychology has been undergoing a shift to competency-based education (Hatcher et al., 2013). After articulating the multicultural frame, the authors will describe moments in a group psychotherapy class where one was the instructor and the other a student.

Social Construction

Social constructionism is a movement in the social sciences, particularly sociology and social psychology, that points to how our experiences are constructed rather than determined in advance as part of the natural working of biological processes (Elder-Vass, 2012). In this chapter, social construction is considered as an ideological challenge to various "taken for granted" realities around cultural identities that have sociopolitical consequences (Gallagher & Gergen, 2011). For example, the statement that race is socially constructed is a truism. In the United States, this constructed ideology of race (Smedley & Smedley, 2005) began in the seventeenth century with the legal establishment of slavery: Europeans, Whites, and Native Americans, and continuing into the nineteenth century, Asian immigrants were fitted into this system where phenotypic differences were linked to invented ideas and beliefs about those differences (Smedley & Smedley, 2005). In social constructionism, social identities are produced by the creative activity of individuals to shape and define the environment. These interpretations are externalized and communicated and form the basis of social identities. These have their influence on creators, imparting a consistent recognizable structure on relationships. The process of construction is discourse. In the example of race in the United States, the dominant discourse (on Whiteness and humanity) established slavery. The dominant voice in this discourse is White voice. A constructionist approach presumes an ongoing interaction between dominant discourse and individuals. Individuals position themselves against this discourse in individual ways. Reality is constructed through this interactive process between individual and society into an ever-shifting dominant discourse and personal identity. Constructionist language is the dialectic between society and the individual which shapes worldview/reality. Identities are constructed through discourse: 1) communication between people and the assumptions and meaning the communication reveals; and 2) the social organized ways of interpreting meanings in a given context that define categories of understanding and specify domains in which things are generally accepted as truths. Social construction rejects that psychological knowledge is ever neutral. For example, the mental health field's use of the Diagnostic and Statistical Manual of Mental Disorders (5th edition) ("DSM-V") is an example of social construction and discourse. The use of a diagnosis as articulated by the DSM shapes "normal" and "pathological" perhaps to the exclusion of other ways of meaning making (Pickersgill, 2013).

Social construction is a broad theory of knowledge. One application is the social construction of identity which Davies and Harré (1990) articulated. Social identity is predicated by: 1) the understanding that there are categories that divide, such as male/female/non-binary, teacher/student, race, and others; 2) engaging in discourse based on categories (discourse, again, is defined as all the ways in which people actively produce social and psychological realities)

(Davies & Harré, 1990); 3) positioning one's self as belonging to one category and not another (a good teacher versus a bad teacher; a Christian versus a non-Christian); and 4) ownership of belonging to the category, and positioned perspective. Knowledge is not static but co-created and always in relationship. Davies and Harré's seminal article (1990) develops positioning as the evolving and creative process as each person positions themselves in the discourse, that can be analyzed in conversations. Applying a social constructionist lens on groups, group leaders can alternatively attend to interactions and words spoken in the group as an individual positioning themselves in a discourse, where group leaders and members, and teachers and students, are positioning, along with various emerging, multifaceted categories (or identities) fluidly shifting through a session.

Teaching

Teaching approaches are often adopted implicitly. Some considerations for teaching should include: What is the purpose of education? What should be taught and why? What are the methods for teaching (Feiner, 1998; Yalom & Leszcz, 2005)? Within the field of doctoral psychology training, in which the authors are positioned, a competency-based model of education is shaping accreditation, and consequently how instructors answer these questions. One might say the dominant discourse in doctoral psychology training is a competency-based approach adopted by the accrediting body of APA (Hatcher et al., 2013). Barlow and Roberts (2012) delineate group specialty practice competencies within a competency-based approach. Common competencies across psychology include, among other things: individual and cultural diversity. This is defined as awareness and sensitivity when working with individuals, groups, and communities with diverse cultural backgrounds and unique personal characteristics. Barlow's adaptation of this broad definition is "engaging in the rich diversity that occurs in all groups, given that they are a microcosm of the larger society, with attendant majority/minority group politics." This chapter proposes that social construction, discourse, positioning, and the Multicultural Guidelines (Clauss-Ehlers et al., 2019; American Psychological Association, 2017) are broad and robust tools for understanding and teaching diversity in group psychotherapy.

Multiculturalism

The word multicultural is broadly defined and set within broad contextual factors and intersectionality among group identifiers, and the coexistence of diverse cultures reflecting various reference group identities. Multicultural can embody the coexistence of cultures within an individual, family, group, or organization (Clauss-Ehlers et al., 2019; American Psychological Association, 2017). It serves to guide and inform the practice of professional psychology. The 2017 Multicultural Guidelines (Figure 12.1) set multiculturalism within Bronfenbrenner's ecological model, composed of five nested dynamic systems that interact over time: 1) the microsystem (the most immediate setting that a person is in); 2) the mesosystem (looking beyond immediate setting to the interactions between settings); 3) the exosystem (the impact of settings that a person does not have direct contact); 4) the macrosystem (the culture within which these settings are embedded); and 5) the chronosystem. Along with systems, the guidelines assume a bi-directional model of self-definition and relationships layered within Bronfenbrenner's systems. For example, a teacher of group will: 1) reflect on their bidirectional self-identity in the context of the self-identity of each student in the class; 2) consider the impact of the microsystems which have direct impact on the teacher and students (the department one teaches in, one's family); 3) consider the impact of institutional forces (perhaps licensing and accreditation standards); 4) consider the impact of domestic and international climate; and finally 5) consider the outcomes given the interactions across levels and identity.

Narrative Case

As an application of the social constructionist approach to diversity training, framed within APA multicultural guidelines (American Psychological Association, 2017), I, Carlos, will use experiences in a group class with a student, David, who is also a co-writer for this chapter, and my interactions with different systems. I've also invited David to write about his experience in the class.

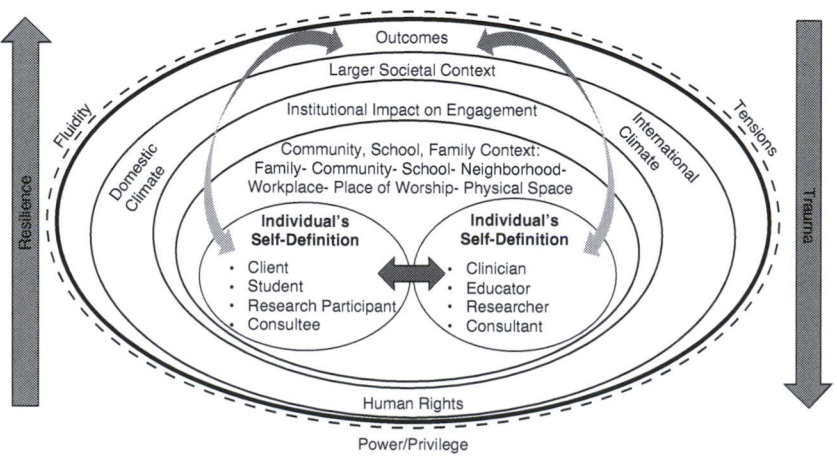

Figure 12.1 The Ecological Model
Source: Courtesy of the American Psychological Association

David's Thoughts

I was honored to be invited by Carlos to co-author this book chapter examining the pedagogy of group therapy through a multicultural lens. The class for me was, as it was for many other students, an important part of my personal and professional development. However, it was also painful. Experiential and interpersonal in nature, the class provided an opportunity to learn about myself from my classmates' and my professor's perspective. This was not always pleasant, but it was an opportunity to understand points of convergence and divergence between my own self-understanding and how I was experienced by others.

I was anxious about participating in this project, too, as I never imagined that I would have something to say about multiculturalism. For most of my life, I never really even thought much about my culture at all. The implicit discourse in my own personal narrative about culture was that when you are American, White, male, cisgender, heterosexual, Christian-affiliated, and able-bodied, you are the norm, and culture is something other people have that makes them different from you. You can learn about their culture, and understanding *their* culture helps you, the dominant majority, make sense of *their* behavior. This, in theory, then helps a person treat others with greater levels of dignity, respect, and fairness. While well intentioned, such a perspective is incomplete and damaging. A failure to address one's own cultural narrative leaves one unconscious to one's own biases and pre-rational convictions.

My own re-education about culture, ethnicity, and self-identity did not start or end with Carlos' class, but it brought me in contact with unknown aspects of my culturally imbedded self-identity and my own various internal discourses – narratives we all use to make sense of the world, to bind anxieties, and orient ourselves to who we are, who we wish to be, who others are, and who they wish to be. Through this process of recounting aspects of my group experience, I hope to highlight the usefulness, and even the necessity of taking interpersonal risks in group therapy education. I also hope to provide examples wherein we can learn more about group dynamics in terms of clashes of diverse, ecological, and concentrically expanding cultures, within and between self and others.

The group experience was a 90-minute, nondirective, interpersonal group comprised of a total of ten students and Carlos. All ten of us belonged to the same doctoral psychology program, were enrolled in Carlos' Group Therapy class, and participated in the group as part of the class requirement. The group took place after the presentation of approximately 90 minutes of didactic material. Carlos taught from a multicultural perspective, but discussed numerous models of group therapy. Psychoanalytically inclined myself, I found our discussion on Wilfred Bion's work with groups most exciting. We reviewed his important ideas about ubiquitous feelings of L (love), H (hate), and K (knowledge), and we explored how each of us are capable of having these kinds of feelings (love and hate) and levels of understanding (knowledge) in relation to one another in a group context (Bion, 1961). We discussed alpha and beta elements, terms Bion used to signify the foundational building blocks of conscious thoughts, just-out-of-awareness unconscious thoughts, and disavowed emotional and psychological elements of thought and feeling. I read Bion on my own time as well, and I tried to understand the basic assumptions Bion believed occurred in any group process – a propensity towards *dependency*, *fight-or-flight* dynamics, and *pairing*. Lastly, I tried to understand the ways in which these processes were occurring within our group.

My adoption of a deeply psychoanalytical perspective in the context of an interpersonal and experiential group class left me somewhat frustrated. I wanted "it" to go faster, whatever "it" was. I wanted things to transpire, I wanted to have transformative moments, and I wanted to see others having the kind of interactions that helped them understand themselves more deeply and holistically. The group seemed cautious. There were interpersonal reflections befitting a group of budding psychologists – thoughtful comments, lots of "noticing," and polite turn-taking. None of this was inherently bad, but I wanted more. My frustration grew as I felt that people filtered their comments and hid from one another to such a degree that only a surface level of engagement was possible, or that they were sharing in vulnerable ways, but often were left without receiving feedback from the group that would have led to deeper personal and collective growth. I was unsettled as well in that it seemed that there had become a right and a wrong way to cathect in our group, and there was a right and wrong way to respond to emotion. I understood this as excessive caretaking that prevented greater understanding. For example, several group members would ask a question of the group. They expressed their uncertainty about belonging, and were tearful as they connected this with moments of pain from their own families and childhoods. The group was quick to comfort, and these individuals appeared comforted. It seemed like textbook Yalom (Yalom & Leszcz, 2005): there was an uncertainty about being in the group, and the group responded in a way that appeared to facilitate greater levels of connectedness and comfort. But I was unsettled by this process, as dialogue about what made them uncomfortable in the first place ceased.

I wanted things to go differently. I can see that this was part of my own "culture" that I brought into the group situation. As noted earlier, reading Bion's *Experiences in Groups* (1961) while taking this group class was a crucial part of my experience and process, and his ideas about the basic assumptions of groups resonated within me in a profound way. Time and time again, these factors seemed to make themselves known. I could feel a pull to *dependency*, to look towards and to rely on Carlos; to *fight/flight*, to challenge, to argue against the prevailing ethos of the group; and to *pair*, to break off with a close friend, to express frustrations and justify my own feelings by allying with another. Perhaps this is also why I felt frustrated with the group while others seemed perfectly content; we looked at the group with different hopes, fears, and expectations.

Something important shifted in my understanding of my own leadership process as well. Bion saw the leader as the group participant with the most serious psychopathology. He believed the dysfunction of the group found a perfect complement in the leader which would arise, and vice versa. I began to think about my strange relationship with leadership, with the term, with people in leadership positions, and with this idea of being a leader. I have longed for leadership positions in the past, not because I wanted to do what those people did, but because I wanted to be known, perceived, loved, and adored in a certain kind of way.

In thinking about these things, I wondered what type of dysfunction exists in me and in the group for those times when I found myself leading? When the pace of conversation in the group would slow, I would often feel a desire to interject my thoughts, to facilitate movement within the group, and to draw others out into the open. I would speak a lot, too. However, throughout the group process, I began to experiment with withholding my thoughts, rather than blurting them out. I noticed different internal and external experiences. There was more silence, silence that was for me uncomfortable. And if the silence lasted long enough, certain people, quieter members of the group, began to share. I was so surprised how long it took some people to become comfortable enough to share. I was saddened to think that these people just needed more time, and that I had potentially made the group unsafe for them by sharing without restraint or regard for how others might be feeling. I also imagined that these quieter individuals did not share to break the tension, as I so often did. They shared, I think, because it was finally safe enough for them to do so, when perhaps they could trust that they would not be taking any time from anyone else.

It was painful but important for me to learn to say less. In hearing the voices of colleagues that do not normally speak out in class, I heard new stories. My worldview became richer, more informed. Yet, I felt increasingly anxious as well, as though in holding back I was being denied something I wanted. Desire and anger flashed within me; I wanted something. I wanted to say the answer to whatever question was asked; I wanted to solve every problem presented. I wanted to push the group and deepen the emotional intensity of the group. I wanted to say profound things and feel more magic in the room. As I thought of Bion, I began to understand these strange feelings as my desire to intoxicate myself with something that may obscure the real work that needed to be done. Something unique about my desire (*perhaps an unconscious, out of awareness, implicit desire to exist?*) to flood the group with elements of myself was keeping both me and the group from actually progressing. Even if what I was feeling had been a well-intentioned desire to help and to work, to "throw my shoulder to the plow," something about my actions took up space that made it difficult for others to co-exist. If I solve every math problem, even if I solve it correctly (*never mind that my assumptions of correctness are culturally embedded and reflect implicit White male privilege*), no one else gets to have an experience of solving a math problem. Perhaps they might have solved the same problem with a more creative, more nuanced approach. If I valued the health of the whole group, then this was a real problem. If I interject my thoughts and wisdom – or lack thereof – into every story, social and psychic space is taken wherein others – as well as myself – may have benefitted from the experience of coming into being in a new way.

In my process of holding back, what emerged was a new tension and a confrontation with what Eigen (1981), writing about Lacan, describes as one's lack. I still wanted the group to go deeper, but I was also surprised to find that *dependency, pairing*, or *fight and flight* dynamics of what Bion calls the basic assumptions of the group no longer seemed so prevalent. Were we approximating a work group? If so, was my holding back part of what was co-creating this to happen? In our group, I had been happy to take up space, but I think the group resented that in some way. I was often left feeling as though something was amiss after I shared. And, I don't know that I was helpful to anyone. In taking a step back, I tried to be open to the input of the group, to the influence of the group. The group benefitted by getting to exist in a different way, I think. I benefitted greatly from receiving from the group and from receiving the group as it was. I grieved becoming what I imagined was "less," but I know now that I received far more in the process. The group was not my stage nor my gratification center, though it had been willing to be used by me if needed. A mentor once told me that it is better to knead the dough than to try to make it rise. This, I think, means that there is something about surrendering to the process of growth and development, rather than always trying to rush it along.

Over the course of the following weeks, months, and years, I continued to learn the ways in which the many layers of identity permeated my understanding, augmented my view, and influenced my perspective on "truth" and "reality." In retrospect, I can see that my drive to grasp knowledge of the group was multi-determined – by curiosity, by passion and a desire to help others, but also by fears of being dominated by others – emotionally, intellectually. I brought these things into the group. I also brought in my own deeply personal issues of becoming and belonging – mainly related to who I saw my father to be, and my fantasies of who I believed I was to him. My graduate experience was in part one of "chasing ghosts:" idealized ancestors and a lifetime of "ought to be." These were foundational issues for me. I can see how they shaped my interactions with others and at times made it difficult for me to see social dynamics more clearly. My own culture of achievement and identity formation through fierce individuation, on one hand, and a deep fear of exclusion from the group and of wounding the other with my own individuation, on the other, has for many years left me confused about my own sense of ambition, expectation, duty, and desire. Mine is an ecology-of-self wrought with a sense of inadequacy and a lack of a sense of significance and belonging. Here again we see the collisions between the culture of self, of family, of school, of race, etc.

Something that I think is really important to communicate about the group process was the disenchantment we were left with that, for me, ultimately made room for new personal and professional growth. There is no Wizard of Oz; there is no complete dissolution of boundaries; there is no perfect merger experience. The growth is in coming to grips with the way our fantasies can never play out; coming to grips with our disappointments in the way our lives have turned out, the way others fail us, and the way we fail others as well as ourselves. All of this leads to empty but solid ground, ripe for new growth. Death of fantasy makes room for life in reality.

Carlos' Thoughts

Students who have taken my group psychotherapy class inform me that it was an important and formative/transformative class for them. But I am also aware of the barriers to a productive group. I format the class with a combination of didactic and experiential components. Half the class is didactic, and the other half is a learning group. For the class with David, I showed Shakti Butler's *Cracking the Codes: The System of Racial Inequality* (Butler et al., 2012) to prime them for attentiveness to issues of race and other diversity markers.

In addition to my role as assistant professor for the Group Psychotherapy class, I also had an administrative position: Director of Clinical Training for the program. I was responsible to oversee and administer clinical training from the admission process, through practicum and through the completion of internship. I helped implement two diversity competencies – understanding the dynamics of power based on group identity markers through the Addressing Model (Hays, 1996) and Bronfenbrenner's (1996) Ecological Model. Combining these two models (American Psychological Association, 2017), among others, create unlimited opportunities to examine the impact of power, relevant discourses, and positions. For example, I can be oblivious to the power, discourse, and positions I am entangled in as a teacher. A common and persistent theme is students' positioning themselves as not aligning with departmental values and culture, and experiencing alienation from the community. Given my role as an administrator, I can be seen as an agent of the department and aligned with the department's values. This positioning leads to a challenge in trusting that the experiential/learning group is safe. My identity as a teacher even seems more salient than my identity as a Person of Color. Spirituality/religiosity is another salient identity marker in group processes: Identification as a Christian or non-Christian is salient because of the religious identity of the institution. I also identify as an interpersonally oriented and psychoanalytically informed clinician/professor, a "minority" position in the department. I tried to address concerns about safety and institutional positioning/discourse by not evaluating participation in group, and structuring experiential groups to explicitly discuss how each student positions themselves to the department's culture and values. I disrupted group process by commenting on the purpose of my interventions, or tying interactions among students to terms and theory.

When I invited David to contribute to the chapter, I had several thoughts. By virtue of his intellect, his earnest engagement in his training, his maturity, and his grasp of psychoanalytic concepts and even group concepts felt threatening to me. Even though I was the professor of the group course (and thus had power/authority/expertise), there were threats to my identity by virtue of his personal qualities (e.g. knowledge about group process that I don't know, and thus threaten me). In general, I'm in an ongoing process of understanding and being conscious of the impact of internalized racism, among other identity markers. My identity as a teacher and Person of Color were salient to my interactions with David. There were many brief verbal interchanges between David and me in the class. In a discussion of diversity, he referenced a psychoanalyst who writes about diversity (Davids, 2011). Though a short communication, I thought and felt several ways. He was engaging me in the discourse of diversity and positioning himself and psychoanalysis as having credible and relevant contributions. Internally, I had positioned myself as someone who doubted the credibility of psychoanalytic approaches from a multicultural lens (Harré, 2012). The interchange with David, along with written work exploring psychoanalytic perspectives on diversity, further assuaged this doubt. He was positioning himself in relation to the institution as a student drawn to psychoanalytic approaches, against the health psychology/behavioral health approaches that were predominant.

With his contribution to this chapter, the richness of social constructionist model emerges. On one level, his experience can be described from social construction within Bronfenbrenner's systems. He positions the group as a "bad" group, describing what emotions were acceptable, filtered thoughts, and absent feedback, to name a few things. However, a shift occurred for him. Reflecting on his understanding of group leadership through his readings of Bion, he opened to new positions in new discourses with other group members around leadership. He wrote: "I have longed for leadership positions in the past, not because I wanted to do what those people did, but because I wanted to be known and perceived and loved and adored in a certain kind of way." I can imagine the multiple discourses along different social identities that are motivated by the longing he describes based on his identity markers: "American, White, male, cisgender, heterosexual, Christian-affiliated, and able-bodied."

Application

In social constructionism, identities are constructions. Categories such as straight, gay, Asian, White, teacher, student, Christian, and atheist do not have essential meanings. Our knowledge and understanding of these identities are constructed through a lifetime of discourse and positioning. When teachers teach, they are engaged in discourse, and position themselves and others: educational institutions, professional organizations, students, professional peers. By virtue of their power and authority, teachers may inadvertently practice oppressive teaching approaches (Freire, 1996). Awareness and sensitivity to discourse and positioning in their own multiple overdetermined, sometimes contradictory, social identities can ameliorate the drift to an oppressive educational approach dominated by a single discourse. In addition to the personal reflective work that teachers can engage in to deepen awareness and sensitivity, teachers can also engage in and teach students how to analyze the positioning in interactions among students, either in a classroom or an experiential training group. Additionally, setting positioning analysis within an ecological model (American Psychological Association, 2017) highlights how flexibly positional analysis can be used to understand personal and social identities.

Conclusion

The scope of teaching about diversity issues in group can often be narrow. A student might assume that taking a class, or a lecture in a class, prepares them sufficiently to appreciate and be technically skilled with diversity issues; or, predicting the settings a student will practice, declare that diversity is not relevant. The scope of what is taught about diversity is expanded by tying diversity issues to social construction theory. If social construction's tenet that knowledge is constructed is taken seriously, then writing this chapter and the act of teaching must be understood from a social construction perspective. By providing a narrative, what is written is set within an ecological model: situated in the field of psychology and taught at a Christian university. As such, even reading the chapter is an exercise in attending to discourse and positioning.

References

American Psychological Association (2017). Multicultural Guidelines: An Ecological Approach to Context, Identity, and Intersectionality. Retrieved from: http://www.apa.org/about/policy/multicultural-guidelines.pdf.

Barlow, S., & Roberts, M. C. (2012). An application of the competency model to group-specialty practice. *Professional Psychology: Research and Practice*, 43(5), 442–451.

Bion, W. (1961). *Experiences in groups, and other papers*. New York: Basic Books.

Bronfenbrenner, U. (1996). *The ecology of human development experiments by nature and design*. Cambridge, MA: Harvard University Press.

Butler, S., Butler, R., Huyler, Y., Jelal, L., DeGruy, J., McIntosh, P., Wise, T. J., World Trust Educational Services, et al. (2012). *Cracking the codes: The system of racial inequity*. Oakland, CA: World Trust Educational Services.

Clauss-Ehlers, C. S., Chiriboga, D. A., Hunter, S. J., Roysircar, G., & Tummala-Narra, P. (2019). APA Multicultural Guidelines executive summary: Ecological approach to context, identity, and intersectionality. *American Psychologist, 74*(2), 232–244, doi:10.1037/amp0000382.

Davies, B., & Harré, R. (1990). Positioning: The discursive production of selves. *Journal for the Theory of Social Behaviour, 20*(1), 43–63.

Davids, M. F. (2011). *Internal racism: A psychoanalytic approach to race and difference* (1st ed.). Basingstoke; New York: Palgrave Macmillan.

Eigen, M. (1981). The area of faith in Winnicott, Lacan, and Bion. *International Journal of Psychoanalysis, 62*: 413–433.

Elder-Vass, D. (2012). *The reality of social construction*. Cambridge; New York: Cambridge University Press.

Feiner, S. E. (1998). Course design: An integration of didactic and experiential approaches to graduate training of group therapy. *International Journal of Group Psychotherapy, 48*(4), 439–460.

Freire, P. (2000). *Pedagogy of the oppressed* (30th anniversary edn). New York: Continuum.

Gallagher, S., & Gergen, K. (2011). The social construction of self. In S. Gallagher (ed.), *The Oxford handbook of the self*. Oxford: Oxford University Press.

Harré, R. (2012). Positioning theory: Moral dimensions of social-cultural psychology. In *The Oxford handbook of culture and psychology*. Oxford: Oxford University Press.

Hatcher, R. L., Fouad, N. A., Campbell, L. F., McCutcheon, S. R., Grus, C. L., Leahy, K. L., & Roberts, M. C. (2013). Competency-based education for professional psychology: Moving from concept to practice. *Training and Education in Professional Psychology, 7*(4), 225–234, doi:10.1037/a0033765.

Hays, P. (1996). Addressing the complexities of culture and gender in counseling. *Journal of Counseling & Development, 74*(4), 332–338.

Pickersgill, M. D. (2013). Debating DSM-5: diagnosis and the sociology of critique. *Journal of Medical Ethics, 40*(8), 521–525, doi:10.1136/medethics-2013-101762.

Smedley, A., & Smedley, B. D. (2005). Race as biology is fiction, racism as a social problem is real – anthropological and historical perspectives on the social construction of race. *American Psychologist, 60*(1), 16–26.

Yalom, I. D., & Leszcz, M. (2005). *The theory and practice of group psychotherapy* (5th ed.). New York: Basic Books.

Yu, J., Sorkin, A., & Redford, P. (2001). Somebody's Going to Emergency, Somebody's Going to Jail. *The West Wing* (television series).

13 Intersection of Race and Gender
Women of Color Leading Groups

Pratibha Kumar and Sheela Reddy

Most organizational studies literature on Women of Color (WoC) discusses the "double jeopardy" of gender and race, but it is mostly centered on quantitative representation within organizations. According to Krivkovich et al. (2018), within the U.S., WoC comprise 17 percent entry-level positions as compared to 31 percent of White women in entry-level positions. They occupy 12 percent and 8 percent manager and senior manager/director roles respectively, compared to their White cohort at 27 percent and 26 percent. At the vice president and higher ranks, WoC hover at about 5 percent, whereas this figure is over 20 percent for White women. Despite an impetus to increase representation of WoC in corporate America, they are still underrepresented with dismal percentages.

Beyond representation, discussions on hiring WoC do not account for retention, development, and promotion, either in entry-level positions or in top leadership. Black, Hispanic, and Asian American women's participation in the workforce is projected to increase rapidly by 2024 (Bureau of Labor Statistics, 2019). Regardless of the steady increase, the literature hardly focuses on the intersections of race and gender in terms of advancement, leadership, and working styles. Within the available research, the majority is focused on African American women, and other categories of WoC, based on race and ethnicity, national origin and citizenship, class, sexuality and sexual orientation, disability status, take the backseat. The focus on African American women is predictable because they make up the largest racial segment of working women in the U.S., but the resulting discussion leaves behind other racial-ethnic categories of women that are projected to increase rapidly in the next five to ten years. Hence, it is imperative that institutional and public discourses on "Women of Color" are not limited to one or two racial categories, but include all. Also, such conversations should not be merely a lip service, checking of a box, or tokenism toward diversity, but a serious and pragmatic deliberation on empowering WoC leading in organizations, and promoting true gendered diversity in the workplace.

In this chapter, we will examine WoC's barriers to leadership, social identities, organizational group dynamics, and reflections on advancement.

The scope of this chapter allows for a discussion on race and ethnicity – how racial, ethnic, and cultural identities of African American, Asian American, and Hispanic women interact with the dominant American organizational dynamic. Additionally, we elaborate on the heterogeneity and nuances within WoC and its implications for leadership.

Systemic and Structural Barriers

WoC encounter barriers of self and others' perceptions, misconceptions, objectification, stereotypes, and discrimination in the workplace. Pervasive are assumptions about their language, accents, appearance (skin color/tone, hair), personality, values, and leadership skills. This pigeonholing perpetuates the myth that WoC are a monolith; that they all have the same experiences and ignores the complexities among women within each racial-ethnic group. A recent study found salient career barriers for WoC in higher education, than White women, due to racism (Kim & O'Brien, 2018). These educational barriers were sexism and racism for African American women, lack of confidence/skills for Asian American women, and lack of financial resources for Latinas. With significant roadblocks in attaining undergraduate degrees, WoC likely have fewer opportunities entering the labor force and achieving high-ranking positions in the business world. At both entry-level and managerial positions, there are few women executives, and even fewer WoC, in corporate America (Krivkovich et al., 2018). Fairfax's (2005) reflection on the representation of minoritized women in high-ranking executive positions moving up to corporate board positions is bleak. It is unlikely to see many WoC in C-suite positions because women, especially WoC, are grossly underrepresented in middle and higher management positions. Consequently, most board appointments transition from high-level executives, and there are very few WoC in such positions; only 5.8 percent of them occupied board seats in Fortune 100 companies in 2018 (DeHaas, Akutagawa, & Spriggs, 2009). This demonstrates that there are tremendous race- and perception-related barriers for WoC in higher education and reaching entry-level and managerial positions, and progressing to high-level executive ranks and board directorships.

Due to historic Black women's reactions to (White) feminism, they have been synonymous with the term WoC for the last few decades in the U.S. Going beyond this black and white binary recognizes other segments of non-White (and African American) women. This lack of genuine inclusion is the greatest barrier for two of the fastest growing female demographics in the workforce, which in itself is a form of gendered racism. Since the discourse on leadership is mostly androcentric and Eurocentric (Souto-Manning & Ray, 2007), there is a dearth of research on how WoC cope with isolation and alienation in the harshly competitive and sexist environment of corporate America.

For African American women, colorism has serious effects on their perception of themselves as well as how others perceive them – White people as well as African Americans. Professionally, lighter skin color determines availability of more favorable opportunities, advantages, and social mobility, as well as psychological benefits such as self-worth, self-esteem, and social outcomes (Hall, 2017). The darker the skin of an African American woman, the more severe are the stereotypes – less intelligent, loud, suspicious, untrustworthy, less educated, "ghetto," "militant," and so on. Consequently, this means lighter-skinned Black women enjoy positive perceptions by others and more privileges compared to dark-skinned women. This indicates that nuances pertaining to WoC go beyond race and ethnicity, and discrimination and inclusion are linked to the color of women's skin (Nassar-McMillan, McFall-Roberts, Flowers, & Garrett, 2006). Hall (2017) and Nassar-McMillan, McFall-Roberts, Flowers, and Garrett (2006) also associate colorism to racial identity and self-perception – since darker Black women feel their self-worth is associated with their skin tone, there is likely to be a decrement in self-esteem and efficacy in organizations. In addition to colorism, Black women encounter everyday racism and microaggressions such as having to prove themselves, lower expectations from others, credibility concerns, and preconceived notions prior to interactions (Spence, 2006). Regarding variations in skin tones, self-identified mixed-race women have to prove their blackness every day.

It is not surprising that race and ethnicity also complicate perceptions of gender among Asian American and Native American women. Like Arab or Muslim Americans, Asian Americans are treated like a homogeneous group by the dominant American society – Whites and other races alike. The "racial lumping" of all Asians as one group ignores cultural values of pan-Asian people from Southeast Asia, Far East, and the Indian subcontinent. Ignoring, isolating, and othering of Asian and Asian American women put them in the "forever foreigner" category (Liang & Peter-Hawkins, 2017), making it more crucial to reveal the differences of attitudes, values, and behavior among Asian American women. The term "foreign-born" (commonly used for Asian American immigrants) is problematic because it insinuates that those born outside the U.S. have no place in mainstream American institutions (Bui, 2013–2014). What keeps Asian Americans at the margins of invisibility and exclusion from racial inequality and justice discourses (Liang & Peter-Hawkins, 2017) is the model minority thesis – educated, hardworking, and self-reliant immigrant group that does not chip away the welfare system of the country. Since it is the most invisible of all the minoritized groups, it is least studied by social scientists. The double jeopardy of being an Asian American is that it is not considered an underrepresented group by federal and state agencies because of its educational background, career aspirations, and economic standing. Since Asian Americans tend to make a great example of overcoming racial prejudice and discrimination and climbing the social ladder, they are used to depict that there is no systemic racism in the country; and that all other minority groups should follow in the footsteps of Asian Americans (Liang & Peter-Hawkins, 2017; Sy, Tram-Quon, & Leung, 2017).

Apart from the "good" model minority stereotype of Asian American women, the most prominent are their hyper-sexualized images emanating from the post-Chinese Exclusion Act of 1882, when Asian women were trafficked to the U.S. for the enjoyment of wealthy White men (Leung, 2017). On the other end of the spectrum, there is the "war bride" image, resulting from American men bringing them back to the U.S. from Asian countries, which leads to the ever-pervasive stereotypes of being nurturing, docile, submissive, family-oriented, and people-pleasing. Some other assumptions and stereotypes of Asian American women are that they lack charisma, assertiveness, political savvy, authority, leadership, self-promotion skills, and self-efficacy (Bui, 2013–2014; Liang & Peter-Hawkins, 2017; Spence, 2006). Their looks, language, and accents further lead to their Orientalization and exoticization. Often, their female and Asian American identity takes precedence over their leadership roles. In reality, that's true for all WoC; their ethnic and racial identities come before their organizational ones. Structurally, instead of placing each of their social identities in separate silos, WoC and their multiple identities should be viewed as a composite whole.

Although 5.8 percent of the current U.S. population is Asian (U.S. Census Bureau, 2018), they make up 12 percent of the professional workforce. However, only 2.4 percent of Asian women held management position in 2018 (Catalyst, 2018). A San Francisco Bay Area technology company survey found that between 2007 and 2015, Asian Americans were the largest cohort of professionals in the technology industry. Nevertheless, they were less likely to become managers and executives (Gee & Peck, 2017); Asian women particularly were least likely to become executives. In contrast, the number of Black executives increased by 43 percent and Hispanic by 24 percent. According to them, race was a significant factor in maintaining the glass ceiling. Leaders in the U.S. are typically expected to be assertive, dynamic, inspirational, expressive, and leading teams with confidence and authority. Most likely, Asian Americans prefer to train in more technical professions that require skills that guarantee a certain income because it is a cultural norm versus focusing on management or leadership skills (Sy, Tram-Quon, & Leung, 2017). Asian Americans who immigrated to the U.S. or who were raised in families that maintain cultural values such as humility, respect for elders, and maintaining harmony may behave in ways that seem submissive, avoiding conflict, deferring to leaders, and not expressing divergent ideas. Sy, Tram-Quon, and Leung (2017) state that submissive behavior is not perceived as leader-like, and that behaviors of some Asian Americans may create barriers to success. However, it may be a double-edged sword – Asian Americans who exercise their agency are perceived as aggressive and reifying a counter stereotype.

For Hispanic women, one of the biggest organizational barriers is the assumption that, regardless of national origin and racial and cultural identity, they are treated alike (Holvino, 2010; Spence, 2006). Unfortunately, most research on Hispanic and Native American women's leadership focuses on political participation and efficacy, and very little from an organizational leadership standpoint. This gap in literature creates the vicious cycle of fewer women from these two racial-ethnic categories rising up to positions of leadership in organizations; the fewer Hispanic and Native American women leaders in academia and industry, the less research and literature there is. Since, historically, Hispanic women have worked as immigrant laborers with or without appropriate legal status, their role in the American workforce has been limited to serving in the secondary labor market, characterized by low pay, part-time/temporary positions, and high turnover. Hence, although Hispanic women make up a large part of the labor force – 18 percent of all women in 2015, according to the Bureau of Labor Statistics (2019) – their presence in lower- and upper-management positions is miniscule. Little published research on Hispanic women's experiences in the corporate world points toward biases and discrimination emanating from their language, accents, country of origin, cultural values, etc. (Hite, 2007).

Institutional discrimination is a well-known reality experienced by all WoC at several stages of their organizational lives. While discrimination can prevent certain racial and ethnic minorities from being hired or treated equally at a job, ethnic harassment is direct verbal, nonverbal, and exclusionary behaviors that target the ethnicity of an individual (Schneider, Hitlan, & Radhakrishnan, 2000). These behaviors can be subtle, indirect, or direct, such as racial slurs, ethnic comments and jokes, and stories that highlight stereotyped beliefs among others. Consequently, these behaviors are associated with varying levels of psychological stress in ethnic employees. Higher levels of ethnic harassment are linked to lower levels of well-being. Exclusion, which is a form of ethnic harassment as well as a microaggression, is related to lower life satisfaction and health problems. Other forms of racial microaggressions in the workplace are exclusion from representation; diversity absent from a company's strategic plan; "ghettoization" or using Black people for less-desirable markets; tokenism; assumptions of criminal status; ascription of intelligence; assumed aggressive disposition; and "mammy" expectations from Black women (Holder, Jackson, & Ponterotto, 2015). These microaggressions manifest themselves through verbal messages and nonverbal gestures. In order to overcome the systemic and institutional barriers and cope with the masculine and dominant cultural value system, WoC need tremendous support in order to advance to top leadership positions. Most recommended strategies for women in general are providing them with opportunities of mentoring, training, sponsorship, and other professional development. These professional advancement platforms do not address the complexities of disparate cultural identities of WoC or how WoC can leverage these identities in becoming effective leaders. The following section is an analysis of social identity and group leadership dynamics and how it specifically relates to developing leadership skills of WoC.

Social Identity and Group Dynamics

Psychological literature has begun to examine the intersection of race and gender pertaining to WoC's organizational participation and leadership. Specifically, implications of how women's intersectional identities may manifest in a group setting as well as how they can leverage their diverse worldview to develop into more competent leaders has not been discussed. Women are socialized into developing relational leadership style, which is a trait embraced in contemporary executive leadership landscape. To elaborate further, we will explain theories of WoC's group identity – social identity theories and Leader–Member Exchange (LMX).

Leadership is individual, social, and a group process. Social identity theory (Tajfel & Turner, 1979) is a cognitive theory which posits that "individuals tend to classify themselves and others into social categories, and that these classifications have a significant effect on human interactions" (Nkomo & Cox, 1996, p. 339). Individuals further decide which social category, out of one's gender, race, class, sexual orientation, skills, and ability, is more salient to their identity at any given time. Salience of social identities is also dynamic and dependent on interactions in a group (Sanchez-Hucles & Davis, 2010). Alderfer and Smith's (1982) embedded intergroup relations theory elucidates two types of groups within an organization – identity group and organizational group. The identity group is based on shared genetics, sociopolitical experiences, and the organizational group is based on factors such as task, work experience, and status within an organization. Each group shares similar worldviews as the other members of the group. An individual's perception and functioning in the team is based on a combination of these two group memberships, but identity group worldviews precede that of the organizational group membership.

The individual in any identity group may also have differing worldviews within that identity group based on their individualized historical, familial, and organizational interactive experiences (e.g. Native American woman A might have different worldviews than Native American woman B). Stages of racial identity development models explain how worldviews can change based on the current developmental stage of an individual (for more on racial identities, see Carter, 1995). Atkinson, Morten, and Sue's (1979) Minority Identity Development (MID) Model of racial identity states that individuals belonging to race or ethnicities different from the majority culture will go through several stages of incorporating racial attitudes and preferences into their social identity. In the initial stage of the MID model – conformity – there is a preference for the majority group's values and presence of negative attitudes toward one's own racial-ethnic group. This stage is followed by dissonance, which is characterized by confusion, resistance, and immersion wherein the individual rejects the majority culture and has positive views about their culture of origin. The next stage is introspection, wherein the individual examines benefits of the dominant as well as ethnic culture. The final stage is awareness – an integration of values and beliefs of both cultures. In this stage confusion decreases and the individual feels self-fulfilled.

People in the earlier stages of MID (conformity) relate more to the majority culture and are less likely to identify with their own racial group's identity. They also have negative attitudes toward those individuals who are similar to them ethnically, and may be at a different level of racial identity development. An individual in the dissonance and/or immersion stage may be more likely to identify with their own social group and have positive interactions with group members who look similar to them. Individuals at higher stages of racial development (introspection and awareness) identify with their ethnic group as well as the majority culture, developing a composite multicultural identity. This is linked to more flexibility in thinking and positive attitudes toward their culture of origin, the majority culture, and other cultures (Carter, 1995).

In a study examining qualities that contributed to the success of Asian Americans, all respondents found that cultural acumen contributes to successful leadership. Cultural acumen includes being aware of similarities and differences between self and dominant (western) cultures, and knowing how one's cultural beliefs impact leadership behaviors (Sy, Tram-Quon, & Leung, 2017). Developing cultural acumen, integrating one's ethnic and dominant beliefs, and incorporating expected leadership traits of the dominant culture not only contribute to success in leadership (individual) but also help meet the goals of the group (collective). An example of this would be an Asian American woman engaging in a productive conflict with her supervisor by dismissing her cultural values of deferring to elders for the benefit of the team and the organization. Being aware of one's complex social identities and achieving higher levels of racial identity development makes for an effective group leader.

The aggregate identity of a Woman of Color would, therefore, be the intersection of multiple social group identities, organizational group identity, racial identity, and individualized experiences which affect her perceptions and interactions in a group. The beliefs and attitudes associated with these multiple identities will be projected onto a group influencing how a Woman of Color leads. On the other hand, beliefs and attitudes of group members affect how a Woman of Color perceives herself and behaves in an organizational group (Kivlighan, Marsh-Angelone, & Angelone, 1994). Leader–Member Exchange (LMX) theory (Dansereau, Graen, & Haga, 1975) and related research provides an additional framework for WoC to leverage their complex identities and increase their efficacy as leaders.

LMX theory postulates that leaders show preferential treatment toward their subordinates; some subordinates receive more benefits and are more able to influence the leader more than others. LMX is greater with subordinates who are perceived as more competent (Dansereau, Graen, & Haga, 1975) and perceived as similar (Linden, Wayne, & Stilwell, 1993). Linden, Wayne, and Stilwell (1993) also found that demographic similarity did not predict LMX. Dose's (1999) study explored the relationship of moral and work values to LMX and Team Member Exchange (TMX) – effectiveness of team members' working relationship and reciprocity among them. Perceptions of work ethic similarities and environmental preferences (job security, type of surrounding, teamwork orientation) predict LMX more than demographic similarities. Actual similarity of ethical beliefs and work environment preferences predict TMX (Dose, 1999). This study is valuable in that it suggests that more than demographics (visible differences), the quality of exchange between the leader and subordinates is mediated by the perception of similarities. High LMX behavior is characterized by communicative behavior (problem-solving, supportive, and coaching) and accommodating behavior (negotiating and civil disagreement), while low LMX behavior is characterized by polarizing behavior (conflict, competitiveness, power, and control). When LMX is low the group member may be more likely to communicate via the leader versus collaboratively amongst each other (Yalom, 1995). High LMX is linked to higher job satisfaction, more commitment to organizational outcomes, and higher team performance (Kivlighan & Coleman, 1999). Nishii and Mayer's (2009) study further examined the relationship between mean LMX, LMX differentiation, diversity, and turnover. Low LMX differentiation is characterized by a leader's behavior showing the employees that they accept their group members equally and provide a psychologically safe environment for interpersonal sharing. They also encourage group members to accept each other as part of the in-group. High LMX differentiation is characterized by leaders who are selective, having high-quality relationships with some members and low-quality relationships with others (exclusionary behavior). This study showed that when the mean LMX is high and there is high LMX differentiation, there is more turnover in a diverse group. When the mean LMX is high and there is low LMX differentiation, there is less turnover in diverse groups. Conclusively, LMX research suggests that diverse group members perform better and remain in organizations if leaders have high-quality social exchange with team members, are equally attentive to all group members, and encourage inclusivity in the group.

A study of 25 successful female leaders in politics (Cantor, Bernay, & Stoess, 1992) revealed three important characteristics – competent self (feelings of self-confidence), creative aggression (ability to speak out and take initiative), and woman power (determination to make the world a better place). Their values included taking work seriously, maintaining high standards of integrity, being considerate and respectful to staff, and encouraging communication. Women's leadership was not about their own power but empowering others – hearing others' opinions, inspiring consensus, being of service, and promoting gender equality. These women authentically integrated stereotypical female qualities such as caring, but with assertiveness and achievement-oriented behaviors. Some of these beliefs were also expressed by several Chinese women in a study wherein they described themselves leading like mothers and grandmothers, being firm but supportive (Cheung & Halpern, 2010). They recognized that this kind of leadership integrated their communal beliefs of caring and accountability, which proved effective. In a similar vein, Faircloth (2017) also describes her journey from being unhappy in her job as a leader to being a more satisfied authentic leader when she integrated her Indigenous beliefs to the expectations of a leader in predominantly White academia.

As suggested by the aforementioned theories and studies of successful female leader, WoC who have accepted their multiple identities lead authentically with self-confidence and have better quality interactions with their team members. They have better understanding of their own and other people's multiple and complex social identities, and hence they are more likely to be inclusive and effective. The theories also imply that exploring a team's diverse belief systems, finding similarities between themselves and their team members, developing a common value system, creating a safe environment, and encouraging healthy communication are ways in which WoC could become more effective group leaders.

Conclusion

This chapter looked at the nuances of WoC barriers to their advancement, and group dynamics that can help them leverage their cultural values in an organizational setting. WoC who have integrated their multiple identities have much to offer to organizational growth. Institutional culture needs to account for the nuances of WoC. Mere awareness is not key to their advancement. Tailor-made specialized professional development programs that help WoC integrate multiple identities, develop confidence, and leverage their unique leadership styles will benefit both the organization and WoC. Apart from providing a healthy, diversity-friendly climate, institutional policies need to be reconsidered. In order to truly address leadership of WoC, it is important for organizations to address issues of marginality, voice, agency, and social transformation in strategic planning. More platforms need to be invented for WoC to effect coaction and coalition with not only other WoC, but also with White men and women and Men of Color. These avenues will give them opportunities to be heard, and we know that both representation and voice lead to greater inclusion. Individually empowered WoC will collectively empower all women in an organization, which in turn would lead to institutional efficacy and empowerment (Gutiérrez, 1990).

Appendix A

Identity and Leadership Workshop[1]

Below is a suggested workshop that can help women leaders of color become aware of their identities, develop confidence, and integrate their identities with that of their team and organization.

In the presence of a qualified organizational or developmental group psychologist (moderator) administer the following two instruments and moderate the discussion with the leader and their team. Group norms such as non-judgment, taking turns, being respectful, and confidentiality need to be established.

- The Social Identity Wheel (Arizona State University Intergroup Relations Center)
- Kluckhohn and Strodtbeck's adapted Value Orientation tool and score (Kluckhohn Center, 1995; Kluckhohn & Strodtbeck, 1961)

Sample questions to help increase WoC awareness and team cohesion:

- How was the experience of completing this information?
- Did you discover something you did not already know? If so, explain.
- What are your most salient identities? Describe.
- What are your most salient values? Describe.
- How are your identities similar or dissimilar to your organizational identity?
- How are your values similar or dissimilar to your organization's values?
- Find someone in the room who has a similar identity/values.

  a   How do individual and collective identities align with organizational mission and vision?

- Find someone in the room who has a different identity/values than you.

  a   Can you find commonalities?
  b   What can people with different identities/values bring to the work that will be helpful?
  c   How can you work with someone whose identity/values are different than you?

Sample questions to help WoC leverage their identity in leadership:

- How can you leverage your salient identities as a leader?
- How does your value orientation contribute to leadership?

- What identity do you need to develop to feel more confident?

Suggested exercise to strengthen confidence in WoC:

- To develop confidence, the WoC leader completes the strength finder's test (Rath, 2007) and has the moderator explore the results of the test.

    a With a coach or mentor, formulate a plan to use the strengths discovered, combined with their social identities and value orientations in leadership.

Note

1 © 2019 Confidential and proprietary Reddy, S. & Kumar P.

References

Alderfer, C. P., & Smith, K. K. (1982). Studying intergroup relations embedded in organizations. *Administrative Science Quarterly*, 27(1), 35–65.

Arizona State University Intergroup Relations Center (n.d.). Social Identity Wheel: Adapted from "Voices of Discovery." Retrieved from https://www.mcgill.ca/engage/files/engage/social-identity-wheel-handout.pdf

Atkinson, D. R., Morten, G., & Sue, D. W. (1979). *Counseling American minorities: A cross-cultural perspective*. Dubuque, IA: W.C. Brown.

Bui, T. (2013–2014). Shaping the mainstream as an Asian American women: Politics within politics. *Asian American Policy Review*, 24, 24–30.

Bureau of Labor Statistics (2019). Labor force statistics from the current population survey. Retrieved from: https://www.bls.gov/cps/cpsaat11.htm.

Cantor, D. W., Bernay, T., & Stoess, J. (1992). *Women in power: The secrets of leadership*. Boston, MA: Houghton Mifflin.

Carter, R. T. (1995). *The influence of race and racial identity in psychotherapy: Toward a racially inclusive model*. Oxford, England: John Wiley & Sons.

Catalyst (2018). Quick take: Women in management. Retrieved from: https://www.catalyst.org/research/women-in-management/.

Cheung, F. M., & Halpern, D. F. (2010). Women at the top: Powerful leaders define success as work + family in a culture of gender. *American Psychologist*, 65 (3), 182–193.

Dansereau, F., Graen, G., & Haga, W. J. (1975). A vertical dyad linkage approach to leadership within formal organizations. *Organizational Behavior & Human Performance*, 13(1), 46–78.

DeHaas, D., Akutagawa, L., & Spriggs, S. (2009). Missing Pieces Report: The 2018 Board Diversity Census of Women and Minorities on Fortune 500 Boards. *Harvard Law School Forum on Corporate Governance and Financial Regulation*. Retrieved from: https://corpgov.law.harvard.edu/2019/02/05/missing-pieces-report-the-2018-board-diversity-census-of-women-and-minorities-on-fortune-500-boards/.

Dose, J. J. (1999). The relationship between work values similarity and team-member and leader-member exchange relationships. *Group Dynamics Theory and Research and Practice*, 3(1), 20–32.

Faircloth, S. C. (2017). Reflections on the concept of authentic leadership: From and Indigenous scholar/leader perspective. *Advances in Developing Human Resources*, 19(4), 407–419.

Fairfax, L. M. (2005). Some reflections on the diversity of corporate boards: Women, People of Color, and the unique issues associated with Women of Color. *St. John's Law Review*, 79(4), 1105–1120.

Gee, B., & Peck, D. (2017). The illusion of Asian success: Scant progress for minorities in cracking the glass ceiling from 2007–2015. Ascend Pan Asian Leaders. Retrieved from: http://c.ymcdn.com/sites/www.ascendleadership.org/resource/resmgr/research/TheIllusionofAsianSuccess.pdf.

Gutiérrez, L. M. (1990). Working with Women of Color: An empowerment perspective. *Social Work*, 35(2), 149–153.

Hall, J. C. (2017). No longer invisible: Understanding the psychosocial impact of skin color stratification in the lives of African American women. *Health & Social Work*, 42(2), 71–78.

Hite, L. M. (2007). Hispanic women managers and professionals: Reflections on life and work. *Gender, Work and Organization*, 14(1), 20–36.

Holder, A. M. B., Jackson, M. A., & Ponterotto, J. G. (2015). Racial microaggression experiences and coping strategies of Black women in corporate leadership. *Qualitative Psychology*, 2(2), 164–180.

Holvino, E. (2010). Intersections: The simultaneity of race, gender and class in organizational studies. *Gender, Work and Organization*, 17(3), 248–277.

Kim, Y. H., & O'Brien, K. M. (2018). Assessing women's career barriers across racial/ethnic groups: The perception of barriers scale. *Journal of Counseling Psychology*, 65(2), 226–238.

Kivlighan, D. M., & Coleman, M. N. (1999). Values, exchange relationships, group composition and leader member differences: A potpourri of reactions to Dose (1999). *Group Dynamics Theory Research and Practice*, 3(1), 33–39.

Kivlighan, D. M., Marsh-Angelone, M., & Angelone, E. O. (1994). Projection in group counseling: The relationship between members' interpersonal problems and their perception of the group leader. *Journal of Counseling Psychology*, 41(1), 99–104.

Kluckhohn Center (1995). *User's manual for the Value Orientation Method*. Bellingham, WA: Kluckhohn Center for the Study of Values.

Kluckhohn, F. R., & Strodtbeck, F. L. (1961). *Variations in value orientations*. Evanston, IL: Row, Peterson.

Krivkovich, A., Nadeau, M., Robinson, K., Robinson, N., Starikova, I., & Yee, L. (2018). Women in the workplace 2018. McKinsey & Company. Retrieved from: https://www.mckinsey.com/featured-insights/gender-equality/women-in-the-workplace-2018.

Leung, K. E. (2017). Microaggressions and sexual harassment: How the severe or pervasive standard fails women of color. *Texas Journal on Civil Liberties & Civil Rights*, 23(1), 79–102.

Liang, J. G., & Peter-Hawkins, A. L. (2017). "I am more than what I look alike": Asian American women in public school administration. *Educational Administration Quarterly*, 53(1), 40–69.

Linden, R. C., Wayne, S. J., & Stilwell, D. (1993). A longitudinal study on the early development of leader-member exchanges. *Journal of Applied Psychology*, 78(4), 662–674.

Nassar-McMillan, S., McFall-Roberts, E., Flowers, C., & Garrett, M. T. (2006). Ebony and ivory: Relationship between African American young women's skin color and ratings of self and peers. *Journal of Humanistic Counseling, Education and Development*, 45(1), 79–94.

Nishii, L. H., & Mayer, D. M. (2009). Do inclusive leaders help to reduce turnover in diverse groups? The moderating role of leader-member exchange in diversity to turnover relationship. *Journal of Applied Psychology*, 94(6), 1412–1426.

Nkomo, S. M., & Cox, T. (1996). Diverse identities in organizations. In S. R. Clegg., C. Hardy, & W. R. Nord (eds), *Handbook of organization studies* (pp. 338–356). London: Sage.

Rath, T. (2007). *StrengthsFinder 2.0: Discover your CliftonStrengths*. New York: Gallup Press.

Sanchez-Hucles, J., & Davis, D. (2010). Women and Women of Color in leadership. *American Psychologist*, 65(3), 171–181.

Schneider, K. T., Hitlan, R. T., & Radhakrishnan, P. (2000). An examination of the nature and correlates of ethnic harassment experiences in multiple contexts. *Journal of Applied Psychology*, 85(1), 3–12.

Souto-Manning, M., & Ray, N. (2007). Beyond survival in the ivory tower: Black and Brown women's living narratives. *Equity & Excellence in Education*, 40(4), 280–290.

Spence, B. (2006). Diversity dialogs. *National Association for Female Executives Magazine*, 10–12.

Sy, T., Tram-Quon, S., & Leung, A. (2017). Developing minority leaders: Key success factors of Asian Americans. *Asian American Journal of Psychology*, 8(2), 142–155.

Tajfel, H., & Turner, J. C. (1979). An integrative theory of intergroup conflict. In W. G. Austin, & S. Worchel (eds), *The social psychology of intergroup relations* (pp. 33–47). Monterey, CA: Brooks/Cole.

U.S. Census Bureau (2018). Quick facts: United States. Retrieved from: https://www.census.gov/quickfacts/fact/table/US/PST045218.

Yalom, I. D. (1995). *The theory and practice of group psychotherapy* (4th ed.). New York: Basic Books.

International Perspectives in Group Psychotherapy

14 A Social Intervention for Court-Ordered Adolescents – The Family: People Helping People Project

David F. Allen, Keva Bethell, Denie Fountain and Marie Allen Carroll

Introduction

The Bahamas is an archipelagic nation situated between the southern tip of Florida and Cuba. The population of approximately 400,000 is 85 percent Afro-Bahamian and Haitian descent, with 15 percent made up of European, Asian, and Latin American. After democratically achieving Black majority rule, The Bahamas obtained its independence from Great Britain in 1973. The countrywide crack cocaine epidemic of the 1980s and its sequelae led to a serious familial and community disintegration manifested by burgeoning murder (Figure 14.1) and violent crime rates, domestic violence, child abuse, and poverty. Crack cocaine, one of the first drugs to feminize drug addiction, resulted in addicted mothers being absent from the home, leaving children to fend for themselves (Jekel, Allen, Podlewski, Clarke, Dean-Patterson, & Cartwright, 1986; Allen & Jekel, 1991). This led to the formation of violent youth gangs that terrorize the community. The average age of a murderer in the Bahamas is between 16 and 25 years and involves young men who have been traumatized by abuse and social deprivation.

In 2016, the authors approached the Court Social Workers to refer adolescents (aged 10–15 years) involved in minor violent crimes such as bullying, disorderly behavior, fighting, gang turf wars, and other destructive behaviors. Based on a carrot–stick approach, if the adolescent cooperates, they are released from their legal obligations. But if they refuse, they suffer the full consequences of the law. In this chapter, a pilot study of the court-referred adolescent program is presented.

Description of Program

Clients are referred to the program by social workers, probation officers, and guidance counselors in conjunction with the courts. The goal is to intervene in the lives of troubled adolescents to prevent them from entering a life of crime and violence. Once referred, an intake interview is scheduled for the adolescent and a parent/guardian in which the program is described and a thorough history is taken. Attendance is mandatory and the length of the program

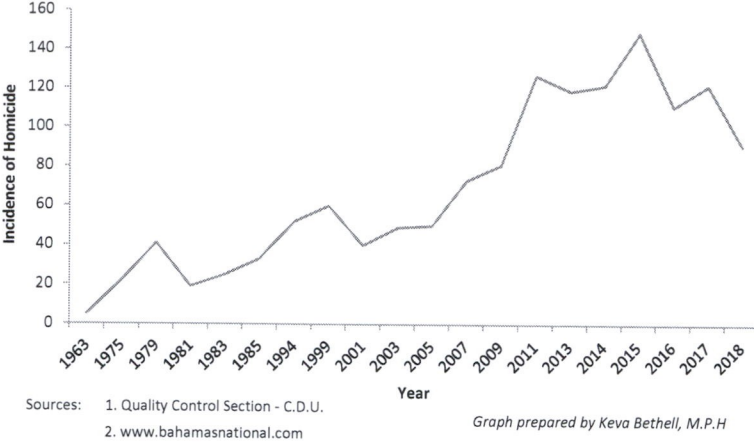

Figure 14.1 Incidence of Murders in the Bahamas (1963–2018)
Source: Graph prepared by Keva Bethell, M.P.H

ranges from six months to two years, depending on the severity of their situation. Because many youth carried knives, screwdrivers, and other weapons
which were used for protection, participants had to be screened prior to
entering the program. Meeting twice a week, Mondays and Thursdays from
4:00–5:30pm, the adolescents would share their stories of trauma and shame in
the presence of two facilitators. Their parents were mandated to attend a
separate meeting on Wednesdays from 4:00–5:30pm. On average, 20 adolescents attended each session and 10 parents (mostly mothers) attended the
parent group. This combination of the adolescents and their parents enabled a
better understanding of their problems and domestic situation. The parent
group assisted parents in understanding their adolescent's language, behavior,
and anger patterns. Our program offered the parents a safe environment to
share their concerns regarding their teens. Many parents were frustrated and
felt distant from their child. But, after listening to other parents, they began to
realize they were not alone in their challenges. Facilitators were able to teach
parents the language of their child, the language of mind and heart. Once the
mind connection began, the heart would follow. Parents came to realize the
love and time they give or do not give their children can make or break them.

For most court-ordered adolescents, family life is non-existent or
extremely chaotic. Many of the adolescents referred to the program have
experienced some type of childhood abuse/trauma (either physical,
sexual, or verbal) from a parent/guardian or other relative. While some of
their grade point averages (G.P.A.) were unknown to the program facilitators, those that were known were very poor and ranged from 0.5–1.00.
Because of the low educational achievement of most of the participants, a
trained teacher was hired to come in once a week to teach basic literacy
and math skills. Males and females were equally represented in the court-
ordered group (1:1). Most of the adolescents attended regularly and felt

very connected to the program. In fact, some of them would arrive one and a half hours early because they felt the program was a safe place. The adolescents displayed attention and behavioral issues but facilitators were adept at maintaining good dialogue and participation. The group process was made more difficult by the gang dynamics amongst some participants. After each meeting, the participants would often gather in their various gang groups to ensure their safe journey home.

Both therapists who facilitated the groups were Afro-Bahamian, committed Christians, and trained in psychotherapy. The male facilitator was a former gang leader who after being reformed obtained a college education. The facilitators, in many ways, were mother and father figures to these adolescents. The program is unique because "while leaders are clearly leaders and facilitators in the group, they are also community members exposed to similar trauma, violence, and community fragmentation" (Abernethy, Allen, & Allen-Carroll, 2017). According to one female facilitator:

> Our group sessions stand in the place of a family environment, where family members gather around the table to talk. With a listening ear, we are ready to absorb the pain, hurt, frustrations, and joy of the youth. What at-risk youth really need is a positive environment where they can recover and learn positive strategies to manage their anger and other emotions. Structure, discipline, and self-control are very important to these adolescents.

The idea was if facilitators could therapeutically impact traumatized adolescents/children (aged 10–15 years) involved in minor violent incidents, these youth could be deterred from committing more serious violent crimes in later years.

Method Used in Pilot Study

Over a period of one year (April 2016–May 2017), the facilitators submitted 81 praxes reports describing each session. These reports were analyzed for pertinent themes. To measure levels of trauma, post-traumatic stress disorder (PTSD), and depression of adolescents coming into the program, during the initial intake interview adolescents completed the Adverse Childhood Experience (ACE) questionnaire, the post-traumatic stress disorder (PTSD) questionnaire, and the Beck Depression Inventory (BDI).

Results of Pilot Study

Thematic Analysis

A thematic analysis of 81 group praxes submitted by the facilitators over the period of one year (April 2016–May 2017) was carried out (Figure 14.2). The

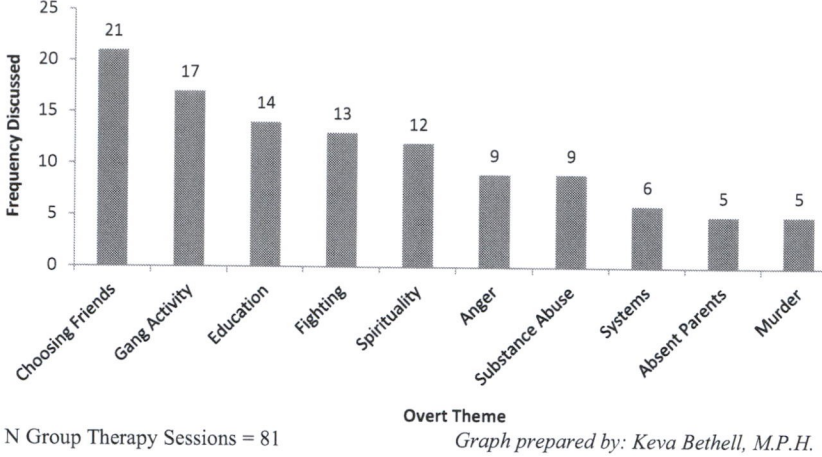

N Group Therapy Sessions = 81   *Graph prepared by: Keva Bethell, M.P.H.*

Figure 14.2 Overt Themes
Source: Graph prepared by Keva Bethell, M.P.H

leading theme discussed in the sessions was association with friends. The adolescents explained that friendship to them is about safety and not loyalty. For example, when asked how they felt about six teenage girls murdering one of their friends, they were not surprised. According to them, friendship may mean they are close today but if an altercation occurs, it could explode into violence. Sadly, some of the participants live under serious threats because of gang involvement. They have shown us pictures of hitmen dressed in hoodies sent to their phone. The gang often represents the masculine part of the single-parent family. In other words, the gang is a perverse rescuer in that it promises the participants relief but at the same time exposes them to greater danger and destruction (Brenneman, 2012).

Often, it takes a long time in the group before they share what is really troubling them. For example, one participant was in the group for a year before he shared that he witnessed a young man being murdered. Some of the adolescents showed a lack of empathy and remorse. After a severe stabbing at one of their schools, one of the young men was asked if he felt sorry for the victim. He said "Why should I? He's not one of my boys." The implication was that unless there is a direct association, there's no reciprocal empathy. When discussing education, many of the participants expressed no desire to continue their education. They did not believe they would live long enough to make it worthwhile.

ACE *Questionnaire*

A cohort of twenty-five (25) court-ordered adolescents was administered a 10-item questionnaire to measure their adverse childhood experiences (ACE) (Adverse Childhood Experience Questionnaire). Any score greater than three (3) is significant. The higher the score, the greater the impact of life experiences (Reavis, Looman, Franco, & Rojas, 2013). The results indicate that eight (8) of the participants (31 percent) scored four (4) or higher on the ACE questionnaire (Table 14.1). According to Dr Elinore McCance-Katz:

> young people who have experienced trauma are more likely to develop mental health conditions such as anxiety, depression, and substance use disorders. Young people exposed to trauma also have an increased probability of developing physical problems such as cardiovascular diseases later in life.
>
> (Greenberg, 2018)

Post-Traumatic Stress Disorder (PTSD)

A cohort of twenty-three (23) court-ordered adolescents (15 males and 8 females) were administered a questionnaire to measure post-traumatic stress disorder (PTSD) (Post-Traumatic Stress Disorder Self-Test). The original questionnaire was altered slightly to make it more understandable for the adolescents. We used our clinical judgment to assess their level of traumatization and violence potential.

The results indicated that three (3) of the adolescents did not have PTSD; seven (7) had moderate PTSD; and thirteen (13) had severe PTSD. Test results indicated that 87 percent of the adolescents in the program had moderate or severe PTSD (Table 14.2). These results are significant because they support our hypothesis that many of our adolescents who are brought before the courts for minor infractions are in fact so traumatized that they

Table 14.1 Participant Scores on the Adverse Childhood Experiences (ACE) Questionnaire

ACE Test Score	Number of Participants
0	2
1	9
2	3
3	3
4	4
5	3
6	0
7	1
8	0
9	0
10	0

Table 14.2 Participant Scores on the Post-Traumatic Stress Disorder (PTSD) Questionnaire

Post-Traumatic Stress Disorder (PTSD) Score	Number of Participants
2	2
3	1
4	2
5	1
6	1
8	2
9	1
10	3
11	1
12	2
13	2
14	1
16	1
17	2
19	1

have a bona-fide diagnosis of post-traumatic stress disorder. This means that they have flashbacks, murderous rage, poor impulse control, and feel hopeless about their life and future (George & Berger, 2013; Walkup & Rubin, 2013). As a result, when they are enticed, either by an individual, gang, or personal desire, they may do the most destructive acts. These results are similar to what is being recorded by emergency centers dealing with violent injury in Chicago, Atlanta, and Detroit.

Beck Depression Inventory (BDI)

A cohort of twenty-three (23) court-ordered adolescents were administered the Beck Depression Inventory (BDI). The BDI showed that more than half (52 per cent) of the adolescents suffered from moderate to severe depression, involving deep-seated anger and rage. Seventeen (17) percent suffered from borderline clinical depression, 9 percent have a mild mood disturbance, and 22 percent have normal ups and downs (Table 14.3).

These scores indicated that the adolescents in the court-ordered group come with significant levels of post-traumatic stress and depression. Any treatment program must take these factors into consideration. Five individual case studies highlight these findings.

Table 14.3 Beck Depression Inventory (BDI) Test Results

Beck Depression Inventory (BDI) Score	Number of Participants
1–10	5
11–16	2
17–20	4
21–30	6
31–40	6
>40	0

Case Vignette #1

The adolescent with the highest PTSD (Post-Traumatic Stress Disorder Self-Test) score (19) was a female (aged 13 years) who showed strong destructive traits. She scored 38 on the BDI (Beck's Depression Inventory) indicating that she was severely depressed, with strong suicidal ideation. This participant claimed that she had given up on life and nothing mattered to her. On the other hand, her grade point average (G. P.A.) was 3.78, demonstrating that she had high intelligence and was doing well in school. She was cared for by her mother but had little attachment to her. She did not know her father and had no siblings. She was referred to the program by her mother (not the courts) due to her cutting behaviors. This phenomenon is not uncommon in adolescents who have deeply repressed anger with emotional numbness. The cutting and witnessing of blood is a masochistic defense which distracts youth from the pain of their depression and isolation (Peterson, Freedenthal, Sheldon, & Andersen, 2008).

Case Vignette #2

A male (aged 16 years) scored thirteen (13) on the PTSD questionnaire (Post-Traumatic Stress Disorder Self-Test), indicating severe PTSD. He was referred to the program by the courts for fighting. He scored 40 on his BDI (Beck's Depression Inventory), which indicated severe depression. Being of Haitian descent and now living as a minority in the Bahamas may have been a contributing factor to his depression. He believed that every young Bahamian male was out to get him. His parents were separated and he was especially angry at this father. He was overtly hostile and showed no signs of remorse or regret for his participation in fighting. Sadly, he claimed he lived in a constant state of fear of being stabbed or murdered. However, he would often say that he was willing to die if he was pushed to fight for his rights. During one of the therapeutic sessions, he was smiling while describing how he caused grievous harm to another person. This was a serious prognostic sign for further destructive, violent behavior. Despite his incongruent affect while describing violent behaviors he committed, this same young man was mannerly and respectful, though extremely angry.

Case Vignette #3

A female (aged 14 years) scored twelve (12) on the PTSD questionnaire (Post-Traumatic Stress Disorder Self-Test), indicating severe PTSD. She was referred to the program by the courts for fighting. She scored 23 on her BDI (Beck's Depression Inventory), which indicated moderate depression. She was extremely impulsive and could change her affect to become violent within seconds. She could remain aggressive, and if not encouraged to change, she could easily self-destruct. She was from a dysfunctional home and displayed a high level of anger. She was failing in school and her grade point average (G.P.A.) was 1.89. At the time, she was reading at a sixth-grade level, with little to no comprehension. Her attention span was also extremely short. In an instant, she could vacillate between actively participating in the session to sitting slumped on a chair as if falling asleep. She would often express anger towards her mother and stepfather for their lifestyle. She claimed both parents were alcoholics and that her stepfather was physically abusive.

Case Vignette #4

A male (aged 15 years) scored eleven (11) on the PTSD questionnaire (Post-Traumatic Stress Disorder Self-Test), indicating that he was severely traumatized. He also scored 32 on the BDI (Beck's Depression Inventory), which indicated a score in the severe depression range. He was referred to the program by the courts for fighting. At the time of his referral, he did not seem to have the capacity to understand the danger and vulnerability of his behavior. Although his grade point average (G.P.A.) was unknown, his reading ability was at a third-grade level. He had dropped out of school and was assigned to another institution for learning but refused to attend based on his Haitian nationality and gang affiliation. Being a minority, he was paranoid that Bahamian young males wanted to attack and hurt him because of his nationality. He had explosive anger and expressed no remorse or empathy for hurting others. In fact, he boasted of continuing this fight should they ever cross paths again.

Case Vignette #5

A male (aged 14 years) male scored nine (9) on the PTSD questionnaire (Post-Traumatic Stress Disorder Self-Test), indicating moderate/severe PTSD and 20 on the BDI (Beck's Depression Inventory), indicating borderline clinical depression. He presented as very angry and moderately depressed. He was referred to the program for fighting and causing harm. His two brothers had been murdered. He was a leader in the gang and had a cruel revenge streak. For example, he threatened to kill his mother because she wanted him to get a haircut. This young man was diagnosed with severe post-traumatic stress disorder. He was extremely impulsive with deep-seated murderous rage and could easily murder another person. In cases like these, the adolescent meets individually with the male facilitator – a reformed gang leader who has special expertise in dealing with young men in this predicament.

Outcomes of the Program

Since the inception of the program, there have been 49 adolescents who have fulfilled the requirements of the program and have been released from their legal obligations. Thirty-eight (38) of the adolescents or their parents/guardians were contacted via telephone and asked a series of questions (Table 14.4). Eighty-four (84) percent of those contacted indicated that since their release from the program, they had not had any trouble with the law. Almost 50 percent of them were able to secure employment. Only 37 percent of them were still enrolled in secondary school, some had left and others had graduated. Of particular note is that one participant had a Grade Point Average (G.P.A.) of 1.70 when he first started the program. Since successfully completing the program, he has graduated from secondary school. According to his stepmother, he graduated with a G.P.A. of 3.75. Seventy-six (76) percent of them said they no longer struggled with substance abuse. For those who still used, the drugs of choice included: marijuana, cocaine, and bidi. One parent indicated that her son was addicted to smoking cigarettes. Another parent disclosed that her son had to be admitted to the state mental hospital for severe cocaine abuse.

Table 14.4 Reponses to Questions Asked during Follow-up Calls

	Yes	No	Not Sure
Trouble with the law?	5	32	1
Employed?	18	20	0
Attending School?	14	24	0
Substance Abuse?	9	29	0
Better decision making/anger management?	33	3	2
Better manages emotions?	33	4	1
Better choices in terms of friends?	29	7	2
Experienced any trauma?	29	6	3

Eighty-seven (87) percent of the adolescents said since their release from the program that they had better decision making, anger management skills, and were better able to manage their emotions. Seventy-six (76) percent said they now made better choices in terms of friends. Seventy-six (76) percent had not experienced any trauma since being released. However, one individual said there was a death in his family, another said he was almost ganged up by a group of men, and a third said there was a murder in his home. When asked about any noticeable changes, responses included: more goal-setting, attending church, less angry, all positive actions, more respectable, much better person, and helps out more. When asked for suggestions on how to improve the program, the majority of the participants indicated that the program was fine for them. Some suggested that we go to the schools to appeal to the students and another suggested that we get more parents involved.

According to Lewis there is a direct correlation between serious childhood abuse and murder in later teenage years (Lewis, 1992; Lewis 1998). Therefore, by simulating a positive family, The Family: People Helping People Project is an effective resocialization intervention based on empirical data. Research studies carried out on participants in The Family Project provided evidence that participants had a significant decrease in feelings of depression, suicidality, anger, and vengefulness. Involvement in illegal activity and abusive relationships also decreased. There were significant increases in intimacy with others, self-esteem, benevolence, quality of family relationships, gratitude, and forgiveness (Allen, Allen-Carroll, Bethel, & Manganello, 2015; Allen, Allen-Carroll, Bethell, & Manganello, 2017; Abernethy, Allen, & Allen-Caroll, 2017).

Universal Application

The hurt child, in any culture, is a smoking gun because a hurt child becomes a dangerous adult. According to the Contemplative Discovery Pathway Theory, children traumatized early in life are deprived of the three basic instinctual needs: safety (survival/security), connection (affection/esteem), and empowerment (power/control) (Keating, 2006). As a result, they develop impacted hurt leading to shame, with deep feelings of abandonment, rejection, and humiliation. Shame (**S**elf **H**atred **A**imed at **ME**) is so painful to the human psyche that the brain, through a series of neuro-mechanisms, develops a defensive Shame False Self characterized by self-absorption, self-gratification, and control to protect the person from the negativity of shame (Allen, 2010; Allen et al., 2014). On the streets, the adolescents describe shame as being "dissed." When they win a gambling game or a turf war, they feel empowered. But when they are further shamed by experiencing abandonment, rejection, and humiliation, they experience murderous rage and enter the Evil Violence Tunnel. In this tunnel, they become destructive to themselves (masochistic/suicide) or others (sadistic/homicide) (Figure 14.3). This destructive behavior is triggered by provocation, loss, and intoxicating substances (e.g. strong alcohol such as brandy, cocaine, marijuana, and liquid ecstasy) (Allen, Bethell, & Allen-Carroll, 2016).

Like many adolescents in the United States and other cultures, those in the court-ordered program were born into difficult circumstances and have estranged or non-existent relationships with the parent/guardian. Most lack a father figure in their lives. Due to their traumatization, they have insecure, disorganized attachment to their parents or caretakers (Duke, Pettingell, McMorris, & Borowsky, 2010). Their decisions are mostly influenced by friends or gang members (Siegel, 2013).

Some of these adolescents have been sexually abused by a family member, leaving them extremely traumatized and shamed. Others have witnessed traumatic events such as the murder of a close friend or relative. Unfortunately, exposure to trauma, especially witnessing violence, is the norm for delinquent youth in juvenile detention (Abram et al., 2004). Some of the participants are grieving the loss of a parent or sibling and their lives are characterized by mood swings, distrust, and depression. The dream of being empowered has been shattered because they are failing in school and feel hopeless about the future. Their trauma leads to severe anger which they self-medicate by abusing substances, stealing, and

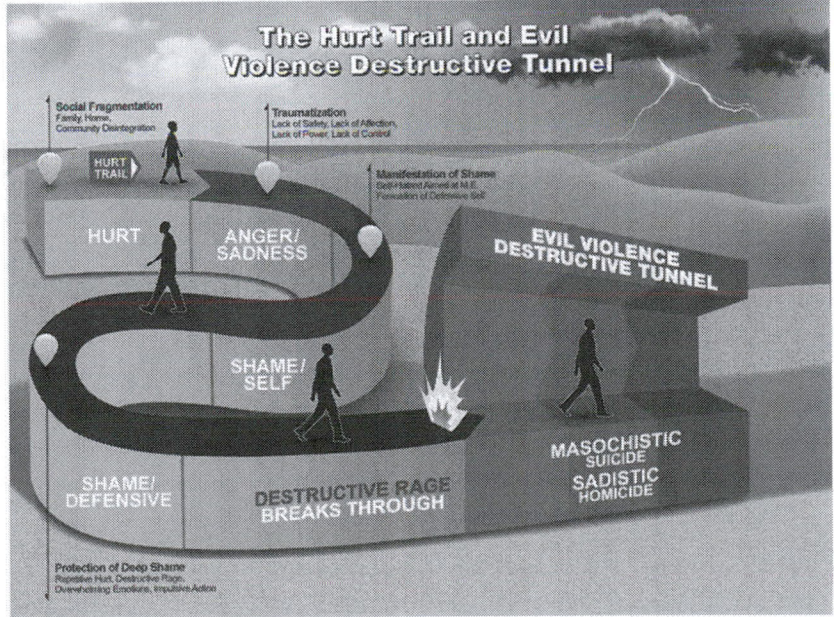

Figure 14.3 The Evil Violence Tunnel

fighting. Many of them have experienced the Evil Violence Tunnel and have been violent towards themselves (self-mutilation) or attempted to fatally wound others.

An article posted in *The New York Times* stated that childhood adversity can chemically change the way the brain works. The author warned that childhood trauma is one of the most important things that shape criminal behavior in adulthood. Her evidence-based research led to the conclusion that long before many inmates were perpetrators, they were victims. In reference to this, she advised that when interviewing inmates, we should shift the question from "What is wrong with you?" to "What happened to you?" (Burch, 2017).

Those working with teens in child welfare custody in the United States asserted that current psychiatric diagnoses of treatment for teens are limited. Medical charts may track multiple hospitalizations and medications but fail to trace traumatic pain. The authors of an article in *Psychiatric News* stated that complex PTSD will soon be added to the International Classification of Diseases and the symptoms will include: behavioral dysregulation, mood and anxiety issues, and attention and memory problems. As many teens who are traumatized are guarded and dismissive, the authors suggest that a tri-factor approach be implemented in assessing them: respect avoidance, respect resilience, and expect ambivalence. A respectful and validating approach can help to uncover the underlying issues, referred to as the "second story," according to the authors. Consequently, this "trauma-informed, developmentally appropriate approach can change the way the teen views himself or herself and the capacity to connect with others, change patterns of behavior and take control of the future" (Gerson & Heppell, 2019). In contrast to these findings, facilitators in The Family program work with the individual participants and not their psychiatric diagnoses.

The importance of offering this court-ordered program for juvenile offenders is to prevent them from entering the penal system, which can be more punitive than rehabilitative. Author Danielle Sered states that "imprisonment isn't just an inadequate tool; it's often enormously counterproductive – leaving survivors and their communities worse off." Prison deprives those incarcerated of the opportunity to heal, be human, and break the cycle of violence (Sered, 2019). There have been circumstances in which both the perpetrator of the violent act and the victim have been referred to our program for therapy. As such, The Family: People Helping People Project can be compared to The Restorative Circle, a meeting in which offenders sit with their victims and a trained facilitator in an effort to support those in conflict. According to an article in *The New York Times* by Michelle Alexander, a perpetrator is greatly impacted if they take full responsibility for what they have done and commit themselves to specific actions to repair themselves and others. The author stated that "a growing body of research strongly supports the anecdotal evidence that restorative justice programs increase the odds of safety, reduce recidivism, and alleviate trauma." In keeping with Dorothy Lewis' hypothesis that the perpetrators were once victims themselves, Alexander, citing Danielle Sered, concludes that:

> Violence is driven by shame, exposure to violence, isolation and instability to meet one's economic needs – all of which are core features of imprisonment ... Nearly everyone who committed violence has first survived it. Studies indicate that experiencing violence is the greater predictor of committing it.
>
> (Alexander, 2019).

Conclusion

According to the Diagnostic Criteria from DSM-5, adolescents with Oppositional Defiance Disorder (ODD) tend to be angry, easily annoyed, resentful, argumentative with authority figures, and spiteful (American Psychiatric Association, 2013). All the adolescents discussed seem to have different forms of ODD, as defined by the DSM-5. The major issue that stands out is the traumatized nature of their lives. If this early trauma is not addressed, it will lead to more destructive behavior such as murder in later teenaged years. We recognize that the program is a work in progress. One limitation of the pilot study thus far is that the adolescents are always under threat of serious violence or being killed. For instance, one of our participants only attended the program three times. When the facilitator called to follow up on him, his sister informed her that he had been murdered. There is evidence cited in our follow-up study that the program enhances resocialization and reduces violent behavior. For example, a young girl referred to the program for fighting had a special preference for attacking males because of her deep-seated anger toward her father. On the verge of being expelled from school, she was referred to the program for anger management and conflict resolution. Having a positive transference toward the female facilitator, the facilitator encouraged her to visualize her face in times when she felt violent. Returning to school, she was challenged to fight when a male student hit her. Picking up a chair to hit the student in the head, she envisioned the facilitator's face encouraging her not to fight. Putting the chair down, she walked away. The principal, who was watching unobtrusively from his office, was greatly impressed and asked the young girl what happened. She told him that remembering the facilitator's face and love for her prevented her from attacking the student. Very impressed, the principal reported this episode to the program administrator. As a result, he allowed the participant to repeat the grade to improve her grade point average in order to graduate. Presently she is a changed person, her G.P.A. is 2.90 and she is about to graduate from secondary school.

In conclusion, these early results are encouraging and motivate us to do more to develop the quality and quantity of the program. Major issues to still be addressed are the development of compassion fatigue or burnout of the facilitators, the recidivism rate of the participants, and the need for a longitudinal follow-up of many more participants to ascertain the program's effectiveness.

Acknowledgment

This work is funded by the Templeton World Charity Foundation.

References

Abernethy, A. D., Allen, D. F., & Allen-Carroll, M. (2017). Adapting group therapy to address real-world problems: Insights from groups offered in the Bahamas. *International Journal of Group Psychotherapy*, 68(2), 1–18.

Abram, K. M., Teplin, L. A., Charles, D. R., Longworth, S. L., McClelland, G. M., & Dulcan, M. K. (2004). Posttraumatic stress disorder and trauma in youth in juvenile detention. *Archives of General Psychiatry*, 61(4), 403–410.

Adverse Childhood Experience (ACE)Questionnaire (n.d.). Retrieved from: http s://www.ncjfcj.org/sites/default/files/Finding%20Your%20ACE%20Score.pdf in June 2017.

Alexander, M. (2019, March 3). Reckoning with violence. *The New York Times*.

Allen, D. F. (2010). *Shame: The human nemesis*. Washington, DC: Eleuthera Publications.

Allen, D. F., & Jekel, J. F. (1991). *Crack: The broken promise*. London: MacMillan Academic and Professional Ltd.

Allen, D. F., Allen-Carroll, M. A., Bethell, K. Y., & Manganello, J. A. (2015). Community resocialization via instillation of family values through a novel group therapy approach: A pilot study. *Journal of Psychotherapy Integration*, 25 (4), 289–298.

Allen, D. F., Allen-Carroll, M., Bethell, K. Y., & Manganello, J. (2017). An instrument for assessment of longitudinal community resocialization through a group process intervention. *Journal of Trauma and Treatment*, 6(01).

Allen, D., Bethell, K., & Allen-Carroll, M. (2016). Anger and social fragmentation: The Evil Violence Tunnel. *Journal of Psychotherapy Integration*, 27(1), 79–92.

Allen, D. F., Mayo, M., Allen-Carroll, M., Manganello, J. A., Allen, V. S., & Singh, J. P. (2014). Cultivating gratitude: Contemplative discovery pathway theory applied to group therapy in the Bahamas. *Journal of Trauma and Treatment*, 3(3).

American Psychiatric Association (2013). *Desk reference to the diagnostic criteria from DSM-5*. Arlington, VA: American Psychiatric Association.

Beck's Depression Inventory. Retrieved from: https://www.bmc.org/sites/default/ files/For_Medical_Professionals/Pediatric_Resources/Pediatrics__MA_Center_ for_Sudden_Infant_Death_Syndrome__SIDS_/Beck-Depression-Inventory-BDI. pdf in June 2017.

Brenneman, R. (2012). *Homies and hermanoes: God and gangs in Central America*. New York: Oxford University Press.

Burch, A. D. (2017, October 15). A gun to his head as a child. In prison as an adult. *The New York Times*.

Duke, N. N., Pettingell, S. L., McMorris, B. J., & Borowsky, I. W. (2010). Adolescent violence perpetration: Associations with multiple types of adverse childhood experiences. *Pediatrics*, 125(4), 778–786.

George, D. T., & Berger, L. (2013). *Untangling the mind: Why we behave the way we do*. New York: HarperCollins Publishers.

Gerson, R., & Heppell, P. (2019, April 5). Beyond PTSD: The complexity of diagnosis and treatment for teens in child welfare custody. *Psychiatric News*, 54 (7), 14–15.

Greenberg, R. (2018). SAMHSA Child mental health event promotes trauma-informed approach. *Psychiatric News*, 53(12).

Jekel, J. F., Allen, D. F., Podlewski, H., Clarke, N., Dean-Patterson, S., Cartwright, P. (1986). Epidemic free-base cocaine abuse. Case study from the Bahamas. *Lancet*, 1(8479), 459–462.

Keating, T. (2006). *Open mind open heart: The contemplative dimension of the Gospel*. New York: Continuum International Publishing Group.

Lewis, D. (1992). From abuse to violence: Psychophysiological consequences of maltreatment. *Journal of the American Academy of Child and Adolescent Psychiatry*, 31(3), 383–391.

Lewis, D. O. (1998). *Guilty by reason of insanity*. New York: Random House.

Peterson, J., Freedenthal, S., Sheldon, C., & Andersen, R. (2008). Nonsuicidal self injury in adolescents. *Psychiatry*, 5(11), 20–26.

Post-Traumatic Stress Disorder Self-Test. Retrieved from: http://www.ptsd.ne.gov/pdfs/ptsd.pdf in June 2017.

Reavis, J. A., Looman, J., Franco, K. A., & Rojas, B. (2013). Adverse childhood experiences and adult criminality: How long must we live before we possess our own lives? *The Permanente Journal*, 17(2), 44–48.

Sered, D. (2019). *Until we reckon: Violence, mass incarceration and a road to repair*. New York: The New Press.

Siegel, D. J. (2013). *Brainstorm: The power and purpose of the teenage brain*. New York: Penguin Group.

Walkup, J. T., & Rubin, D. H. (2013). Social withdrawal and violence – Newtown Connecticut. *The New England Journal of Medicine*, 368(5), 399–401.

15 Group Interpersonal Psychotherapy in the Context of Poverty and Gender

Toward a Culturally Sound Adaptation of IPT-G to Socioeconomically Disadvantaged and Depressed Lebanese Women

Salaheddine Ziadeh

Cultural adaptation of psychological interventions is far from uniform. Practices vary and emerging theoretical formulations are diverse. In this vein, practitioners may benefit from an integrated model and practical guidelines for adaptation. While the present chapter edges in that direction, it doesn't pretend to complete the picture. The main objective is rather to sensitize the reader to key notions in the area of cultural adaptation, drawn from theory and practice. These notions I attempt to elucidate using Group Interpersonal Psychotherapy as treatment example and socioeconomically disadvantaged Lebanese women suffering with depression as population. Context is critical to any adaptation; this includes sociocultural factors, such as poverty, gender, and local culture. A culturally sound adaptation may also benefit from a broader examination, involving the intervention itself and its mechanisms of change.

Background

Seven women entered the room, a former classroom turned into a therapy space, itself a room in an apartment building annexed to another to form a community health care center. It took more than two decades to come through, in this poor and marginalized part of the old city, reviving hopes that something good can happen after all. It was the group's eighth and final session. A mix of feelings filled the air as the women walked to their chairs, arranged in a circle.

It was an all-women group: Single headships belonging to a *kafala* (i.e., sponsorship) group at a conservative community in northern Lebanon. To qualify for sponsorship, the women must have had no income or male support. The *kafala* offered them a basic medical care package and, occasionally, some food and clothing. The majority had dependents, but some were childless. Some lived alone; others, in crowded dwellings with extended family. They came in contact with us in the context of an exploratory study on psychological distress in socioeconomically disadvantaged women.

Central Population Characteristics

Our group came from a specific Lebanese population, at the intersection of womanhood and poverty. In what follows, we discuss gender and poverty before turning to local culture.

Poverty

Poverty isn't a simple attribute but a central aspect of identity and experience; it alters one's way of life and comes with a heavy set of challenges and limitations, including mental health issues and barriers to care. Scholars and researchers have long recognized poverty's potent effects. Several studies were allocated to women living in poverty (see Grote, Swartz, & Zuckoff, 2012). And, in the larger population, one finds a salient association between poverty and depression: A meta-analysis of 56 studies showed people with low socioeconomic status (SES) to be at a greater risk for depression than those with high SES (Lorant, 2003). Although the relationship (expressed in probabilistic terms) doesn't implicate causality, it doesn't preclude it either; poverty can contribute to depression either directly or indirectly.

To be poor is one of the greatest strains that a family can experience; it not only causes stress but also limits one's ability to cope (Eamon, 2001). More distress, in turn, can make the family poorer. This assertion is consistent with the observation that individuals with severe psychological distress often experience deterioration in functioning, resulting in a downward social drift (Mossakowski, 2014). Thus, under stress, the poor are at risk of becoming more dysfunctional and poorer.

There is a significant association between economic deprivation and psychological distress (e.g., Knitzer, Theberge, & Johnson, 2019; Thanakwang, 2013). The stress from both poverty and deterioration in coping and functioning may impact families in many ways, one of which involves maternal mental health (e.g., depression). If impacted, the mother's ability to care for her family is further reduced, which can trigger or exacerbate her condition.

Chronic stressors that pervade the lives of poor women are various and often infringe their basic needs. They include: food insufficiency; crowded and/or inadequate housing; community violence and crime; societal discrimination; unemployment and under-employment; substance use problems; limited mobility; and, at times, imprisonment or incapacitation of significant others (Markowitz & Weissman, 2012). Moreover, there are barriers – practical, psychological, and cultural – that limit or block the women's access to care.

Markowitz and Weissman (2012) identified some barriers to health care. On a practical level, there is cost, lack of insurance, inconvenient clinic locations, limited service hours, transportation difficulties, and child care problems. On a psychological level, one notes stigma, negative experience with services or providers, and the incapacitating effects of illness (e.g., depression). On a cultural level, one encounters problems such as provider's cultural incompetence, insensitivity or blinders to community-sanctioned coping resources, and to the centrality of family.

Gender

Depression is the leading cause of disease burden in women – but not in men – worldwide (Albert, 2015). That women are more likely to develop depression than men is "one of the most replicated findings in epidemiological studies" (Grigoriadis & Robinson, 2007, p. 247). A number of studies produced a 2:1 ratio, leading scholars to conclude that women were twice as likely as men to develop depression in their lifetime (Hyde, Mezulis, & Abramson, 2008). This finding transcends culture, nationality, and ethnicity (Weissman, 1996); it points to gender.

The above finding, however, isn't constant across the life span. In fact, it is only around age 13 that gender difference in depression rates become remarkable, reaching the 2:1 ratio in late adolescence (Nolen-Hoeksema, 2001). To explain this trend, scholars have offered several perspectives, two of which are the "stressful life events" and "reactivity to stress" models (p. 173). The first model ties the emergence of gender difference to power, in that most societies give less power to women, thus increasing the odds of negative experiences and chronic strains. The second perspective attributes the difference to women's reactivity to stress, both in terms of biological response and coping style. To be sure, the two models aren't mutually exclusive. In fact, an integrated model may be conceived where stressful experiences and reactivity to stress feed off each other, in a reciprocal causation paradigm (Nolen-Hoeksema, 2001).

Until gender and psychopathology are fully deconstructed and understood, we cannot be sure of the exact contribution of gender to depression, independent of sociocultural factors. What remains certain, however, is that being a woman comes with certain correlates that vary in magnitude and influence with operating sociocultural factors, which themselves intersect with gender.

Research on depression provides a plethora of findings that show an intersection of gender with sociocultural factors. For example, one finds a high prevalence of depressive symptoms in mothers on low income (e.g., Hobfoll, Ritter, Lavin, Hulsizer, & Cameron, 1995; Miranda et al., 2003; Siefert, Bowman, Heflin, Danziger, & Williams, 2000; Siefert, Heflin, Corcoran, & Williams, 2001, 2004) and young minority women (Kessler, 2003). In a review, Kumar, Supriti, Kumar Nehra, and Dahiya (2013) explain: "Pressures created by their multiple roles, gender discrimination, and associated factors of poverty, hunger, malnutrition, overwork, domestic violence, and sexual abuse, combine to account for women's poor mental health" (p. 59). That being said, higher prevalence of depression in women doesn't preclude biological factors, some of which may be potentiated or suppressed by sociocultural and/or other environmental factors.

Lebanese Culture

Lebanese culture may be described as "high-context," "poly-chronic," and close-quartered (Hall, 1989). People tend to be indirect in their communication, yet expect the implicit part of their message to be understood. Relationship with "the clock" is somewhat liberal: Multiplicity of what can be done in an hour is rather the norm, and professional meetings don't necessarily start and end on time. Typically, the Lebanese don't separate time from relationship, or business from person. They resemble Latins in their use of space (e.g., they stand close to one another). When socializing, it is not unusual for two or more people to draw their chairs closer or sit closely to convey friendliness and/or specialness. When waiting for service, the Lebanese cluster informally, striking conversations (some personal) with others in their proximity.

Family

In the "collectivist" (versus "individualistic") culture of Lebanon, identities are largely based on group affiliation (Haboush, 2005). The family holds a central place and is characterized by interdependence and diffuse boundaries. To maintain family ties and traditions, provide emotional and material support to relatives, and defer to one's elders are common exigencies in Lebanese society. Family structure is predominantly patriarchal (Haboush, 2005); parenting tends be moralistic and authoritarian, with stricter rules for girls than boys (Dwairy & Pedersen, 2006).

Gender Roles

Lebanon remains largely a male dominant society, but women are increasingly assuming more powerful positions. Fathers have the ultimate say in most matters, but mothers still enjoy some power by virtue of the central role they play – e.g., maintaining family ties and stability (Haboush, 2005). Children are socialized into fairly traditional gender roles, with the expectation that they stay home until marriage. Divorce is generally frowned upon, especially among women.

Expression of Emotions

Context-dependent, emotional expression is typically constricted in public, except on special occasions (e.g., weddings). Cultural values, such as respect and propriety, modulate such expression. To express frustration is more accepted. Men express anger with some ease, whereas women tend to be more reserved and internalizing. Women share their deep feelings almost exclusively with intimate female confidantes. Saving face and/or fear of losing social status force many to project an air of normalcy. Much emotion is expressed in behavior, and typically lines up with social expectations and norms.

Mental Health and Illness

Traditionally, mental illness has been associated with shame and stigma—perhaps because it runs contrary to a "good presentation." Conditions with visible signs (e.g., psychosis) are shunned, whereas a non-psychotic depression may be explained away as "tiredness" (*taab*) or "grief" (*zaal*). What determines social acceptance of an illness is the extent to which it can be subsumed into a familiar context that is socially non-threatening. In this context, somatization is an acceptable form of being unwell.

The family is typically the first line of management when it comes to mental illness (Abi-Hashem, 2014). Parents or relatives first try to manage the "problem" themselves. Then the family may seek out physicians and/or religious scholars (e.g., *sheikhs*); some may take vitamins, drink, or consult psychics to cope (Abi-Hashem, 2014). Usually, there is a preference for "medical" (versus "psychological") explanations, and for medication over therapy. The Lebanese expect authoritative and expert guidance, clear and concrete structure, engaged attitude, and personable interaction; they do not respond well to speedy diagnoses and pressured evaluations (Abi-Hashem, 2014).

Interpersonal Psychotherapy

Initially developed to treat depressed patients, Interpersonal Psychotherapy (IPT) has been successfully used to treat many disorders in various parts of the world (Weissman, Markowitz, & Klerman, 2018).

Overview

Informed by attachment theory (Bowlby, 1999) and the interpersonal school of psychiatry (e.g., Sullivan, 1953; Meyer, Winters, & Mac-Bowers, 1957), IPT is characteristically relational. A central tenet is the association between psychopathology and context: Symptoms arise in, and are maintained by, a specific socio-personal context. In treatment, the focus is on the present, and the interpersonal context is conceptualized in terms of "problem areas" (e.g., dispute).

Disruption in the availability of important attachments, through an interpersonal "problem," is likely to compromise interpersonal functioning and result in illness (Weissman, Markowitz, & Klerman, 2018). IPT for depression aims to repair interpersonal functioning, first by understanding the context in which depression arose and what presently maintains it. Such elucidation provides a framework for therapist–patient collaboration. Treatment is time-limited, focused, and progresses in three phases – i.e., initial, intermediate, and termination. Phase-specific strategies and various techniques are used to restore and promote interpersonal functioning, consolidate gains, and even inoculate patients against future relapse.

The IPT therapist works actively and strategically to instill hope. He or she advocates for change while being non-judgmental, supportive, and validating. He or she promotes skill acquisition, agency, and autonomy while recognizing the incapacitating effects of depression. The therapist encourages affect expression and uses techniques, such as communication/decision analysis role play, to build skills and facilitate change. In group, the IPT facilitator additionally works at group cohesion, linking patient problem areas, and "harnessing member-to-member relationships" (Wilfley, MacKenzie, Welch, Ayres, & Weissman, 2000, p.162).

Group IPT for Depression

IPT was first adapted to group modality by Wilfley et al. (2000), thus providing a model protocol to use with other disorders (e.g., depression). The intervention consisted of 16–20 group sessions, preceded and followed by individual meetings, in addition to a mid-treatment individual session. Subsequent protocols shortened the intervention (e.g., eight sessions) and largely preserved its approach and structure, but dropped the mid- and post-treatment sessions.

In the pre-group meeting, the therapist gets the patient's history and learns about their experience and the interpersonal context within which symptoms emerged. The therapist establishes the "problem area(s)" most associated with the current episode, shares their "formulation" with the patient, and prescribes "the sick role" – a process whereby he or she validates the patient's experience, bringing it into a socially sanctioned context (i.e., the medical model), and prescribes rest. The "sick role" has the virtue of alleviating the patient's associated guilt or shame; it calls for self-care and legitimizes help-seeking (Wilfley et al., 2000). The patient also learns that their illness is treatable and discusses with the therapist the type and course of treatment, and what to expect and do on the way to recovery.

The therapist also completes the "Interpersonal Inventory," whereby he or she identifies the patient's significant others and specifies the nature of their interactions with them, their expectations from them, satisfying and dissatisfying aspects of these relationships, and what they want to change or keep the same (Weissman, Markowitz, & Klerman, 2018). The inventory provides a specific context for the patient's illness and their interpersonal functioning, as well as a map for focused therapeutic work. In collaboration with the patient, the therapist establishes treatment goals and encourages them to share these goals with the group, explaining the latter's function, structure, and rules.

Group IPT (IPT-G) comes with some advantages. For one, there is the synergizing power of group, where members work together to help one another and resolve issues (Wilfley et al., 2000). There is also the inherent capacity to normalize and reduce isolation. Further, in gathering to discuss illness, the group provides a *de facto* endorsement of the "sick role" (Weissman, Markowitz, & Klerman, 2018). An "interpersonal lab" also opens up, wherein patients work on relationship difficulties, learn from each other, recognize and accept the experience of others, apply what they learn to their own lives, and bring their experience back to the group (Wilfley et al., 2000). Thus, patients resolve their problems.

Problem Areas

Within the theoretical frame of IPT, depression may be triggered by one or more interpersonal events disrupting (or threatening to disrupt) central personal attachments (Weissman, Markowitz, & Klerman, 2018). This can be in the form of a death, interpersonal dispute (overt or covert), or role transition.

Grief – a common experience following the loss of a loved or important person – is to be distinguished from simple mourning and refers mostly to complicated loss. The group offers an ideal space for processing grief in an open and supportive environment, and allows, at least in part, for the re-establishment of lost connections (with the deceased) via the group.

As regards "interpersonal disputes," the heart of the matter resides in the non-reciprocity between the patient and a significant other around their respective roles in the relationship (Wilfley et al., 2000). If the two are at an impasse, then the therapist tries to bring them into "renegotiation." Absent this option, the therapist moves towards dissolution. In the process, the patient identifies and re-examines their expectations, modifies them or learns to communicate them more effectively, and/or draws on available support (e.g., mediation) to resolve the conflict. The therapist and other patients can support this process through the "interpersonal lab" (e.g., help the patient spot dysfunctional patterns).

Changes in one's life circumstances can trigger depression in the context of one or more role transition(s), such as pregnancy or retirement, and related pressure to adapt. This is true of positive and negative change, inasmuch as both types take the person out of the familiar, alter one's attachment system, and typically require new skills (Weissman, Markowitz, & Klerman, 2018). The therapist helps the patient identify what has been lost and what might be gained, mourn the old and embrace the new, and develop the necessary skills to succeed in the new role. Group members can contribute to all aspects of this work, drawing on their experience and providing support.

Cultural Adaptation

At the turn of the century, cultural adaptation of mental health interventions was already a driving force (see meta-analysis by Griner & Smith, 2006). A review of these adaptations, however, shows them to be anything but uniform (Bernal, Jiménez-Chafey & Domenech Rodríguez, 2009). Nevertheless, commonalities can be found. In this vein, Griner and Smith (2006) identify four approaches: 1) incorporating the patient's cultural values into treatment; 2) matching patient and therapist on spoken language and/or ethnicity; 3) tailoring interventions to the patient's circumstances and increasing care accessibility; and 4) using client community resources and cooperating with local supports. This summary lets through the plurality of perspectives, mirroring that of the field.

Bernal, Bonilla, and Bellido (1995) may be credited with the first unifying framework for cultural adaptation through their EVM or "Ecological Validity Model" (Rosselló, Bernal, & Rivera-Medina, 2008). Another framework is the "Formative Method for Adapting Psychotherapy" (FMAP), a ground-up community-based developmental model that uses collaboration with the target population to develop and test cultural adaptations to therapy (Hwang, 2009). Both the EVM and FMAP identify areas for adaptation: Eight in the former (e.g., language, content, goals) and six in the latter (e.g., cultural beliefs about illness, differences in the expression and communication of distress). However, the FMAP goes beyond "domains" to provide "principles" and "rationales" for adaptation. One such principle is to differentiate between "culture-general" and "culture-specific" constructs when providing psychoeducation. For example, assertiveness is culture-specific and cannot be presumed optimal across cultures: In some Asian societies, it may be too direct and disrespectful (p. 372). One drawback of the FMAP is that it needs to be generated for each cultural group; the published model was developed for Asian Americans.

A more recent model by Domenech Rodriguez, Baumann, and Schwartz (2010) adds a process component to content. In this community-centered approach, adaptation follows a tri-phasic process, with an *a priori* version that gets subsequently field-tested. The model was developed for a Latino population in the context of parent training and wasn't tested in a clinical population.

IPT and Adaptation

Central to cultural adaptation is evidently the intervention itself. Expert recommendations on adapting IPT include the following (Weissman, Markowitz, & Klerman, 2018, pp. 209–210):

1   Include at least one member who is familiar with the target culture, on the adaptation team
2   Know how the illness (e.g., depression) presents clinically in the target population and how it is understood
3   Determine the acceptability of available interventions, given the culture
4   Keep in mind that while problem areas are universal, intervention techniques may be culture-bound
5   Recognize that boundaries are culture-dependent when considering patient privacy and family involvement

Interestingly, none of these principles are specific to IPT or get to its mechanisms of change.

Adapting IPT to Socioeconomically Disadvantaged Women

To successfully adapt IPT to the Lebanese population, one should go beyond local culture (i.e., Lebanese) to central characteristics. This includes poverty, inasmuch as it permeates and shapes the women's everyday perception and experience.

Certainly, IPT has proved effective in treating depression in poor women, and across a wide range of presentations (e.g., Crockett, Zlotnick, Davis, Payne, & Washington [2008], pregnant mothers; Miller, Gur, Shanok, & Weissman [2008], mothers with postpartum depression; Zlotnick, Miller, Pearlstein, Howard, & Sweeney [2006], new mothers). Yet, there is room for improvement. In this vein, some IPT adaptations targeted barriers to care and service utilization (e.g., Talbot & Gamble, 2007; Grote, Swartz, & Zuckoff, 2007), getting at issues of engagement, collaboration, and retention.

Evidently, barriers to care must be considered in any treatment adaptation, especially in a population where they face a multitude of challenges. First, IPT needs to demonstrate its relevance to the complex, acutely, and chronically stressful culture of living in poverty (Markowitz & Weissman, 2012). This can be achieved by addressing basic material needs and by reducing treatment burden (e.g., shorter and flexible intervention). There also needs to be a resolution of psychological barriers to care (e.g., explicitly address treatment ambivalence and depression stigma from the outset) and demonstrate IPT's cultural relevance (e.g., incorporate culturally based coping strategies).

One sensible adaptation to the socioeconomically disadvantaged is "Enhanced IPT-B" (Grote et al., 2009). Its relative brevity (eight sessions) reduces the patient's practical barriers (e.g., financial and time constraints), and its engagement session tackles the patient's ambivalence and major barriers (Markowitz & Weissman, 2012). Of the measures to increase IPT-B's relevance, Markowitz and Weissman (2012) identify:

1   Stigma reduction (e.g., conduct therapy in a large primary care facility)
2   Maximizing treatment continuity by using alternate methods of delivery (e.g., telephone sessions when patients cannot attend in person)
3   Extensive outreach to re-engage the patient whenever they miss a session;
4   Adding a management component (e.g., facilitate access to needed social and legal services so basic needs don't get prioritized over therapy)

As exemplified above, poverty and other contextual aspects must be addressed in any adaptation. After all, there is an ethical responsibility to factor in the culture, values, and context of the people clinicians treat (Trimble & Mohatt, 2002); and the "cultural compatibility hypothesis" tells us that "treatment is more effective when compatible with client culture patterns" (Tharp, 1991, p. 802). In practice, however, adaptation runs the risk of critically altering the original intervention or being reduced to "cosmetics" – changes that make it culturally correct but only in form.

Adaptation and IPT's Mechanisms of Change

Arguably, successful adaptation presupposes knowledge of the treatment's active ingredients and its mechanisms of change – lest adaptation undermine the intervention. This holds true, regardless of where one stands on the "universalistic" versus "cultural compatibility" debate. Although proponents of the former posit that treatment mechanisms are universal, and therefore adaptation to specific cultures is unjustified, none pretend that modifying an intervention doesn't change its effectiveness.

IPT is thought to operate through four mechanisms (Lipsitz & Markowitz, 2013): 1) enhancement of social support; 2) reduction in interpersonal stress; 3) processing of emotions; and 4) improvement in interpersonal skills (p. 1139). Within this framework, emotional processing and improved interpersonal competencies operate problem resolution, whereas reduction in interpersonal stress and strong social support bring therapeutic change.

Although "identifying mediators [of change] may lead to refinements and improvements in IPT and enhance its application in a range of clinical populations" (p. 1144), no such study has been attempted. In other words, one cannot be certain of what mediates change. Nonetheless, a yet-to-be-confirmed theoretical framework may still be useful, especially when informed by fieldwork experience.

IPT's Field Adaptation

The Ugandan study by Clougherty, Verdeli, and Weissman (2003) constituted the first adaptation of group IPT for depression (Weissman,

Markowitz, & Klerman, 2018). IPT-G-U, the adapted treatment, retained the intervention's basic structure with some modifications. The language was simplified (e.g., role transitions were renamed "life changes"); and, therapist–patient transactions were scripted so that non-clinicians could use it. Group sessions were reduced to eight. One problem area (i.e., "Interpersonal Deficits") was dropped, inasmuch as Ugandan people are practically never alone. Women and men were treated in separate groups, eight to ten participants each. Cultural relevance was enhanced with feedback from Ugandan staff and culture-fluent people.

The effectiveness of Uganda's adapted IPT-G was demonstrated by at least two clinical trials involving over 500 participants in total (Bolton et al., 2003, 2007). Both "IPT-G-U" (adapted to Ugandan culture) and "Enhanced IPT-B" (adapted to socioeconomically disadvantaged women) are examples of successful adaptation to a specific "culture."

Successful implementation of IPT (and IPT-G) in other regions of the world, pragmatic considerations, and the "collectivistic" nature of the culture, motivated my own work with Lebanese *kafala* women. Yet, the complex sociocultural context – that had poverty, gender, and local culture at its core – called for a sensible adaptation. A number of things were helpful in this regard: Familiarity with the culture, prior experience practicing individual IPT with Lebanese patients, conscious effort to adapt treatment to patients' needs, feedback from my Lebanese assistants and patients, and clinical judgment. The intervention was based on the World Health Organization and Columbia University's (2016) protocol for the treatment of depression. A validated version of the PHQ-9 (Kroenke, Spitzer, & Williams, 2001) was used to measure progress.

In retrospect, this author believes that areas of cultural adaptation satisfied Bernal, Bonilla, and Bellido's (1995) model in terms of ecological validity. As regards "Persons," the treatment team enjoyed cultural fluency and I had worked with economically disadvantaged people. In terms of "Metaphors," we used stories and parables from the patients' cultural background to enhance cultural relevance, increase a sense of belonging, and strengthen motivation. For "Concepts," problem formulation and psychoeducation about depression were made in language that was familiar and de-stigmatized. As regards "Content," family/community resources and methods of coping were identified and drawn upon, with some emphasis on spirituality and cultural wisdom. In the pre-group session, patients were asked what they wished to accomplish, aligning what they wished for with treatment "Goals." In terms of "Methods," great care was taken to accommodate patients' day-to-day realities, in scheduling the group, for example, and to reduce treatment burden (e.g., asking them to commit to eight sessions versus 16–20). As regards "Contexts," IPT-G was conducted in a primary health care clinic in the community where patients lived. As to "Language," all members of the treatment team spoke Lebanese; moreover, PHQ-9 questions were audio-recorded in the spoken local dialect to enhance comprehensibility and overcome reading problems.

A preliminary quantitative analysis to test treatment effectiveness showed statistically significant (within-group) improvement in PHQ-9 scores. Therefore, IPT-G "as-we-practiced-it" helped our group get better. However, what constituted our intervention?

The Intervention

To be sure, the steps described above helped make the intervention more culturally relevant. But, was relevance the sole operator of success?

An examination we conducted at the time revealed some group features, which might have potentiated the intervention. The first can be described as "expressiveness" – i.e., the group as outlet where the patient is heard. There is also the related mechanism of "empowerment," in the context of asserting one's presence and claiming one's share in a group. A third feature is that of "authoritative re-scripting," where the doctor gives the patient permission to rest and take care of herself, or prescribes (e.g., via "role play") ways to speak and act differently. Fourth, there is "strength in number," where participants feel the power of the group, coming together in support of one another. Fifth, there is "safety," whereby patients transcend their initial reservation about being in group (e.g., betrayal of confidence). Finally, there is "experiential reversal" where participants experience in group something opposite their usual experience, heavy with sadness and stress.

In the context of change mechanisms, the third and fourth features (described above) are consistent with the theorized "social support;" the first lines up well with "building interpersonal skills" and (perhaps) "emotional processing," whereas the last two mitigate "interpersonal distress." These mechanisms, it should be noted, are neither independent nor culture-free. Social support, for instance, extends to emotion regulation inasmuch as "emotions are largely processed and regulated within relational systems" (Lipsitz & Markowitz, 2013: p. 1140) like a group; and, how a system regulates emotion is, in turn, shaped by culture. Therefore, adaptation may touch the intervention's core.

There were also factors that probably undermined our work. For instance, challenging circumstances threatened patient engagement and retention. To illustrate, one patient had to drop out because she had her disabled husband, father, and son fall ill within the same week, as she was their sole caretaker. A number of patients were also illiterate. So, for assessment, we had to create visual analogs with audio recording in our weekly administration of the PHQ-9. In terms of clinical presentation, a complex picture characterized the women – e.g., somatization and history of physical abuse and/or neglect. Further, there were practical, psychological, and cultural barriers – not only to access and use of care, but also to social growth and functioning (e.g., gender-based role restrictions). In group, there were concerns with privacy and risk to one's public image, which is consistent with the weight given to "good presentation" in Lebanese culture.

Given the aforementioned challenges, we devised a set of guidelines for therapists working with socioeconomically disadvantaged and depressed Lebanese women (Ziadeh & Ribeiro, 2018), some of which are reproduced below:

1 Ensure adherence to confidentiality (e.g., reiterate the importance of maintaining confidentiality; ask participants to avoid identifiers; monitor and explore related feelings)
2 Attend to hard patient realities (e.g., poverty). In this vein, you may help them create venues to make ends meet (e.g., skill training centers; trade) and encourage networking and skill building
3 Strive for inclusiveness (e.g., make sure everyone gets to talk every session, even if it isn't in depth), to counter marginalization and redress power
4 Increase cultural relevance (e.g., use cultural parables, proverbs and folk stories). To help build group cohesion, for instance, we would recount the parable of the loving father who, on his deathbed, advised his children to stick together like a bunch of arrows – broken individually but not together
5 Draw on patients' value systems to shore up resilience (e.g., encourage and support protective spiritual practices and beliefs, such as prayer and the value of hope and patience).
6 Monitor and manage risk (e.g., in terms of suicidality, use the last item on the PHQ-9 to invite disclosure of harm-related ideation/ behavior and to destigmatize the experience)

The above recommendations, far from being complete, convey the general picture: Our work is still emerging.

Discussion

The various models and perspectives presented above portray the complexity of cultural adaptation. Within this complexity, one finds intersecting elements. One emergent finding is the need to attend to context in treating different populations. There also emerges a research agenda that extends from theory to implementation, from context to treatment proper, cutting through many conceptual and practical spheres.

Recommendations on how to culturally adapt IPT to economically disadvantaged women suffering with depression, in Lebanon, cannot be based on culture fluency alone. The intersection of multiple identities and experiences makes such an undertaking at best misguided. In fact, poverty permeates the lives of women striving to make ends meet in ways that cut across their personhood and life choices, including self-care and therapy utilization. Under the chronically stressful circumstances of poverty, treatment may be perceived as just one more burden (Markowitz & Weissman, 2012); and, despite the brilliance of any proposed intervention, if such barriers aren't addressed, we cannot really speak of a sound adaptation.

Theory itself may be insensitive to sociocultural context. It may also hold culture-specific values that make it less apt for cross-cultural use. An intervention's mechanism may be modulated – e.g., potentiated or neutralized – by cultural factors. Even when it comes to "universal" mediators, their activation or mode(s) of action may be culture-bound. How social support, for instance, operates isn't necessarily the same in every culture. The same goes for conflict resolution, in that collectivistic cultures tend to be more compromising and solution-oriented than individualistic ones (Holt & DeVore, 2005). "How would things look like when a problem is resolved?" and "How do we know that it was?" are two questions that therapists should keep in mind. A patient's input is a must.

Cultural adaptation cannot be but collaborative and accommodating of patients' worldviews and values. Interdependence and spirituality should be considered; engagement and retention, prioritized; barriers to attendance, removed. A culturally sensitive approach tailors treatment to specific sociocultural contexts, thus increasing the congruence between the patient's cultural experience and treatment properties (Hall, 2001). This begins, perhaps, with the very perception of mental health (e.g., bias and stigma).

Language around mental health is another important area for successful adaptation. Expressions of distress must be examined and understood in their sociocultural context. A culturally sensitive therapist adopts the patient's own language around illness, thereby enhancing engagement. Another aspect of language pertains to research itself: How the researcher positions and sees him/herself – e.g., as agent of change who collaborates with the host community to balance their "needs" with "scientific integrity" (Bernal, Jiménez-Chafey & Domenech Rodríguez, 2009, p. 365); and, how that gets to the larger paradigm of the adaptation itself, or its meta-context.

Cultural context not only pertains to patients, but also to therapists and therapies. How a therapist approaches a problem area is culture-dependent. IPT's classic strategies for grief, for instance, include speaking about the positive and negative aspects of the patient's relationship with the deceased. In American culture, this seems straightforward. However, in Lebanon, where it is customary to speak well of the dead, this may prove problematic. A more culturally sensitive approach would be to explore "the difficult moments" with the deceased (Verdeli, Clougherty, & Weissman, 2018).

In group therapy, there is the added layer of how a specific culture intersects with group structure (e.g., same-sex group), rules (e.g., confidentiality), norms (e.g., information disclosure), and processes (e.g., therapist–patient transactions). Group dynamics and perceptions change in the context of culture. What constitutes "group cohesion?" What does "being supportive" or "working together" mean and look like? The complexity takes on a more daunting aspect when we add within-group heterogeneity to the mix.

Methods of adaptation, even when adequate, don't speak to group interpersonal processes. Traditional IPT leaves the therapist–patient relationship out of the equation (Stuart & Robertson, 2012) and, in group, member-to-member interpersonal processes aren't typically focused on. The intervention's short duration seems prohibitive in this regard. Yet, when it comes to adaptation, failing to examine group or cultural dynamics and processes leaves it incomplete. Indeed, an area that hasn't received adequate attention in the field of cultural adaptation is that of process. By this, I mean three things: 1) cultural adaptation as process (versus content); 2) interpersonal processes pertinent to adaptation; and 3) the intersection of the first sphere with the second, at the group, sociocultural, and meta-context levels.

Conclusion

A primary challenge in writing about cultural adaptation is that culture permeates everything human. In the context of therapy, one faces this challenge in multiple spheres – e.g., psychopathology and diagnosis, social structure and values of the target population, and culture-bound variables of the intervention itself. Just because a treatment was shown to be effective in a population, it doesn't follow that it is for all; conclusions about mediators of therapeutic change may not necessarily apply equally – or at all – across different cultural groups.

Cultural adaptation cannot be separated from the sociocultural context within which treatment is deployed; and, this truth cuts through all layers involving the intervention, from acceptability to implementation. In this context, available models of cultural adaptation aren't equally useful. The Ecological Validity Model, for example, may increase the correspondence between an intervention and its host population by matching them to key dimensions, but it largely stays at the level of content and ignores process. Further, where other models may provide guidance on how to adapt an intervention, they typically limit themselves to methods (e.g., collaboration with stakeholders). By and large, the interpersonal remains unaddressed. The latter point is especially relevant to group therapy.

A well-adapted intervention goes beyond the limits of the treatment proper and reconstitutes itself in the service of the people it aims to benefit. Optimal cultural adaptation is comprehensive, collaborative, flexible, and meta-contextualized. In this vein, I propose to expand our view of cultural adaptation beyond "tool" adjustment to the making of "what is helpful," given the strengths and limitations of concerned people and the affordability and bounds of their specific sociocultural reality. Such are the ethos and ways of a culturally sound adaptation.

References

Abi-Hashem, N. (2014). Cross-cultural psychology and counseling: A Middle Eastern perspective. *Journal of Psychology and Christianity*, 33(2), 156–163.

Albert, P. (2015). Why is depression more prevalent in women? *Journal of Psychiatry & Neuroscience*, 40(4), 219–221, doi:10.1503/jpn.150205.

Bernal, G., Bonilla, J., & Bellido, C. (1995). Ecological validity and cultural sensitivity for outcome research: Issues for the cultural adaptation and development of psychosocial treatments with Hispanics. *Journal of Abnormal Child Psychology*, 23(1), 67–82, doi:10.1007/bf01447045.

Bernal, G., Jiménez-Chafey, M., & Domenech Rodríguez, M. (2009). Cultural adaptation of treatments: A resource for considering culture in evidence-based practice. *Professional Psychology: Research and Practice*, 40(4), 361–368, doi:10.1037/a0016401.

Bolton, P., Bass, J., Betancourt, T., Speelman, L., Onyango, G., & Clougherty, K. et al. (2007). Interventions for depression symptoms among adolescent survivors of war and displacement in Northern Uganda. *JAMA*, 298(5), 519–527, doi:10.1001/jama.298.5.519.

Bolton, P., Bass, J., Neugebauer, R., Verdeli, H., Clougherty, K., & Wickramaratne, P.et al. (2003). Group interpersonal psychotherapy for depression in rural Uganda. *JAMA*, 289(23), 3117–3124, doi:10.1001/jama.289.23.3117.

Bowlby, J. (1999). *Attachment*. New York: Basic Books.

Clougherty, K. F., Verdeli, H., & Weissman, M. M. (2003). *Interpersonal psychotherapy adapted for a group in Uganda (IPT-G-U)*. Unpublished manual available from M. M. Weissman, New York State Psychiatric Institute.

Crockett, K., Zlotnick, C., Davis, M., Payne, N., & Washington, R. (2008). A depression preventive intervention for rural low-income African-American pregnant women at risk for postpartum depression. *Archives of Women's Mental Health*, 11(5–6), 319–325. doi:10.1007/s00737–00008–0036–0033.

Domenech Rodríguez, M., Baumann, A., & Schwartz, A. (2010). Cultural adaptation of an evidence based intervention: From theory to practice in a Latino/a community context. *American Journal of Community Psychology*, 47(1–2), 170–186, doi:10.1007/s10464–10010–9371–9374.

Dwairy, M., & Pedersen, P. (2006). *Counseling and psychotherapy with Arabs & Muslims*. New York, NY: Teachers College Press.

Eamon, M. (2001). The effects of poverty on children's socioemotional development: An ecological systems analysis. *Social Work*, 46(3), 256–266, doi:10.1093/sw/46.3.256.

Grigoriadis, S., & Robinson, G. (2007). Gender issues in depression. *Annals of Clinical Psychiatry*, 19(4), 247–255. doi:10.1080/10401230701653294.

Griner, D., & Smith, T. (2006). Culturally adapted mental health intervention: A meta-analytic review. *Psychotherapy: Theory, Research, Practice, Training*, 43(4), 531–548, doi:10.1037/0033–3204.43.4.531.

Grote, N., Swartz, H., Geibel, S., Zuckoff, A., Houck, P., & Frank, E. (2009). A randomized controlled trial of culturally relevant, brief interpersonal psychotherapy for perinatal depression. Psychiatric Services, 60(3), doi:10.1176/appi.ps.60.3.313.

Grote, N., Swartz, H., & Zuckoff, A. (2007). Enhancing interpersonal psychotherapy for mothers and expectant mothers on low incomes: Adaptations and additions. *Journal of Contemporary Psychotherapy*, 38(1), 23–33, doi:10.1007/s10879-10007-9065-x.

Grote, N., Swartz, H., & Zuckoff, A. (2012). Interpersonal psychotherapy for women with depression living on low incomes. In J. C. Markowitz, & M. M. Weissman, *Casebook of interpersonal psychotherapy* (1st ed., pp. 296–320). Oxford: Oxford University Press.

Haboush, K. L. (2005). Lebanese and Syrian families. In M. McGoldrick, J. Giordano, & N. Garcia-Preto (eds), *Ethnicity & family therapy* (3rd ed., pp. 468–486). New York: Guilford Press.

Hall, E. (1989). *Beyond culture*. New York: Anchor Books.

Hall, G. (2001). Psychotherapy research with ethnic minorities: Empirical, ethical, and conceptual issues. *Journal of Consulting and Clinical Psychology*, 69(3), 502–510, doi:10.1037//0022-0006x.69.3.502.

Hobfoll, S., Ritter, C., Lavin, J., Hulsizer, M., & Cameron, R. (1995). Depression prevalence and incidence among inner-city pregnant and postpartum women. *Journal of Consulting and Clinical Psychology*, 63(3), 445–453, doi:10.1037/0022-006x.63.3.445.

Holt, J., & DeVore, C. (2005). Culture, gender, organizational role, and styles of conflict resolution: A meta-analysis. *International Journal of Intercultural Relations*, 29(2), 165–196, doi:10.1016/j.ijintrel.2005.06.002.

Hwang, W. (2009). The formative method for adapting psychotherapy (FMAP): A community-based developmental approach to culturally adapting therapy. *Professional Psychology: Research and Practice*, 40(4), 369–377, doi:10.1037/a0016240.

Hyde, J., Mezulis, A., & Abramson, L. (2008). The ABCs of depression: Integrating affective, biological, and cognitive models to explain the emergence of the gender difference in depression. *Psychological Review*, 115(2), 291–313, doi:10.1037/0033-295x.115.2.291.

Kessler, R. (2003). Epidemiology of women and depression. *Journal of Affective Disorders*, 74(1), 5–13, doi:10.1016/s0165-0327(02)00426-00423.

Knitzer, J., Theberge, S., & Johnson, K. (2019). Reducing maternal depression and its impact on young children: Toward a responsive early childhood policy framework. Retrieved September 16 2019 from https://academiccommons.columbia.edu/doi/10.7916/D86T0WCV.

Kroenke, K., Spitzer, R., & Williams, J. (2001). The PHQ-9. *Journal of General Internal Medicine*, 16(9), 606–613, doi:10.1046/j.1525-1497.2001.016009606.x.

Kumar, P., Supriti, Kumar Nehra, D., & Dahiya, S. (2013). Women empowerment and mental health: A psychosocial aspect. *Delhi Psychiatry Journal*, 16(1), 57–65.

Lipsitz, J., & Markowitz, J. (2013). Mechanisms of change in interpersonal therapy (IPT). *Clinical Psychology Review*, 33(8), 1134–1147, doi:10.1016/j.cpr.2013.09.002.

Lorant, V. (2003). Socioeconomic inequalities in depression: A meta-analysis. *American Journal of Epidemiology*, 157(2), 98–112, doi:10.1093/aje/kwf182.

Markowitz, J. C., & Weissman, M. M. (2012). Interpersonal psychotherapy: Past, present, and future. *Clinical Psychology and Psychotherapy*, 19(2), 99–105, doi:10.1002/cpp.1774.

Meyer, A., Winters, E., & MacBowers, A. (1957). *Psychobiology*. Springfield: Charles C. Thomas.

Miller, L., Gur, M., Shanok, A., & Weissman, M. (2008). Interpersonal psychotherapy with pregnant adolescents: Two pilot studies. *Journal of Child Psychology and Psychiatry*, 49(7), 733–742, doi:10.1111/j.1469–7610.2008.01890.x.

Miranda, J., Duan, N., Sherbourne, C., Schoenbaum, M., Lagomasino, I., Jackson-Triche, M., & Wells, K. (2003). Improving care for minorities: Can quality improvement interventions improve care and outcomes for depressed minorities? Results of a randomized, controlled trial. *Health Services Research*, 38(2), 613–630, doi:10.1111/1475–6773.00136.

Mossakowski, K. (2014). Social causation and social selection. In *The Wiley Blackwell encyclopedia of health, illness, behavior, and society* (pp. 2154–2160). Hoboken: Wiley.

Nolen-Hoeksema, S. (2001). Gender differences in depression. *Current Directions in Psychological Science*, 10(5), 173–176. doi: 10.1111/1467–8721.00142

Rosselló, J., Bernal, G., & Rivera-Medina, C. (2008). Individual and group CBT and IPT for Puerto Rican adolescents with depressive symptoms. *Cultural Diversity and Ethnic Minority Psychology*, 14(3), 234–245, doi:10.1037/1099–9809.14.3.234.

Siefert, K., Bowman, P., Heflin, C., Danziger, S., & Williams, D. (2000). Social and environmental predictors of maternal depression in current and recent welfare recipients. *American Journal of Orthopsychiatry*, 70(4), 510–522, doi:10.1037/h0087688.

Siefert, K., Heflin, C., Corcoran, M., & Williams, D. (2001). Food insufficiency and the physical and mental health of low-income women. *Women & Health*, 32 (1–2), 159–177, doi:10.1300/j013v32n01_08.

Siefert, K., Heflin, C., Corcoran, M., & Williams, D. (2004). Food insufficiency and physical and mental health in a longitudinal survey of welfare recipients. *Journal of Health and Social Behavior*, 45(2), 171–186,doi:10.1177/002214650404500204.

Stuart, S., & Robertson, M. (2012). *Interpersonal psychotherapy: A clinician's guide* (2nd ed.). Boca Raton: CRC Press.

Sullivan, H. (1953). *Collected works*. New York: W.W. Norton.

Talbot, N., & Gamble, S. (2007). IPT for women with trauma histories in community mental health care. *Journal of Contemporary Psychotherapy*, 38(1), 35–44, doi:10.1007/s10879–10007–9066–9069.

Thanakwang, K. (2013). Poverty, perceived economic strain, and psychological distress among Thai older adults. In W. J. Yeung, & M. Yap, *Economic stress, human capital, and families in Asia* (1st ed., pp. 151–168). Dordrecht, Netherlands: Springer Netherlands.

Tharp, R. (1991). Cultural diversity and treatment of children. *Journal of Consulting and Clinical Psychology*, 59(6), 799–812, doi:10.1037//0022–0006x.59.6.799.

Trimble, J., & Mohatt, G. (2002). Coda: The virtuous and responsible researcher in another culture. In J. Trimble, & C. Fisher, *The handbook of ethical and ethnocultural populations and communities* (pp. 325–334). Thousand Oaks: Sage Publications.

Verdeli, H., Clougherty, K. F., & Weissman, M. M. (2018). Interpersonal Psychotherapy (IPT) for persons affected by the Syrian crisis in Lebanon. An adaptation derived from *The clinician's quick guide to interpersonal psychotherapy* by M. M. Weissman, J. C. Markowitz, & G. L. Klerman (2007). Oxford: Oxford University Press.

Weissman, M. (1996). Cross-national epidemiology of major depression and bipolar disorder. JAMA: *The Journal of the American Medical Association, 276* (4), 293–299, doi:10.1001/jama.1996.03540040037030.

Weissman, M., Markowitz, J., & Klerman, G. (2018). *The guide to interpersonal psychotherapy* (updated and expended edition). Oxford: Oxford University Press.

Wilfley, D., MacKenzie, K., Welch, R., Ayres, V., & Weissman, M. (2000). *Interpersonal psychotherapy for group.* New York: Basic Books.

World Health Organization, & Columbia University (2016). *Group Interpersonal Therapy (IPT) for Depression (WHO generic field-trial version 1.0).* Geneva: WHO.

Ziadeh, S., & Ribeiro, M. D. (2018). *Examining Interpersonal Psychotherapy within group and cultural contexts.* Presentation, APA Convention, San Francisco.

Zlotnick, C., Miller, I., Pearlstein, T., Howard, M., & Sweeney, P. (2006). A preventive intervention for pregnant women on public assistance at risk for postpartum depression. *American Journal of Psychiatry, 163*(8), 1443–1445, doi:10.1176/ajp.2006.163.8.1443.

Section VI

Other Perspectives and Endings

16 Wheelbarrows

Outing Myself

Nan Narboe

Risk flavors therapy. The biggest risk is walking through the door; showing up in the first place; showing up as yourself, as someone who sees what you see and knows what you know and hurts where you hurt. Riskier still is group therapy – eight people, ten people, a dozen people. More can go wrong. Or right.

"If this line represents all of recorded time," said the man who taught a yearlong course in Roman history, drawing a chalk line across the blackboard then over the edge of the blackboard and across the walls, all the way around the classroom, "then this" – here he held his forefinger and thumb an inch and a half apart – "is what we will spend the year considering."

An inch and a half is my range too. As a Gestalt therapist, my allegiance is to the observable; the particular; to verbs instead of nouns: this happened and then that happened. Speakers speak, listeners listen, interrupters interrupt, each element an inch-and-a-half section of the chalk line that surrounds the room and contains us all (Polster & Polster, 1973).

A woman in the group speaks blandly, looking at no one. The man next to her scowls. He opens his mouth and then shuts it again. Another man shifts in his chair. What's going on? Why doesn't anyone help her? Does the sense of depletion, the unspeakable emptiness circling the room, originate with the speaker or with those of us listening?

Another group member mentions a topic that rarely interests me, but I lean forward, attentive, eager. I look around the group, trying to gauge other people's involvement. I assess their posture, their breathing. Are they engrossed or am I the only one?

The Advantage of Group Therapy

The advantage of group therapy is the abundance of listeners. A single response can be idiosyncratic, more descriptive of the listener than the speaker, but not the response of an entire group. The more diverse the listeners, the more encompassing their responses. In one group, wild west individualism prevailed until two Midwesterners insisted that fitting in had its uses. Objections gave way to mumbles as the gay Midwesterner told us he had been chased home from school day after day for being a sissy and then chased back outside again, the better to fit his mother's prescription for Boy.

As a young therapist, I read the room and asked a cutter – a woman whose wrists were wreathed with scars, a woman still bandaged from yet another run to the emergency room – if, over the weekend, she had done anything else: something that was, well, *interesting*.

It was a logical question, once I counted the number of times we'd all heard the same story. The set of knives, surgical steel, that her mother had sent her for Christmas: the blood, the towel, the emergency room. We had lost interest. Maybe, despite her shiny scars, the woman with the hospital I.D. tag still circling her wrist had lost interest too. When I asked if she'd done anything interesting over the weekend, the woman stopped breathing. To console myself, I counted. One, two, three – there were three people in the group she trusted, three people she knew cared about her. If my question had wounded her, she'd turn to them. She took a deep breath and told us a different story, one about something else she'd done over the weekend. She also stopped cutting herself.

This week, a woman told the therapy group that her father is dying. She told us and there was no response, which surprised me. Generally what she says moves us and what we say moves her, and the results change everybody – the way textbooks on group therapy say it is supposed to. "He plans to hang on until his wedding anniversary," she told us. "Next week." Between her and her father, she told us, nothing more needs to happen. She has said all she has to say to him, he has said all he has to say to her. All that remained was waiting, watching. We waited. We watched. We *became* her, silent and tender and helpless. Five of us listened with mouths slightly open, three with mouths closed. She sat back, satisfied, and we did the same.

At our best, Gestalt therapists are literal. We do not dispute whether the unconscious exists; we just shrug and say we've never seen one. Actions, we can see. Sounds, we can hear. Someone tells a story and I listen, tracking with my inch-and-a-half viewfinder:

How does the speaker move, speak, breathe?
What happens to me as I listen?
Where, exactly, do those sensations lodge in my body?
Does the sensation persist?
Who else is listening? How are they affected?
What is the rhythm between speaker and listeners: percussive, easy, disjointed?
When does the speaker lose our attention?

Here is where experienced therapists – and experienced group members, for that matter – have the advantage. We know the times we are likely to exit for reasons of our own, so we can gauge when our exits are the speaker's doing. When she first entered the therapy group, the woman whose father is dying believed no one could hear her. She lived in the world of the child who had no words for what had been done to her. She spoke with the expectation that she would not be heard, her expectation a baffle that absorbed the few sounds she managed to make.

Gestalt therapists put our faith in the specific. We believe in William Carlos Williams' famous dictum:

so much depends
upon
a red wheel
barrow
glazed with rain
water

So much depends upon the particular, upon the *way* a thing happens. Clients prefer laughing to crying, but both are observable events that occur on an out-breath. Laughter can be soul-satisfying, habitual, or somewhere in between. So can tears; rage; playfulness. Any emotion, any psychological state, can be welcomed or resisted. That's the reason to focus on the way people do things. That's the reason my viewfinder is so small: so I can track whether a sigh completes a sensation or merely stirs it (O'Sullivan, Ekman, Friesen, & Scherer, 1985).

Tuesday night, 6pm. I open the door to the waiting room. Group members file past, into my office. They get a cup of tea, find a chair. Risk appears as soon as the group gathers. People fiddle with the venetian blinds, grab a cushion for their backs, try to get comfortable; close their eyes, scrub their faces with their hands; take audible breaths.

Group therapy takes nerve. Fortunately, it develops nerve as well. The rewards of reaching out accumulate and start to compete with the risks. The woman whose father is dying has been in the group long enough to believe that we want to treat her well. We make mistakes, of course, but ignorance is an interpretation she can now consider. When she feels overlooked, she can tell us – and believe that we want to do better.

Forgetting and Remembering

I forgot the chickens:

so much depends
upon
a red wheel
barrow
glazed with rain

water
beside the white
chickens

I generally forget the chickens. Everybody does – everybody forgets parts of what they remember. Forgetting is a given, as is having access to certain words and feelings but not others. Nobody's history is completely available to them; nobody has a full range of expression. What is notable is the way people forget, the which–where–when–what of their forgetting, which brings me back to breath. Your breath. Right now – the shallow way you are breathing. Gestalt therapists attend to breath for the same reason poets attend to rhythm: it leads to the next place.

A member of the group inhales, and pauses. Exhales, then pauses. The pattern continues. "Say what you have to say without first holding your breath," I suggest, and out come the witty remarks, the pained reservations: the words and emotions the speaker habitually excludes. Or (*woo-woo alert!*) someone else starts to feel them. When the need to forget is sufficiently potent, when survival required going blank, abandoned emotions can take up residence inside another member of the group, a phenomenon theorists refer to by various names: induced feelings, joining (Ormont, 1992), projective identification (Jacobs, 2006), emotional leakage (Wojciechowski, Stolarski, & Matthews, 2014).

The woman whose father is dying told the group a dream. In it, she was a little girl watching an unknown grown-up drown a litter of kittens. Afterwards, she looked woozy and a man in the group who paints houses for a living looked even worse. Eventually, the house painter asked her, "Are you feeling spacey and frightened, kind of scrunched down, like you're scared you're gonna get hit?" Her eyes widened. That was exactly how she felt.

The house painter picks up other people's internal states and feels them as his own – much as he wears the splattered colors of whatever house he's painting. Once it occurs to him that the emotions he's feeling are not his own, and he can identify whose emotions they are, he's okay. Well, mostly okay. That night, when it was almost time for the group to end, his face was still a funny color. When I asked him how he was doing, he snapped at me. "I suppose you're going to tell me," he sneered, "that if I sat up straighter and put my feet on the floor I wouldn't feel as spacey?"

I extended my legs and slumped down in my chair to replicate the way he sat slumped in his. "Why would I say that?"

The house painter grumbled and planted his feet firmly on the floor. After a few minutes, his face cleared, and the group ended. The house painter doesn't yet have a reliable method to name the sensations he feels, to place them, and let them go. Years of his life have been lost to amorphous states that are the curdled residue of other people's emotions, sensations he picks up unknowingly and then gets lost in. It can happen to therapists too: the wheelbarrows and the chickens and the rain add up, crowding our internal experience.

"Tell us what you have to say," I urge the woman whose father is dying. "It's not important," she says, and group members tease her. "How would you know?" asks a man dear to her, a man who kept an eye on her during the years she sat silent and quaking. She joins in the laughter. She swallowed what she had to say for so long that she no longer knows what it is, let alone the importance of saying it. Eventually, she remembers. She remembers wanting her father to notice her, to see that she was burning with fever: six years old, sitting silent at the top of the stairs, flannel nightgown tucked under her bare feet. Feeling her throat swell shut, scared it would close completely, scared she would die. Now, it is her impulses that die. She closes her throat against the sensation of having something to say. I prompt her – with a question, a raised eyebrow. Out comes something smart, something funny, something poignant and on point; something everyone in the room turns to hear.

Experienced bakers recognize the moment a soufflé puffs into full formation. A similar sense allows experienced group therapists to tell when members of the group have something to say. The therapist then observes what they do next: wait to be called on, shake their head "no," look agitated but remain silent, interrupt, vacate their bodies. There are as many responses to the urge to speak as there are people in a group and each carries with it generations of family history.

Therapists bring with them their History

Beginning therapists want explicit directions. Therapy is so like and so unlike other human endeavors that it takes years to distinguish between the requirements of a role (psychotherapist), an approach (Gestalt or whatever modality), and the roles and approaches learned as a child in a family. When I was a beginning therapist, a voice I thought was my own told me, repeatedly, insistently: "You can't say that!" When I needed to say, "You did *what?*" I couldn't. When I needed to say, "I'm so sorry," I couldn't. True, my austere Scandinavian forebears shook hands from a distance – firmly, once – but everyone has a voice that shushes them. Everyone has a history that limits how much of what they observe and feel and intuit they get to say.

For me there was an additional hurdle: I wasn't born to the professional class I wanted to enter. It took me years (and second-wave feminism) to recognize that "professional" and "white male" were near synonyms, that one of the voices in my head was an imaginary Episcopalian. I had degrees, but other people's *grandparents* had them. From better schools. My folks had a hardware store. I was merchant class, a striver. An outsider. Best play it safe (Allison, 2013).

People in group therapy learn to say the obvious. To say, "You look agitated," to say, "This bores me," to say, "I'm scared for you." People in therapy groups learn to override the conventions of social speech. When someone's voice thickens with tears, you're supposed to look away, change the subject, back off. Members of a therapy group learn to keep going, or to back off – and announce that they're backing off. Members of a therapy group learn to say the things that nobody says. To say, "You didn't answer my question," to say, "You just stopped breathing," to say, "Where did you go just then?" To say the things that confound people's expectations.

Wheelbarrows

While typing the Williams poem the way I first remembered it, a wheelbarrow showed up on my front porch, one I had never seen before. A wheelbarrow. On my porch. I saw it when I got up to stretch my legs. I'm not talking metaphor here, I'm talking porch. I'm talking wheelbarrow.

I could be grateful, I suppose. Had I remembered the poem correctly, I might have had chickens on my porch as well. But I'm not grateful, I'm pissed: pacing, muttering, struggling to catch my breath. I don't know what to do with myself – a sensation I remember from childhood, the weepy aftermath of trying to tell my literal-minded mother about something that moved me.

Fortunately, the sensation is one I also recognize from doing therapy. Something outside the ordinary tugs on my shirt: Over here, it says. Look at this.

The wheelbarrow is unpainted, its wood weathered gray, the kind of wheelbarrow that people who like frilly curtains fill with petunias and put on their porch. My husband is an antique dealer; maybe somebody left the wheelbarrow for him.

He doesn't know a thing about it. He calls the neighbors a block away, the ones who built a wishing well in their front yard. Maybe they ordered the wheelbarrow for their porch and it got delivered to ours by mistake? No. He checks with the police. No wheelbarrows reported missing.

Advice

In the next group session the house painter said he uses anger to break out of feeling other people's feelings, to return to himself. This makes sense to me: Anger is highly defining. So is advice. Both therapists and therapy group members tend to give advice when they want to fend off feeling what the speaker is feeling – despairing, anxious, isolated. Whenever they start to feel crowded by all that goes unsaid. By all the wheelbarrows they don't know what to do with.

The woman who supervises the staff at a group home for battered women says this is something she always has trouble getting new staff to understand. Battered women so clearly need protection that newcomers find the temptation to advise them irresistible. If a battered woman is about to make another mistake, a life-threatening mistake, shouldn't you stop her? But then, isn't that what her batterer does? Stop her before she makes another mistake?

The house painter worries that he will make mistakes, say things that don't make sense. Some of his concern is courtesy. He doesn't want to burden others. But some of it is the oddity of what he perceives. "Say what you have to say," I urge him one evening, "whether you can make sense of it or not."

"But some of it is really weird."

"So?"

The wheelbarrow appeared on my porch the next day. It created in me sensations similar to the ones the house painter feels. First I marveled that there *was* a wheelbarrow on my porch, and then I went to annoyance. The damn wheelbarrow was too weird to talk about and too weird *not* to talk about. Hearing myself mutter, I came closer to understanding the house painter's dilemma: whether or not to put into words the odd things he notices and the even odder things he imagines. Things like this have happened to me before. I hear other people's songs in my head. Their dread fills my chest. I dream dreams so unlike my own as to be in another language.

"It requires a certain physiology, along with a culture that allows for such things." The Russian Orthodox priest was talking about a boy from Hong Kong who had seen a recently deceased patriarch of the church – white beard, tall hat, black robe – waft through the church basement.

I have the physiology and I have cultivated the susceptibility; culture is where it gets tricky. I know better than to natter on about ghosts – in fact, I can hear a disdainful upper-class voice tell me not to. Like many who travel between classes, I learned to split the difference, using my senses to discern what clients experience without revealing their earthy origins. "Only those in the lower class mention their bodies."

In this instance, although there was an actual wheelbarrow on my literal porch, I hypothesized that the wheelbarrow represented the way that suddenly, inexplicably, things appear in the house painter's internal landscape: How startling he finds them, how little he knows what to do next. Which is to say that together he and I created a representation – the wheelbarrow that every therapist and every client cobble together – of his dilemma inside me. Well, on my porch.

Group therapists have more data to help them sort the thoughts they think and the sensations they feel into those that belong to them and those that do not. Group members have more data too, and more help sorting what they experience. All their lives, the house painter and the women whose father is dying have thought the errant thoughts and felt the stray emotions of others. Group therapy gives them – and me – a place to sort them. A way to clear our porches.

Outing Myself

My wiring, along with the attentiveness that group therapy cultivates, has left me so receptive that I avoid department stores the entire month of December – all that hope and longing and desperation, tied together with a big red bow. For the 30 years that I led groups before the painter joined one of mine, I used the emotions and sensations I picked up from others to guide my work while preserving my privacy. I behaved "professionally." (Like a white male.) On the continuum between "What's going on in your throat" to "I feel as if I'm choking. Do you?" I chose the industry-standard option.

I asked questions that didn't expose me. Out me.

Until I led a group with two members who required something different. The quaking woman and the house painter, each profoundly isolated, both habitually self-attacking, needed to know – what? That they weren't alone? That I "got them" more than they could imagine? I wasn't sure what outing myself would achieve, but I was clear what my priorities were. If the choice was between me saving face and them feeling less peculiar, my face would have to go.

Therapists should violate commonly held boundaries only when they have studied their reasons for doing so and discussed them in supervision. (Langs, 1978). I had thought through the potential cost as well: specifically whether I would scare anyone in the group (no one in it had a psychotic mother) or damage my professional reputation – which is to say, lose potential business. I was being "professional" and I was being "mercantile."

One night the woman brought up her unsatisfying sex life. Two or three of the men in the group had crushes on her; the group as a whole wanted her to have whatever she wanted, including orgasms. At one point, she said she was getting flooded by all the attention and asked the group's permission to talk just with me. (Raised working poor, she is respectful of norms; asking for what she needed was a risk for her.) We moved our chairs to face one another. After we had gone back and forth for about ten minutes, I realized how close to her I felt, how intimate. How sexual.

There are any number of ways to introduce the idea that sexual intimacy is a continuum. But I was ready and she was a seasoned group member. "We've been focusing on your sexuality," I said.

She laughed, sounding both breathy and nervous, the push–pull that kept her from coming.

What allowed me to assume I was experiencing her sexuality and not my own? The same phenomenon that lets me distinguish between my distain – or fearfulness, or generosity – and someone else's. Each person's emotional vocabulary has a timbre all its own. Even when I am in a receptive state and another's emotions resonate in my body strongly enough for me to notice them, they do so bearing that person's distinctive signature (Steinbeis, 2016).

The risk for the seasoned group member wasn't talking about sex; it was asking the group to accommodate her. The risk for me wasn't talking about sex either; it was acknowledging that my body can reflect another person's experience. She hadn't been reared to ask, I hadn't been reared to tell. Group work is generally thought of as risky, but each participant's sense of risk is personal: for one, it's expressing tenderness; for another it's feeling rage; for a third it's sitting quietly.

The house painter appeared at the next group with gray in his hair. He told us he was afraid that he won't do with his life what he is supposed to do. He ran his hand through his paint-flecked hair, smoothing it back, ruffling it forward. He didn't mean some familial or societal *supposed to*. He meant he won't live the one life that is authentically his.

The group is generally pretty good about not giving advice, but this time people bombarded him. You could study philosophy. Or teach high school. High school history. No, the man hollered, holding his paint-speckled hands in front of his face like a catcher. No.

Advice is rarely useful. What is useful is discovering *how* someone makes a problem impossible to solve (Perls, Hefferline, & Goodman, 1951). This is what advice-giving obliterates, and the reason therapists and therapy groups generally avoid it.

"It isn't like you to give advice," I say to the woman who had suggested philosophy. "Or you," I say to the man who had recommended teaching. As I speak, the painter exhales. His chest softens. "As a group," I said, gesturing towards the house painter, "we've gotten used to the idea that sometimes he feels what other people are feeling." The woman with the kitten dream nods. "Maybe tonight we're feeling what it's like to *be* him" (Casement, 1985).

That's when the painter told us that the advice we had given him was the advice he's been given his entire life, advice his father gave him – the father who himself had studied philosophy and taught high school. (Yep, history.) Hand-me-down advice that the painter gives himself, then fends off, just as he did with us: The complicated internal process that he'd been trying, unsuccessfully, to tell us about for months.

We remember by involving others in our efforts to forget. We remember in order to involve others in our efforts to forget (Wang, Placek, & Lewis-Peacock, 2019).

Group therapy creates *senders* and *receivers* as surely as breathing out leads to breathing in. When the woman whose father is dying sat silent and shaking, the man with paint in his hair shook with her (Ekman, 1971). Her shaking she could ignore; his, she could not. (My prompting she could ignore; his she could not.) Members of the group asked her to talk about her silence and the words burst forth: No one wanted to hear her stories, she said, the stories that, even now, gave her nightmares. (The stories her abuser had threatened – with his hands around her throat, her head underwater – to kill her if she ever told.) True, the group said, we don't want to hear such stories. But you can bear to tell them and we can bear to listen. She told her stories and over time new stories emerged.

Last week she told us about singing, full-voice, at her son's wedding.

References

Allison, D. (2013). *Skin: Talking about sex, class and literature*. New York: Firebrand Books.

Casement, P. (1985). *On learning from the patient*. New York: Tavistock Publications.

Ekman, P., & Friesen, W. V. (1971). Constants across cultures in the face and emotion. *Journal of Personality and Social Psychology, 17*(2), 124–129.

Jacobs, M. (2006). *Psychodynamic counselling in action*. London: Sage.

Langs, R. J. (1978). *The listening process*. New York: Aronson.

Ormont, L. (1992). *The group psychotherapy experience: From theory to practice*. New York: St. Martin's Press.

O'Sullivan, M., Ekman, P., Friesen, W., & Scherer, K. (1985). What you say and how you say it: The contribution of speech content and voice quality to judgments of others. *Journal of Personality and Social Psychology, 48*(1), 54–62.

Perls, F., Hefferline, R., & Goodman, P. (1951). *Gestalt therapy: Excitement and growth in the human personality*. Seattle, WA: Julian Press.

Polster, E., & Polster, M. (1973). *Gestalt therapy integrated*. New York: Penguin Random House.

Steinbeis, N. (2016). The role of self-other distinction in understanding others' mental and emotional states: neurocognitive mechanisms in children and adults. *Philosophical Transactions of the Royal Society of London. Series B, Biological sciences, 371*(1686), doi:10.1098/rstb.2015.0074.

Wang, T. H., Placek, K., & Lewis-Peacock, J. A. (2019). More is less: Increased processing of unwanted memories facilitates forgetting. *Journal of Neuroscience, 39*(18), 3551–3560, doi:10.1523/JNEUROSCI.2033-2018.2019.

Wojciechowski, J., Stolarski, M., & Matthews, G. (2014). Emotional intelligence and mismatching expressive and verbal messages: A contribution to detection of deception. *PloS one, 9*(3), e92570, doi:10.1371/journal.pone.0092570.

17 Closing Thoughts

Michele D. Ribeiro

Like all groups, there is a time for termination. Such is true for this text on group psychotherapy in which we will bring closure to our focus on intersectionality and social identities. This chapter will highlight the many ways groups are utilized and how group cohesion and support is a universal need across all cultures and societies. Ultimately, whatever the country, groups help people heal.

Having spent a few weeks participating in two International Learning and Exchange programs (Cuba and Tanzania) with the American Psychological Association's Office of International Affairs, I was able to learn how other countries are providing mental health services within their cultures. One inspiring therapeutic intervention this author witnessed in Cuba was psicoballet. This practice brings groups of people together who have disabilities (cognitive, physical, and genetic disorders such as Down syndrome) to express themselves through the art of dance. The emotional release that occurs in clients is remarkable, not to mention the healing power of agency and strength demonstrated in their movement and performances. The chapter in this text on group art (collaging) for Mothers of Color reminded me of the value of other ways of processing as therapeutic tools for healing, as did psicoballet.

Spending a few weeks in Tanzania afforded me access and time to talk to clients and therapists in sober houses, after school programs for high-risk adolescents, a breast cancer clinic, and orphanages. Support and psychoeducational groups are key treatment modalities that are utilized for mental health treatment and recovery within this culture. Similarly, learning from Kilimanjaro mountain guides, I was exposed to the ways they support each other within subgroups, in managing the deaths of family members, sicknesses, and the general vicissitudes of life. I witnessed how the mostly male guides come together regularly to assist each other emotionally and spiritually in song and prayer. Dr Abernethy within this text speaks to the value of spirituality in groups, reinforcing the strong reliance on religion that I witnessed in the highly Muslim and Christian country of Tanzania.

Having recently walked El Camino in Spain, I observed similar experiences of groups coming together to process divorces, infertility, physical pain, spiritual connection, and general social isolation. A 24-year-old Italian male I met shared how his psychologist prescribed him a walk on the Camino over medications for his generalized and social anxiety issues. He shared how much he appreciated this treatment approach from his therapist. Regardless of culture, individuals, couples, and families from Germany, Italy, France, Spain, Romania, Peru, Brazil, Philippines, Canada, South Korea, Australia, South Africa, and the United States, to name a few, all seemed to coalesce around the desire for community in groups across the boundaries of country and society. All on a pilgrimage toward a common group goal, walking the path of Saint James/Santiago, and finding cohesion and community along *the way*.

Working on a study abroad trip with 800 college students through Semester at Sea, similar needs arose there. Sailing across the Atlantic Ocean from Florida to nine countries in the Mediterranean, students from several countries (but predominantly the United States) attended support groups that were formed on the ship with eight to ten students in each one. The group members shared feelings of homesickness, depression, racism, and anxiety as they ventured into new countries and explored their social identities within these new spaces and contexts.

Serving as manager of a meditation course, the women servers (Carly, Patricia, Emily, and myself) regularly came together as a group, for breakfast and lunch, and shared the many different emotions that were being released as a result of the meditation practice we participated in between hours of serving the student meditators. Compassion and gratitude were at the root of our everyday experiences.

Groups (whether informally through people gathering due to need and proximity, or formally through more structured group therapy processes) provide a space to come together, to share struggles, experience vulnerability, and ultimately bring about some personal healing. This book is about all of these contexts and needs and our work as group therapists to understand the complexity of people and their lives. It is about knowing and learning how to work within the diversity of the world we live in.

This book was an opportunity to share my passion for diversity and to find colleagues and friends who could lead us a little to the edge of what we experience as group therapists, and how to push these boundaries further into the unfamiliar. It is always a gift as an editor to have an idea, think of who could contribute to the material, and then see how all the thoughtful narratives weave together into a whole. In the beginning, I had a strong desire to reinforce practical information with theory, regarding the intersections of social identities and how they show up in group. The other purpose of this book was to encourage more dialogue and consultation with group psychotherapists on best practices when working with people across intersecting and varied identities. Toward this goal, the journey through this book covered many areas, starting from foundations of theoretical concepts and ecological guidelines for practice to an intentional reminder that cultural humility and compassion are the key foundational ingredients to doing this work wholeheartedly. The first two chapters were the forming and norming pieces to our text or the first stage of development necessary in all groups.

The chapters that followed led us into social identities, populations, and practices that can be universally applied, or appropriately adapted, based on context and culture of the group and country. Dr Allen and colleagues, and Dr Ziadeh's work are amazing examples of powerful interventions occurring internationally with disenfranchised populations. Although this book highlighted only two international contexts of group therapy, the globalization of our world will require us to move past Eurocentric frameworks of healing and learn other ways of relating with more sensitivity to cultural contexts.

The final essay artistically depicts the fullness of group, the risks that members take in sharing vulnerability, and the maturation process of leaders and members over time. Although no book can be complete, my hope is that this book, for you as the reader, ignited new excitement for all there is to learn about our clients and ourselves. Perhaps you learned more about a specific social identity or maybe the importance of holding on to the humanity of clients that are either pedestaled or locked away, privileged or marginalized. Whatever your learning curve, my hope is that this resource provides something of importance for you as a group therapist; that it invites meaningful conversations to occur; and that it opens up new insights into your work as a scholar and practitioner.

As all terminations do, this ending creates a new beginning.

Index